*To self-respect, survival of the soul
and
To my husband, Paul*

Courage and Love

Gisela Konopka

Gisela Konopka

Revised Fourth Edition
July 1997

Beaver's Pond Press

Revised Fourth Edition first published July 1997.

Printed in the United States of America.

J   I   H   G   F   E   D   C   B   A

Cover Sculpture: E. Paul Konopka
Cover Drawing: Gisela Konopka
Cover Design: Morris Lundin
Production Coordination 1997: Milton E. Adams

Library of Congress # 88-91411
ISBN 1-890676-05-5

Published in the United States by:

Beaver's Pond Press

5125 Danens Drive
Edina, MN 55439-1465
(612) 829-8818 Email: adamsppo@aol.com

Translated into German and published
under the title *Mit Mut und Liebe*
Deutscher Studien Verlag • Weinheim 1996
ISBN 3 89271 613 7

Table of Contents

Preface

*W*hy write this now? Why want others to know about me? All of us are only small specks in the universe. We have to accept this. Yet, so many asked about my early experiences in another country, another time. Young people want to know why my whole life is dedicated to fighting against injustice, why this basic abhorrence of any arrogance related to race, religion, nationality, sex, age, intelligence or whatever nonsense human beings think makes them superior to others.

What you will read was not written recently, the "memoirs" of an old person. I wrote much of it not too long after my entrance into the United States so as not to forget and to share with others. I was, and still am, questioned frequently as to where I and others took the courage to withstand terror. The answer is complex, and therefore I wrote about the early childhood influences: life, people, reading, the arts. Later came thought-through-conviction, a sense of duty to follow it and the marvelous, strengthening, supportive, demanding power of love. This story is not only my own, but also the story of my husband, Paul, and though it is an account of much horror, it is also one of LOVE!

There are some other, more objective reasons for my wanting this to be read. It is the historian and former anti-Nazi fighter in me who wants to correct misconceptions about this period:

1) The Nazis were not only a dictatorship but also a totalitarian regime of a special kind: consciously, deliberately and systematically they worked toward a total and pervasive breakdown of human dignity of everybody who had any different thoughts from the rulers or who did not belong to the rulers' so-called "master race". All those, and not only Jews, they decided had to be, and were, demeaned and exterminated.

2) It is not true that people did not know of the agonizing Nazi terror though they may not always have known all details. Most everybody knew what the Nazis stood for *before* the Nazis came to power. Their terror tactics showed in street fights, in writings, in threats before they came to final power. The demeaning and torturing of anyone resisting them started immediately after January 1933. Fear pervaded the country. Everybody (I exclude the children) knew about the terror. It was also known outside of Germany. Yet people did not *want* to believe those atrocities, or hoped to be on the side of the Nazis, whom they perceived as invincible.

3) There *was* resistance against the Nazis inside Germany consisting of a variety of people who had a conscience and courage. Those people included Jews (who are unjustly accused of never having resisted), women (who are practically omitted in the history of resistance), and non-Jewish Germans, as well as many of the old labor movements (who also are hardly mentioned). They fought the Nazis out of basically moral convictions and out of abhorrence of racial superiority.

4) The decision to be an active resister meant not only a decision for possible death; that would have been easy. It meant isolation from the whole fabric of a country in which one had grown up: it meant for the young ones a decision not to have children, or not even to marry. It meant giving up any hope for what we would call a normal life.

Finally, I want to convey a basic conviction about human beings:

They carry in them the seeds of destruction as well as great love and giving. It will depend on us, each person within each generation at all times, what we help to bring forth. This is an unending task.

That we have tried, bear testimony, God!
That we have tried and stood defeat and laughter,
that we have worked until we won and after
have tried again! Bear testimony, God!

And when they grinned and spat
and left us weeping
and left us all alone, and left no love,
You, who then must have seen us from above
bear testimony, that we were not sleeping.

Bear witness, when the future judges, God,
that we were wide awake and worked and tried,
and that we conquered, even though we died!
If you are there at all, bear witness, God!

Ruth Peiper (Gisa's sister),
at the age of 20, in exile

Chapter One

Childhood—World War I and Revolution

$\mathcal{F}$irst memories? I don't know whether they are firsts. Oddly, they have to do with leaves. A city girl, grown in the cramped quarters of a Berlin "Mietskaserne"—can one translate this word? They were the ugly high rowhouses built under Wilhelm the II with the typical "Berlin windows," narrow, a pretense at something to let in light. And yet, my first memory seems to be leaves, marvelous branches full of something green and dark red glistening before my hands, my hands reaching for them, trying to touch while the wind sometimes puts them out of my grasp. I sit in a little carriage, pushed by a woman with an ample bosom. I know she is a neighbor and she has taken me out in the twilight and somehow I love her because she put those heavenly moving leaves into my carriage. I feel the incredible joy in me. Has this always stayed with me? I remember that they laughed at me when I was a little older—a five year old—because I never lifted my feet when fall came and the rustling leaves were lying in the streets. Again, I feel the joy of hearing the sound, of feeling the soft swish of them, of seeing those magic colors. And I remember, later, about 12 years old, when a cousin who lived in the tree-less streets of North Berlin came to visit. She got crazy over seeing those trees in our street. She jumped up and down and tried to pull off leaves, and I stood and looked at her with a lump in my throat and so filled with pity—such aching, horrible pity, because she had no leaves at home. Leaves, leaves, they were life and death and beauty even when they were dying. My older sister later showed me how to press leaves, but I did not like to do it. I felt as if I was killing them, imprisoning them, and I loved the freedom of their moving.

My parents were young and poor and struggling. They had this little grocery store which I hated all my life. It made us "a living," but it ate out my father's soul because he had to be subservient to rich clients from the neighborhood—and he was anything other than an accommodating man. It made my mother into a "fretful mouse" who constantly had to apologize for the outbursts of her husband because one had "to make a living." It forced us children to carry out goods to the rich people who were too lazy to pick up even half a pound of butter. I carried small and large packages to them, forced to use the "Hintertreppen," those winding, uncomfortable, ugly stairs in the back of the buildings, reserved for beggars and "delivery persons," all those "inferior" human beings. Sometimes, when I did not have a large load, I tried to sneak into the front, where the stairway had carpets and one did not feel humiliated. But frequently the "Portier," the watchdog of the house, discovered me and forced me to take the back stairs. I was so angry, so hurt. I tried never to meet one of my schoolmates. If you grow up in a class society you may not feel poverty, but you feel the horrible sting of being someone "inferior" and I hated it, fought it, resented it. It continued through all my life.

But all this is later. Early memories, before the age of four, I can date this because at age four World War I broke out and I remember that moment.

I feel the softness of Mother's body when we crawled into bed with her and Father in the early morning on a Sunday. (Years later, when I got out of the concentration camp, I felt it again, this gentle warm flesh, but that time I held her like a child who needed protection. I remember thinking then, "My God, the roles are reversed. She needs my strength, my courage. She is so totally alone." I was alone then, too, but I was supported by my convictions and by Paul's love, though he was far away. We could not even write to each other, but my mother was much more alone. Her husband had died, her children were far away, nobody really was there—and her life had been the family, only the family and reading!) Yes, I felt the soft body protecting me and I always saw her reading or sewing, always, when she did not have to take care of the store, that miserable store! I swore that I would do anything in my life but tend a store.

Before the age of four, Father seemed so tall. I loved his singing, arias from the "Fledermaus" or "Rigoletto," I learned later. His voice was deep and caressing when he sang. His eyes twinkled behind his glasses. I loved him, but I was also very afraid of him. I felt his rages very early. He shouted and struck things with his fists when he was angry and frustrated—and that was often. No, he did not hit only things. He hit mother: he hit us. From very early on, I heard mother apologize for him: "You know, Emil is sick. He has a bad heart. That makes him nervous." She told that to relatives who felt sorry for her, to customers at whom he yelled—and she knew we needed them—and to us, the children cowering in a corner. I "see" in my mind the day he furiously pushed mother, screamed at her and then threw a big frying pan of eggs on the kitchen floor, that was supposed to be our dinner. Suddenly he stood still, then knelt on the floor and started to clean up, moaning.

I slept in the same room with my parents. I heard him try to make love to Mother and I heard her frequent refusals and his angry responses. I had no idea what was going on. I only knew that they were fighting and I always pulled the featherbed over my ears to shut out the horror that invaded me.

Hanna, my older sister, already slept in the other room. I began to become aware of her, because I was so jealous of her. From early on she seemed to be so beautiful, the same long hair like mother's, falling to her knees, the same soft grey, large eyes. What I saw in myself was this straggling, thin hair and those awfully thin arms. I was told later that I had been sick, seriously ill all those years before I went to school. I had all the children's sicknesses, whooping cough, diphtheria, measles and pneumonia; and I did not like to eat. But I did not know that then, I just thought of myself as ugly, especially compared with Hanna, who was singled out by neighbors as the beautiful child.

Two pictures: I lie in bed, wet towels hanging over me and I am so hot. They had packed me in ice and I had screamed knowing I was again that "bad" child. My mother and my aunt Mindzia were sitting at my bed talking. My mother cried, "She's dying, she is dying." My aunt said, "Now it is time." She got up and brought a pail of glowing coal. They put it near my bed and they threw water on it, pushing it around the bed. While the mist arose, they prayed and prayed in Hebrew. I was frightened, I wanted to get up and run away, but I could not. I fell asleep. Today I know that what seemed like witchcraft to them and to me was a sound way of getting more moisture into the air for this child whose whooping cough seemed to kill her.

Another picture: My father taking me by the hand and saying angrily: "Hanna is gone long enough. She is *our* child. Come on, Gisa, we bring her home." It was winter and we went to some people, rich people who loved Hanna. I did not go in, but my father did. And then Hanna came out of that house, dressed in a beautiful, knitted snowsuit and snowcap, all in white, pulling a sled. My God, we usually wore only dresses mother had made for us and we certainly could never buy a sled. There she was, beautiful and so much in demand. I felt very envious and yet very smug. I was father's girl.

There are so many memories, so many pictures and so early. I remember how horrible it was to button one's pants after having sat on the potty and how embarrassing not to learn that fast enough. There was a special day when I was sent to a neighbor because Mother was "sick." When I next saw her, she was lying in bed, but close to her was a baby with lots of dark hair, my new sister, Ruth. I had wanted a brother and had been told to put sugar on the windowsill for the stork who would bring him. Now I was told that it was because of me that this was a girl and not a boy! I had put granulated sugar out for the stork instead of lump sugar. But nobody had told me! Do people know what they do when they tease a child? I knew that Father, too, had wanted a boy and now it was my fault that it did not happen. I cried with shame and guilt and heard them talk about "that Gisa who always cried so much, that child cried when she did not get the right remnants for her doll's clothes, that child cried about everything." And they gave me a kind of nickname, "Gisa with the 'Puppenlappengesicht.' Gisa with the doll-remnant face." I never can look at photos of my early childhood without seeing this sad, sorrowful face. Oh, they never knew that I carried the guilt and fear and sadness of so much, so early in me!

But I loved Ruth from the beginning. Her eyes danced. She spoke early, and both of us older sisters taught her everything we knew. I can still say the long formula for aspirin, (dymetilamidophenil dymetil pyrazolon) which was one of the first I learned after I knew how to read. I taught it to Ruth and loved it when the then three-year old repeated it without hesitation. We two became very, very close friends.

Since we had a store, we had about the only telephone in the apartment house. I constantly was sent "upstairs" to call someone to the phone. I hated it. I was always out of breath when I ran up some stairs. On one of the landings was a huge spot, probably made by some water damage. That spot scared me to death. I knew a fairy tale of "Frau Holle" in which the horrible Mrs. Holle lived in a well and the girl who fell into the well had to help her shake the pillows so that the feathers were flying, that meant that it was snowing on earth. I imagined Mrs. Holle as a threatening witch. For some reason that spot represented the place where she was ready to drag me in. Anytime I had to call someone to the phone, I ran past this spot and arrived home breathlessly. Mother always wanted to know what had happened, but I simply could not tell her nor anyone else. They laughed enough about all the things I saw or imagined! I would lie in my bed and look at the ceiling and saw in the little cracks and patterns, birds and trees and hands. But when I told this once to Hanna, she humiliated me by laughing and telling everybody how crazy I was. And yet, I did see all this!

One day, I was told to call a neighbor to the phone whom we loved very much. We called him "Uncle Paprikastock" because he carried a cane in paprika color. I liked him especially because he never made fun of me (I had become so sensitive to this!), and sometimes he swung me into the air and I loved this. He spoke at the phone with great excitement that day, and after he hung up, he cried, "Mr. and Mrs. Peiper—Mobilmachung!" I never forgot the word. It meant "mobilization." World War I had started. I experienced it quite consciously though I was only four years old. The moment Uncle Paprikastock said the word, my father grabbed his chest. (Later only, much later, did I find out that my father had Angina Pectoris. As a teenager, I was sure that he was simply hysterical.) Mother started to cry. People started to pour into the streets and flags were hoisted. My parents were Austrian-Polish-Jewish immigrants, Father came from Krakow, Mother from Przmysl. They did not see war as something joyful. We had flags, always the Austrian as well as the German. I thought of Kaiser Franz Joseph as a kind old grandpa (which he surely was not) and of Kaiser Wilhelm as glamorous and someone I would love to see, but those impressions came more from the wider environment than from my parents.

I want to tell some about my parents, though I know far too little about them. In those years parents were not really people. They were parents. What I know about them is pieced together from what they told me occasionally, because I was always a very curious child and asked so many questions. They never talked spontaneously of their childhood.

Mother had grown up in Przmysl and she spoke with great love and admiration of her father. I don't know what he did for a living, but I know that his father had been a Torah scribe, a very admired profession. Such a writer had not only to be perfectly versed in Hebrew, he also had to be able to write superb calligraphy. (Both, my older sister and myself learned, enjoyed and did well in calligraphy.) I have pictures of my grandfather, though I never knew my grandparents. He has a gentle face framed by the traditional "payes", the long hair of the orthodox Jew wearing a "yamalca" (a small cap). I secretly kissed that picture. I loved him and dreamed of meeting him some day. I loved it when mother told me how courageous he had been! Once, a special rabbi had come to the little town where he lived. People went out of their homes to kiss his hands. My grandfather did not do this. He said, "Nobody is above anyone else, only God is. One does not kiss another person's hand!" Marvelous music in my early egalitarian ears!

Mother's mother died early, and her father married a woman who was not educated, not interested in books, not interested in the three children she inherited. My mother loved school. But one day, when she was about ten years old, she played with the dry hulls of raspberries and pressed them together into little balls. Some flew up and spattered the wall. As a punishment, she was not allowed to go to school any more. She was apprenticed as a seamstress. All my life my mother has been reading and reading, as if to make up for that deprivation. And, whenever my mother saw a beautiful ball, and had a little money, she just had to buy it for us children. How she loved to play ball with us! I learned to juggle three balls, and I learned it from her. Later, after she had told me that story, I always saw behind the balls the pathetic little pressed bunch of raspberries!

She had two brothers and one sister. All are dead now, some killed by the Nazis. The brothers preceded her to Berlin, which was at that time the great hope for poor Jews from the Eastern countries where cruel pogroms constantly interrupted their lives and where poverty allowed no way out of misery. (The stories about the "Stetl" sound so lovely, but I have no sentimental longing for it. People somehow "live" everywhere under any circumstances, but much of it was a life of degradation, hopelessness and recurring fear.) Mother, 16 years old, shy, with her heavy hair piled on her head so as to look more adult, arrived in Berlin frightened and with murderous headaches. There was her brother! She opened her arms and called to him in Polish. Wham! Instead of the welcoming arms she got a heavy cuff against the already painful head: "Don't you dare speak Polish here! Here one speaks only German." She learned her lesson: The men were in charge and anything Polish was forbidden. We children later chided our parents for never teaching us Polish. The Slav language would have opened another world for us. But my parents spoke that language only when they did not want us to understand what they said. After World War I, two young cousins came to visit from Poland and I finally learned a few words.

Father was the youngest of 11 or 12 children. Both his parents died when he was still very young. He grew up as one of his oldest sister's children, who had eight or nine children. They lived first in Krakow. His father had been a butcher. Father's love was books. Still, who had the money to study? Early in life, he felt anger against all oppression and joined the then-forbidden labor movement. He read Russian, Polish and German socialist literature: he joined some demonstrations that were brutally dispelled. He hated the home in which he grew up. He was a "nuisance" to them, just an additional mouth to feed. He told me that, when they wanted to punish him, they took away his pants (he had only one pair) and he could not go anywhere. All the other children in the family made fun of him. After my father had a stroke at age 52, and not too long before he died, he cried out, "Give me my pants, oh, give me my pants!" I was the only one who understood what those words meant and why there was such agony in his voice. He was back in his childhood and totally impotent, because they had taken those pants away. I don't know how he got to Berlin. He was there earlier than Mother. They got to know each other because the families knew each other: all the immigrants lived closely together. After father's death I found many letters from him to my mother written during the time they were courting. Here was this young 19-year old man who had not been allowed to go to school, writing the most beautiful letters in perfect German and telling her glowingly about his theater visits and his reading of Schiller and Goethe and Shakespeare. He knew more literature than many intellectuals I have met later in life.

The two small rooms in which our family lived were always full of books. He introduced me not only to the classics, but also to the Socialist writers, such as August Bebel and Lilly Braun. He loved to read poetry aloud, mostly to me, something I have kept doing all my life. We earnestly discussed Heinrich Heine when I was eight or ten years old, and he explained to me the fable of the three rings in Lessing's Nathan the Wise when I first did not quite understand. But I know little about his early life.

Back to the outbreak of World War I. Pictures, hundreds of them in my head: cars—there had been few of them previously, now running through our street, almost running over my precious ball, sirens sounding with the special sound of the Kaiser's "Leitmotiv," everybody running out to see the Crown Princess or the flying scarves of the Kaiserin and a funny feeling somewhere in my child's insides to hear the jubilations and see mother cry. Henryk, a cousin from Poland, came to visit. He was of draft age and would soon be in the Austrian army. Henryk affected my life profoundly. I fell in love with him at the age of four, deeply in love. He was lean and beautiful and he was good and he treated me from the first moment on like a person. He watched Hanna build houses and bridges with her "Steinbaukasten" (a kind of Lego). I felt so hopelessly clumsy next to her. But, while he was attentive to her skill, he held me on his lap and I could feel his arms around me and see his face turned to me when I had some-thing to say. Later, when he was in the army, I cried because I was afraid he would be killed. On father's desk was a picture of him with his family, put in a paper envelope. I could not reach it. So, when no one would see me, I climbed on a chair, then on the desk top, took out the picture and kissed him, secretly and tenderly. Nobody, but nobody should know of this! Why was I so afraid—all through my childhood—of being made fun of? I am not sure. But there were many of those secrets, that I had to hide from anyone.

I heard about the poor soldiers in the hospitals and I imagined myself being a nurse taking care of them. I bandaged them and held my hand over their hand and I rocked them the way I loved to be rocked. I always went to sleep with the corners of the featherbed in my arms. I pretended these were poor soldiers I had to protect.

Henryk: He came back healthy from the war and studied medicine. Just after he had passed his final examinations, it was discovered that he had a terminal kidney disease. He came with his parents to Berlin which was supposed to have the best medical care. He was more beautiful than ever with an inner serenity that filled me with awe and love. I was then 15 years old. I knew Hanna and one of my cousins were also in love with him, and I felt they had prerogatives as they were older. This was a period in my life when I had read much and was constantly struggling with religion and philosophy. I cried out to God that he should not let a person like Henryk die, that it was not for me that he had to live, but for mankind. I visited him almost daily in the hospital. It was far away from where we lived. I had to take streetcars which nauseated me: I had to walk much, but I was there, reading poetry to him every day: Ernst Toller and Fritz von Unruh, and dramas, especially Schiller and Shakespeare. Had it meaning to him? I don't know. I only knew that he always made me feel that it was important, that he loved my coming to see him and my reading to him. I wrote a poem, but never showed it to him or anyone,

Du bist ein Gott, kein Mensch;
wenn andre sich in Schmerzen winden

liegst Du still.
Zum Tode, zur ewigen Nacht verurteilt,
predigst Du das Leben.
Wir sind nicht wert, den Staub zu küssen,
den bein Fuss berührte.

Translation:

You are a God, no mortal;
If others would thrash in pain
you lie quietly.
Condemned to death, to eternal night
you preach life.
We are not worth to kiss the dust
which your feet touched.

I walked down the street and prayed, no, bargained with God: "Let him live. I don't want anything from him. Just let him live. If you let him live, I will truly always believe in you. I will keep all your laws, just let him live."

One day I came home from school. Mother put her arms around me, "Henryk died this morning, Gisa." I did not look at her. I ran out of the store, running, running, cold like a stone, blindly saying, "Oh, God, what kind of a God are you? What kind of a God are you?" I felt like breaking in a thousand pieces.

They sat "Shiva" in the dark rooms of one of my very pious uncles: they talked about Henryk as it is custom among Jews. I sat separated from them. I could not shed a tear. I felt alone, excluded from those adults: I hurt and hurt. My Aunt Mindzia, one of father's sisters, the one I always loved, came to me. She put her cheek next to mine (I still feel it—it was something warm I had not felt for days) "Cry, Gitele, cry! You loved him so. Cry, my Gitele." "Gitele," the sweet sound of the Jiddisch diminutive: nobody else called me that. Now it meant love and being a child, not a rebel against God. I threw myself on Aunt Mindzia. I moaned and cried as the women in ancient biblical times, as I would do more than a half century later when he died, Paul, my beloved!

But back to me as the five year old: Father had to go away to war. I heard Mother crying, "But he has a bad heart," and, "What will I do alone with three small children?" Still, Father left one summer day. I sat in front of the store in my child's chair and waved to him. He carried a suitcase in his hand; Mother stood behind me crying, and so I cried too.

She was so pretty, this Mother of mine. Her sister told me, when I was an adult, that people turned their heads when they saw her, this slim young woman with the big grey eyes, the long, long ash blond hair, the fine nose. How we teased her about her obviously not totally Mediterranean heritage. But she was also very strong. I have always known my mother working—sewing, taking care of the store—alone or with Father, but more and more she had to take on the major responsibility. I saw her crying when she had to use a hammer and chisel to open the huge wooden crates in which eggs were delivered to the store at that time, but she did it. She ordered flour and sugar on credit to be able to sell. Later, when Father returned, he was horrified about this. Nothing was allowed to be bought on credit, everything had to be paid in cash, otherwise "we would land in jail," he said. He never even had a bank account. (I learned to write my first check at the age of 32 in Pittsburgh, PA in the U.S.A. by asking my landlady how to do this.) One must not make debts, one must only buy what one can pay for in cash, immediately. He screamed that at Mother. She stood her ground, "We would have starved without credit, and we will not have a store without occasionally buying on credit." It was done as she said. But I, still today, am more of my Father's daughter, though with my head I know that my Mother was right. Buying beyond one's means! Terrible!

One of my uncles occasionally helped Mother. Yet, she worked all day in the store: she sewed all our clothes, and every night she washed and ironed and starched those white, lovely eyelet dresses: "My children will look as good as all those rich children in our street."

Aunt Mindzia's husband was taken prisoner the first year of the war. He had been a jolly, round man. He was my Mother's brother, and Aunt Mindzia was Father's sister. They had four children. Those cousins and we were not only biologically like brothers and sisters, we felt that way. And now that Aunt Mindzia was alone and without a husband, the family became totally part of ours. Some of the cousins always slept and ate with us. How my mother did this, I don't know. The quarters in which we grew up were very cramped, totally misbuilt, as only Berlin apartment houses could be. One entered climbing some steps into the store. On one side of the store was a room which lay over the cellar. A large part of the already small room was taken up by a built-in double table with a window on top of it. I spent practically my childhood on that table. There I kept my dolls, read later my books, dreamt, talked secrets with my friends, or used the table as a jumping pad to jump into my parents' beds which took the rest of the space of that room. At night the table was turned often into a bed where my cousins slept. On the other side of the store was the second room, a little larger, but always dark because it had only a narrow window opening on to the courtyard. There we ate our main meals and at night we had to bring our featherbeds, piled up during the day on those of our parents, to make up on the couch where Hanna slept, on the sofa where I slept, and on a small children's bed brought in for Ruth.

We had a girl who helped carry out the goods for the store, and helped with whatever else had to be done. She also slept in this room, or, when my cousins were there, she slept in a small corridor that branched off the store. That corridor! It was totally dark, but it had a mirror and a small loft. For Ruth and for me it became our secret kingdom. We retired there when we wanted to do something special, especially when we became actors—and we "acted" very early in our lives. We knew hundreds of poems by heart and we acted them out. We were kings and queens, and peasants and later Marquis Posa and Don Carlos in one of Friedrich Schiller's plays. In this corridor we could be anything, and we also hid there when Father was in one of his rages.

The second room opened into the kitchen. I hated that kitchen, and I know why I later fell in love with bright, modern American kitchens. It was dingy: the water drip always produced rust stains that we scrubbed every day. The big coal stove (gas came later) had to be watched all the time. There was a shortage of coal during the war. We wrapped briquets in newspaper to keep the heat a little longer. We also had a "heating box," a box packed with straw in which food could be kept warm. But often food was also kept warm wrapped in some old clothes and put under the feather beds. Under the window was an icebox. That was one part of the kitchen I liked. I often sneaked in to lick the dripping ice. Marvelous! And from the kitchen a door led to the bathroom and toilet. The bathroom walls were always sweating. The paint on the bathtub was always peeling—to my delight! I scratched pictures into it. The oven for a bath was heated once a week. One thing about this ugly bathroom: it was the only place where one could have privacy. That became important later, when I had fights with my father around religion and ideology, and I needed a place alone to cry and to read! I read more Nietzsche and Rilke poetry on the toilet seat than anywhere else!

Yes, and there was the cellar. We kept mostly eggs and later even chickens down there. In the days of my rebellion I wanted badly to move into the cellar to have a place of my own, but father would not hear of it—"No daughter of mine sleeps in a cellar."

But, I am jumping ahead. It is still war and I am not yet in school. One incident stands out in my mind: It is around Christmas. A young woman comes running into the store: "Mrs. Peiper, we have arranged to have charades (living pictures) for Christmas and suddenly the baby that should be the Christ Child is sick. Can we borrow your Ruth for that?" Mother, the pious Jewish woman, did not even hesitate. "Sure, you must have your celebration, but, please, let the two older girls come along to see this." Oh, we were excited! There was my sister, high up on the stage, lying in the crib, the light shining in her big brown eyes, the angels holding glittering gifts up to her. She sat so still, she did not cry. Once she moved, and Mary's beautiful hair moved too. My heart swelled with enchantment. And later they asked whether children wanted to come up and say poems. Hanna always had been shy, but I always wanted to act! There I stood, declaiming before the whole crowd, "From draus, vom Walde komm ich her, ich muss Euch sagen, es weihnachtet sehr." ("Outside, from the woods I come. I must tell you it feels like Christmas.") Mother smiled: people came to admire Ruth. Somehow, I will never understand bigots.

The winter was very, very cold. There was less and less fuel and our clothes were not very warm. I always cried coming from the cold into the warmth; the fingers and toes hurt terribly. Feet and legs were often frozen blue. Mother rubbed them with glycerin and that was added agony. She would dance with us when we came in from the cold to get us warm, that was the best. Then we laughed....

She cried when letters came from my father. One day she cried and jumped and acted really strange. I heard her say, "He is sick, he is coming home! He is coming home!" I did not understand that one could cry with joy and with relief. And father came back, but the war continued.

I went to school. It was not far to go, but I always ran because I was afraid of being late. There was a big clock on the top of the school, but I could not read it. Nobody at that time knew that I was very nearsighted and astigmatic. Hanna made fun of my not being able to read the clock. I still smart seeing before my eyes her drawings of me standing before a clock with my head crooked, indicating that I was "dumb." I was supposed to learn to read, but I could not distinguish the letters. I bent deeply over the "Fibel," the first reader, and Hanna took my braids and bound them to the back of my chair so that I could not do this. I cried, and moaned, "This damned reading!" My family was shocked to have a retarded child on their hands. I don't remember who suggested to get my eyes checked. I don't remember the eye doctor. I remember the shame of wearing glasses and knowing that I was now uglier than ever before, but I do remember the immense joy of reading. Later, mother sometimes sighed, "Stop, stop reading! Oh, God, this is the child who once said, 'This damned reading.'" I loved school. It was like a haven. Nobody yelled there, and nobody made fun of me. And I loved learning, it was so exciting! I loved my teacher in those first grades, a gentle young woman. Sometimes I observed her crying behind the book that she held. My heart went out to her. How do children know? I knew that her fiancee was in the war and she was afraid. And I knew the day she had the letter that told her he had been killed. She was no more the same. She never smiled. And the day the defeated German armies marched back into Berlin, she stood at the school window and cried openly—and I, seven years old, could not do anything, only almost break down with her.

We celebrated victories all the time in the school, but the food got worse. We were lucky that we had a store. The broken eggs were always for us and mother could make miracles out of flour, water and eggs. People stood in long lines before our store to get food. A policeman with a big helmet and a wide blue cape helped keep order and he became our friend. He especially loved Ruth, who played hide-and-seek under that wide cape. But there were goods we had to stand in line for, especially butter, if there was any to be had at all. I was always sent to stand in line because I was little and thin and people often let me go a little ahead of them. The most dreaded words were always, "There is nothing anymore." But I hated standing in line and swore, as I had sworn to never have a store, never to stand in line for anything. One little incident stands out in my mind, because I felt guilty about it for a long time, and at that time I thought I was really a criminal. I had gotten the butter that day. It was wrapped in a stiff waxed paper. I was so hungry for butter. With my teeth I tore open a little corner, pressed out a little butter, licked it off and closed it so that nobody could see it. Oh, this marvelous forbidden fruit! And the torture of conscience, never relieved. Only now I confess!

People looked more and more grey. I hated potatoes; they were blue and sweet from frost. The Russians had been driven into the Mazur lakes in Tannenburg in East Germany. The country celebrated, but in my imagination I saw them drown and I cried. I had terrible dreams: some I still remember: a huge Zeppelin fell into our cellar and burned and the whole street burned. Or: soldiers dug trenches and all the dirt fell on them.

One day Father took me along to carry goods to customers. We had a little wooden wagon. He pulled it and brought the goods into the houses while I waited outside. Suddenly, while he was gone, two huge tanks came rolling down the street, searchlights turning the evening into day. Soldiers sat on them, shouting and singing, waving red flags. I trembled, but I stood watching the precious wagon as I had been told. Father came out of the house, put his arm around me and said, "Don't be afraid, Giselchen, those are not bad people, they don't mean any harm to us. They just want to get rid of the Kaiser who got us into this horrible war." Thus I experienced the great revolution. The Kaiser became a person to despise and make fun of. He was not even courageous: he ran away and asked for pity. Most monarchies in Europe toppled. I never will have any love for kings and queens. They proved to be cowards during those harsh days of the revolution. There was violence in the streets. When I visited my relatives in the north of Berlin, I saw holes in the walls made by gunfire and was told to crawl under a bed when I heard that noise. But I don't really remember fear. I knew it was not directed at us.

Once Father took me for a walk through the Tiergarten, the beautiful large woods in the middle of Berlin. We walked over a bridge spanning the "Landwehrkanal," a channel. He said, "Here they killed Karl Liebknecht and Rosa Luxemburg and threw them into the water. Remember, they were martyrs. I never agreed with them, because they, too, preached violence, but one should not have killed them." They had been leaders of the Spartacus, a radical, communist group, but both of them were really idealists. Later I read Luxemburg's letters written in prison and cried for her because those letters showed a tender soul, feel-

ing with people, but also with animals. She described buffaloes
(or was it steers?) brought into the prison courtyard and how she
felt like crying seeing their large, velvet sad eyes. I cried for
Rosa Luxemburg as I had cried as a small child for Joseph when
his brothers threw him into a pit. Why were people so cruel?

There are so many events, "pictures" in my mind during those
years of 1918 to 1922, age 8 to 12.

There was Hanna, contracting scarlet fever, my beautiful,
admired and secretly envied older sister! I trembled for her life.
The doctor—I hated him because he was always rough, authoritarian, treated all of the family including my parents as if we
were idiots—the doctor insisted that we younger children had to
be removed from the home so as not to contract the illness. Ruth
went to a cousin I loved, beautiful Salzia, who had a slight
speech handicap and whom her parents had forced to marry a
man they thought was best for her. (He turned out to be abusive
and uncaring.) She had been in love with a young doctor, a
Christian, and, coming from an orthodox Jewish home, it was absolutely forbidden that she could marry him. To me she was a romantic heroine and I detested her parents, especially her mother.

I was sent to some neighbors, an older couple without children. I felt totally alone and abandoned. I am sure that those
people were not mean, but they did not understand children. The
woman gave me some big sales catalogs to look at, and when I had
finished, she said, "Now, you did not see everything. Start all
over again." My eyes brimmed with tears. I missed my family
and I hated those long days. Lying in the bed, I turned to the wall
papered with red roses and imagined myself to be in an enchanted
castle, but it did not help. There was a corner window in that
apartment. Until late in the evenings, I sat there staring at the
corner of our street where we lived, which I could see from the
window, and prayed that I could go home soon. Once, my father
came to visit. I hurled myself into his arms with heartbreaking
sobs, "Take me away, take me away!"

"That ungrateful child," the neighbors said. My adored
cousin said I could stay with her...Oh, Salzia, she had such a

miserable life: two beautiful children, but a husband who pushed her around and never took care of her; and finally after the advent of the Nazis, she was deported to Poland and killed. But we did not know the future at the time she let me come to her house and kissed me and made me feel part of the human race again. And a little later I could see Hanna and tell her that she was so beautiful! We two always loved each other and detested each other and fought with each other, occasionally physically. But around the age of 12 I learned about the Stoics in school. I decided that I wanted to be like those, and that changed, at least for a time, my whole behavior. Once Hanna broke a special pen of mine. I was furious, but I said calmly, "It is only a *thing*." And she almost fainted. Gisa, the Stoic!

There was a horrible influenza epidemic shortly after the war. Many people died. All of us had this murderous flu. I see before me Mother, in a long white nightgown, her hair falling to her knees, moving from one bed to another putting cold compresses on us, talking in a soothing voice, even to Father who fretted terribly. "Emil, it will get better. Sleep, Mendele (that was his real name), sleep." Only later I knew that she had been as ill as any of us. And all of us recovered.

There was little and very poor food available. One summer my older sister and I were sent to a children's camp. It was a disastrous experience. The young helper was a gentle and kind woman, but she had to submit herself to the supervisor, a mean, harsh person. We children gave her secretly all kinds of horrible names, always related to her tendency to beat us mercilessly. I was a very shy and conforming child. I was never beaten by her, because I was so afraid of her. The food was abominable. It was not only tasteless, but it was often rotten. One day the cabbage was full of maggots. For the first time all of us, including the young counselor, revolted, sat before our plates and refused to eat. The supervisor threatened a general beating, and forced us to eat the stuff. Obediently, I always ate those disgusting meals and always promptly had to get up from the table and throw up.

Another torture were the evenings. There was an epidemic of head lice. Though we certainly were not responsible for them, all of us were terribly ashamed of having lice. Every night the counselor went with a fine comb over our long hair, killing lice with her fingernails (they made a horrible little noise), and then poured some fluid over our heads that burned the scalp. A towel was wrapped around the head, and we lay crying and crushed in our beds. Who knows whether my constant concern with the treatment of children in institutions had not its root in this summer?

Mother only once, as far as I remember, went on a trip with us, to Kolberg, one of the places at the sea. I have a photo from that time, when she looks pale and thin. She had had a miscarriage, twin boys. It must have been a terrible disappointment, because the whole family wanted some boys with us. We children were not told anything. I learned about it much later, at a time the Nazis were in power and I hear myself saying, "Good, they died early. They would have been killed first, because they were male."

Kolberg was a great experience. I saw the sea for the first time. I wrote letters to my father about it and I wrote poetry. The sinking sun over the sea made me feel so much part of nature. I bent down to the sand, holding it, caressing it and almost kneeling.

Just the year before I had begged my parents to be allowed at one of the high holidays to visit a reform synagogue to which some of my school friends went. We went to an orthodox, small "Schul." I loved singing with the others and once, everyone kneeled and it made me feel good and holy. I told my father about it and he said, "We Jews are a proud people. We are not supposed to bow down before anyone, not even before God." That impressed me and I decided never to kneel again. I wanted to look God into the face. I was very pious and loved all the religious laws. I even fasted on the high holidays, though I did not have to do this as a young child. But even then I began to question a few things. I was told, for instance, that I was not supposed to look at the Torah when it was taken out of its shrine. One of the neighborhood boys who was a "Cohen" (a member of the priesthood) was allowed to be in front with the Torah and be part of removing it. I was furious, "He is dumb and poor in Hebrew. Why is he allowed to see it and not I?" Rebellion started.

Counter forces against the German republic started early to develop. And with it came anti-semitism. The swastika appeared on street walls long before Hitler. We children walked around with small pocket knives to scratch them out whenever we saw them. One day, the swastika appeared big and bold in chalk on the blackboard in school. We knew the girl who had marked it, but she only mocked us when we confronted her. We were a number of Jewish children in that particular school, but there was only *one* Jewish teacher, a woman, and she was only allowed to teach religion in special release time. The German republic had not yet changed those bigot laws. I was elected by all the Jewish girls to seek her out and to tell her about our complaint. There I was, little Gisa, (I was always the second shortest in my class) my braids dangling down, afraid but full of righteous wrath. I finally found her. Her sweet, always sad face looked even sadder. "I don't know what I can do, but I will try. Just go back to your lessons." Well, the homeroom teacher of our grade, tall, thin, erect like a tin soldier, hair always carefully curled, a lorgnon hanging on a chain from her neck, came into the room, rapped her stick for silence and, with the swastika still behind her on the blackboard, said, "It has come to my attention that a certain person in this class has complained to Miss X. Politics do not concern us, and certainly are not supposed to concern you. I will not ever hear about complaints again. I am ashamed of that person." I threw myself over the school desk crying my eyes out. Such injustice! Shamed before the whole class! Not one of those who had asked me to do the complaining came forward to say that she also was part of this. For the first time in my life I experienced treachery and cowardice and being left holding the bag. I cried all the way home. When I told my father, he said, "Now, you have learned. Jews are not supposed to fight. They are only supposed to suffer." Salt into my wounds, and hurt and my first inner questioning of Father's wisdom. Was he right? Why should this be so? And he belonged to the Social Democratic Party and he let me read those books that spoke about the struggle of the working class! No, he could not be right.

School: It became more and more interesting. I could not imagine myself not going to school, not studying. But the class society of Germany still existed in its school system. Poor children went to the "Gemeindeschule," learning their ABC's, and could be beaten by the teachers. Their education ended at age 14. Children whose parents had more means, could go to a school that allowed them to be there until the age of 16, but made entrance into higher education impossible. I was in such a school. But at the age of 11 one could transfer into a Gymnasium, if one had money and the brains. Hanna had already transferred to the Gymnasium. She was excellent in mathematics and natural sciences and had a scholarship. Now I begged my parents to be allowed to try to get into that school too. My strength was in literature and history and languages and I wanted so badly to go on and study. Mother insisted that there was no money for a second child to do that. Even with a scholarship, there was some tuition to pay and books to buy, and such schooling would not earn anything for a long time. Mother insisted that, "any girl can make a living sewing." Oh, God, I could not! I hated sewing. Hanna was good at that too, but not I. I wanted books and books and books. I cried and cried. I literally cried my way into school. I also promised that from the day of my entrance into the Gymnasium, I would pay for all my clothing, shoes, etc., and help in the detested store. I did. I kept my promise. Father finally said, "If a child wants to learn that badly we should let her." I think he was secretly proud of me. And, later, when it was Ruth's turn, there was no question about her transferring into the "Gymnasium."

Childhood memories crowd in on me. I hardly know how to sort them out. I remember the horrible time of major inflation when money was worth nothing. My father admonished me to give the teacher the tuition money immediately because the next day it was worth nothing. Our store made good money only around Passover, when people bought supplies for a whole week in advance. But it was a horrible time for us: Everything that was regularly sold in the store during the year had to be taken out and stored in the cellar to make room for the supplies for the Passover: large rolls of matzot (unleavened bread), flour and some special goodies. The matzots were stapled high up on the walls of the store and the adjoining room. There was no room to play or study, and hardly any to eat. I see we three girls crowded in a corner, I held my finger in my ears so as not to hear Ruth learning English vocabulary or Hanna mumbling Latin. I tried to work on mathematics which at that time I truly enjoyed; that changed later with a poor teacher. The worst of that time was that we got practically no sleep. The goods had to be prepared during the night: flour to be put into one-pound and two-pound bags, orders from customers put into huge boxes, organized and checked. The next day the orders had to be carried out. I fell asleep sitting on the toilet. I cried with tiredness. Once my father kept me away from school for a day. I never forgot the humiliation when the teacher wrote a note, saying that helping in a store was no excuse for staying away from school. It never would have occurred to anyone of us to lie about why we could not go to school.

Yet the Seder evening was pure joy and my favorite holiday. My increasingly social consciousness loved the symbolism of a celebration of liberation from slavery. I loved my father dressed in a "Kittel" (a loose gown) with a silver braided cap on his head, leaning against a beautiful pillow, symbols of being a free man. I loved the playfulness of some of the songs. I imagined the prophet Elijah entering the house and drinking of the wine we reserved for him. For both Seder evenings, each of we three girls was allowed to invite a friend who had no such celebration at home and they were invited to stay overnight. In spite of those tiring days preceding this, we loved talking half of the night. Once my Polish cousins visited us for this. I learned a little Polish and they expressed their pride in the newly created

Poland. How that hurt later when most Poles did not lift a finger
to help Jews when the Nazis deported and tortured them!

Art and friendship, which all through my existence have
made life more livable when it seemed too dark, entered strongly,
forcefully, rewardingly.

Berlin was full of great art, sculpture, painting, dance, and
theater. There were the Greek excavations and the marvel of the
Pergammon altar! There was the Kaiser Friedrich Museum with
the old masters. Dürer and Holbein were my favorites. I found
Raphael a bit too sweet, but then, there was Titian and, oh, the
Dutch painters! The greatest excitement for me was in the
"Kronprinzenpalast" with the then modern art, the impression-
ists and the expressionists! My father did not allow us to take the
streetcar or subway on a sabbath. We lived in the west of Berlin
and the museums were in the north. We walked, approximately
one and one half hours to get there. Then we walked through the
galleries drinking in the beauty and then took the long way back.
It never seemed to be a hardship.

I learned to really understand expressionism through a complete stranger. One day, Hanna and I were looking at canvasses
by Franz Marc and I marveled at his strong colors. There was a
painting of Francis of Assisi, either by Marc or Haeckel, I don't
remember. The saint had a very small body and a big head with
huge sad eyes. With the piping loud voice of my 8 or 9 years I
commented on how awful that was! A man who had walked quite
awhile behind us said in a serious voice, "Now, wait a minute.
The artist wants to *express* something, something he feels when
he thinks of the saint. To him, Francis of Assisi cared little about
his body: it was unimportant to him. But in his head and in his
eyes especially, lie all his caring for men and all the creatures in
the universe. That is what is important about this man. Can you
see it? The artist expresses what he sees and feels and lets us feel
that too. That is expressionism." How marvelous! A miracle! An
adult who took seriously the comments of a little girl and did not
think her too stupid to understand! Only a week later I had a
similar experience: I rode in the streetcar in the evening standing

on the outside platform because I always got nauseated inside. The moon shone and the stars were out. I craned my neck to see. I pointed out to my little sister, Ruth, the various constellations of the stars. Again, a stranger spoke up and showed us other constellations. He also told us about the lenses needed to see more and how those were ground. Adults could care, adults could tell you things, adults did not only make fun of you! It made me feel very happy.

The sad, accusing and strong drawings of Käthe Kollwitz became my standing companions and next to them Ernst Barlach's spiritual sculptures. My greatest wish for my 11th birthday was a folder of Kollwitz' drawings and I got it! I kept it carefully until I had to abandon all this when I had to escape from the Nazis. I have many Käthe Kollwitz copies in my possession now, but I always mourn the first folder I had. She had great influence on me. Later, when I was about 17 years old, I distributed leaflets at a rally against Italian fascism. There I met Käthe Kollwitz. Shyly I approached her and stammered how much her art meant to me. The big dark eyes looked at me seriously, "You are young and you are full of ideals. Good. But remember this also when you get older. Too many people forget." I hope I never will.

The new dance: Mary Wigman (who later, to her shame, became a Nazi.) At that time she was new and exciting and full of promise of a new art form. And Palucca and Laban! The theater: I read later Elisabeth Bergner's autobiography. I can't tell better than she does about the theater of that time. The great actors, Alexander Moissi who made us cry when he presented the onset of mental illness in the "Ghosts," Alexander Granach, Lothar Müthel and so many others! We had little money and we stood for hours in line to get a ticket for the "Olympus," the last rows upstairs in the theater where one had to stand during the whole performance. It was worth the pain to stand 2 hours in line and stand again for 3-5 hours to see the play when Elisabeth Bergner played St. Joan in Shaw's play and Max Reinhard was the director. And to see her in Turandot or the "Chalk Circle!" The HABIMAH came to Berlin and played the strange "Dybbuk." We learned about a new and different art form. I saw the opening night performance of Kurt Weil's and Brecht's "Three Penny Opera." Ruth could sing the songs. I cannot sing a note. I loved them, but I protested his materialism "Erst kommt das Fressen, dann kommt die Moral...." ("First comes food, then ethics.") He probably was right, but at the time I did not agree. I myself was acting in plays at school and in the youth groups. We played Gerhard Hauptmann and Strindberg, Ibsen. We read aloud Lagerloef, Björnstjerne Björnson, and especially Ernst Toller. It was an exciting time, this Berlin of the 1920's when so many new ideas exploded and one began to believe that humanity could change and become better. The school reformers, Wyneken, Geheeb and Berthold Otto spoke and we flocked to their presentations. Actually, it was Hanna who started that and she hated my always tagging along, but I would not miss any of this! Wittfogel spoke about his trip to Japan, about the lovely almond blossoms and about the children dying of neglect, destroyed by child labor.

Chapter Two

Adolescence

*W*ith all this around me, I moved almost imperceptibly into adolescence, one of the painful, beautiful, significant times of my life. Life was already intense, filled with so many questions and concerns, and life offered friendship with its sweet and sour awards. I was then 13 or 14 years old. There was Rollie. We were so close that we constantly walked together, always talking. Rollie's round face and long braids were always next to my small face with the much shorter hair. Rollie had no father and her mother was a "dissident," something like a Unitarian, totally unknown in our environment. (Only later my older sister also had a friend of this denomination.) Well, Rollie began to question my strict religious beliefs: "Man was not created by God," she said. She taught me about evolution. I began to read Darwin and Haeckel. Hanna read it too, but she hid the books when my father approached. I was thoroughly imbued with the ethics of being truthful and showed the books to my father. I thought he would discuss them with me, as we had discussed many other questions. Yet he only got angry and yelled at me. That did not help. Rollie disputed again and again the existence of God. I tried to prove it by saying that God had appeared to Moses and thousands of people had heard Him. Rollie gave explanations for this through natural events. We walked and walked discussing religion. Rollie was the pessimist. I the optimist. I wrote a poem to her:

Sonne, Sonne, Licht, Kraft
In allen Gliedern ist Leben, Leben,
Die Kraft in sich fühlen zu kämpfen, zu ringen
gegen alles, was dunkel, was kraftflos ist.

Leben und Jugend, was will man noch mehr?

Und über allem Sonne, Sonne!

Translation:

Sun, Sun, Light, Strength,
In our total being is life, life,
The strength we feel in us to fight
against everything dark and weak.
Life and youth, what more do we want?
And above everything Sun, Sun!

I loved Rollie, with the sweet intense love of early adolescence. I wanted to pull her out of her dark and unhappy moods. We read Schiller's Don Karlos aloud together. I was always Marquis Posa, the faithful friend who is willing to make sacrifices for the friend. Yet, after a time, Rollie began to turn to others. I lived through the awful experience of rejection not comprehending the "Why?" Pain at that age is just as severe as later and it is increased when one cannot tell anyone about it. I think Rollie moved away from Berlin.

I had another very good friend, Hilde, with whom the discussions about God and the world (Did Mephistopheles really exist? Should we be totally pacifist or should one sometimes allow for violence?) were less disturbing than with Rollie. We walked each other home from school, back and forth, and always arrived home late, to the chagrin of our parents, but we *had* to talk this over. The relationship with Hilde lasted until the end of our school years. (As far as I know, Hilde was later killed by the Nazis. I never heard of Rollie again.)

We read Freud and Adler's teaching and Marx and Bebel. Later, when I started in a school of social work in the U.S.A., it first puzzled me when Freud was taught as a dogma, and then later rejected as if everything he had taught was nonsense. We read him so early and so carefully and discussed pros and cons, never considering him an oracle. For awhile, at about the age of 16, we split into two camps, one Freudian, one Adlerian. I was Adlerian, because at that time I had experienced so much of the authoritarian role of the father, and also because Adler's teaching fitted better with my Socialist convictions. But that did not mean that we did not think quite a lot of Freud too, or that Adler became a God. I remember an incident which I described in my book, *Group Work in the Institution*, to show how important adult recognition of young people is:

> We were a bunch of sixteen-year-old boys and girls in a large urban center in Germany. In a culture that places a great deal of authority in the adult, youth is doubly rebellious, and so we were. We felt that no adult would ever understand us, but we felt happy and well related to our own age group. We were reading a great deal and at the time of the fight between the Freudian and Adlerian schools of psychoanalysis, we were strongly partisan one way or another. At this time, young Doctor Bernfeld announced six lectures on psychoanalysis. We were burning to go, feeling that we were just as well informed as any-

one else, but also knowing that our parents would only laugh at us, and besides, we had no money to pay for those lectures. We thought, therefore, that it was our right to sneak into those lectures without paying and without telling anybody about it. Each of us alone would have been afraid to do this, but as a group we felt justified and secure.

Before the first lecture we were posted at the entrance where the lecturer would enter, since this was not the public entrance, and we tried to go in right behind him. Suddenly Doctor Bernfeld turned. He had seen us and he confronted us directly. I have never forgotten my own feeling. I was absolutely sure that we would now be thrown out in disgrace and that the man of whom we thought very highly would probably laugh at us and call us "children," about the worst insult we could think of. Doctor Bernfeld's first calm words were, "Did you want to hear the lecture?" There was no rush of explanation on our part, but only a suspicious and resistant nodding of our heads. We were sure that if he did not throw us out at this point, he would start with a lot of questions. Instead of that he gave us a long intensive glance, reached into his pocket, and said, "I have a few extra tickets. If you sneak in today, you are not sure you can make it next time. If you want to hear the lectures, it is only valuable if you hear all six of them, so here they are." We could hardly thank him before he had left.

I doubt that Doctor Bernfeld ever had more intense and—I would almost say—more understanding listeners in his lectures than he had during the next six evenings. We did not miss a single one; we took notes. His incredible trusting and understanding gesture had even made it unnecessary for us to show off with this. We met after each lecture and discussed the content. I cannot remember the details of it. But I do remember the amazing feeling of peace that pervaded us, peace with ourselves and peace with "those adults." He had not only prevented the "delinquent act" of entering the lectures without paying for them, but he had restored a great deal of basic faith in an adult environment that seemed hostile to a group of adolescents.

(From Gisela Konopka, *GROUP WORK IN THE INSTITUTION—A MODERN CHALLENGE*, Association Press, New York, 1954, pp 196-198.)

School had so much meaning to me!

I loved my school and I hated it. I loved the knowledge. For instance, Miss Eggert taught literature and art. She asked us eleven-year-olds once to write about the presentation of death during antiquity and the Middle Ages. I wrote and wrote for hours about it. I was totally on the side of antiquity where the major presentation of death was a beautiful youth turning a torch upside down. During the Middle Ages, death had become an ugly and threatening skeleton. How wonderful for me to have to think through the meaning of those times. Miss Eggert explained to us why this had happened. We learned about the terror of pestilence during the Middle Ages. I also encountered for awhile the hostility of some of my Jewish contemporaries because I got very excited about such painters as Dürer, Grünwald and Fra Angelico. They presented Christ, the Apostles, the Crucifixion—and I knew all the New Testament stories and loved them. My young Jewish friends were shocked.

Miss Eggert was also my English teacher, and at that time I did not do so well. I remember vividly that she called me once to stay with her after class. She walked with me up and down the corridor of the school, her arm around me, saying earnestly, "You know you are a good student, and you can do excellent work. One does not throw away one's gifts." She talked about the need for excellence. Somehow it has always stayed with me that there was a demand made on me, but it was made while this usually very stern woman put her arm around me. A scolding would not have motivated me, but this serious appeal to my conscience helped.

I did like mathematics when it was taught by a teacher who loved it. He could even explain Einstein's theories and make them exciting. But later, when we had a teacher who taught mathematics in a dry, unimaginative way, I got terribly bored with it and read a lot of good literature holding the book under the desk. That included reading *Colette*, who was considered quite naughty by many people. She did help me through extremely boring mathematics lessons.

Then there was Latin: Every day, six days a week. I disliked Latin—I feared it. The teacher once told my mother that she hated to look at me during tests because I was looking so sick and trembling and crying. I thought it was stupid to learn a language that nobody spoke. To the horror of all my "learned friends" I regret even today, that I had to spend so much time learning Latin instead of Spanish or Italian.

But what I hated most in school was the authoritarianism of the system and especially some of the teachers' reactionary views. There was, for instance, a young history teacher. I loved history and would have totally enjoyed the classes, but his contempt for young people was disgusting. If he got angry, he threw his books on the table or on the floor and screamed at us. He was handsome but had slightly bowed legs. To get even with him we called him, "Apollo with the Lyra built into his legs." When teachers yelled at us, some of us sat with fists held tight under our desks. Hilde once wrote a little note to me: "Let us promise to each other that we will never forget!" I hope I have not forgotten, and I will always fight against adults who think they can lord it over young people.

The higher we went at school, the fewer students there were in the class. Among them were friends and rivals. There was a strong rival, a girl whose name I have forgotten. She was blond, tall, blue-eyed—everything the reactionary school system cherished at that time, even before the Nazis. She was the darling of most of the teachers. She was also intelligent. We kind of exchanged seats (we were seated according to our grades). Sometimes she was the first one, and sometimes I. That made for harsh rivalry. We each had our followers. I can't remember what we did to each other, but I do remember how angry I was that she was superb in gymnastics and I was not. I tried to jump hurdles and to run as fast as she could, but I did not make it. One of the students, Ullie, did very good cartoons. I can still see them before me: The fat Gisa trying to jump while the other girl only had to lift her beautiful long limbs. The differences were also political—her group was a very German-Nationalist group, reactionary, wishing for the return of the Kaiser; I and my followers were Democrats and Socialists, fiercely loyal to the young Republic. When Rathenau, the German foreign minister who tried to develop friendship between France and Germany and who was one of the few Jews in government, was murdered, the school factions showed themselves openly. There were those who welcomed that murder and there were those of us who mourned. The German Republic demanded that the school authorities call all the students together and give a memorial for Rathenau. In our school there was no teacher who wanted to speak at that memorial. The director, always with a high stiff collar and a strict face, was known to have hated Rathenau and everything he stood for. My Latin teacher, the only Jew in the Gymnasium, was a frightened mouse (early in the Nazi period she committed suicide). Some of us students volunteered to speak but something like that was unheard of! Finally, a little round Latin teacher, just as right-wing as the others, was appointed to give the eulogy. After all these years have passed I still hear her opening sentence, "De mortibus nil nisi bene." Translation: ("About the dead one should only speak good.") We understood this to be an insult.

Perhaps before telling about all the other things in my adolescence I can just as well tell about the ending of school. Actually, the few of us who made the "Abitur" (that's the final examination of the Gymnasium and entrance examination to the university) became quite close. We had gone on several trips together and together tried to defeat the often much too rigid supervisors. I can tell the same stupid stories that all adults tell reminiscing about their youth, about their foolish behavior when they are exposed to adults who don't understand the exuberance of young people. For instance, we made a trip to Bamberg. It has the most beautiful early Gothic cathedral in Germany. Bamberg's cathedral stands high on a hill. We loved the place and were quite reverent when we were inside of it. But something must have triggered our anger because of the continual admonishing that came from the teacher. So, when he turned his back, we seventeen-year-olds took small paper bags of candy that we had with us and threw them into the open window of the church school where a strict-looking nun was instructing children. The paper bags exploded in a burst of candy-rain inside the school. We hid behind the cathedral and thoroughly enjoyed the giggling faces of the children and the angry face of the nun, who leaned out of the window shouting at an unseen enemy. It was a foolish thing to do but oh, how we enjoyed it! This cathedral is one place that I have always yearned for, even when there was nothing I really wanted to come back to in Germany. In the days of exile I never yearned to go back to Germany, except once in a dream. In that one dream, I found myself back in the Bamberg Cathedral seeing its spires and the beautiful rider in it.

During the last years of school I sometimes had the privilege to go with Hanna to the university. She had started medicine there. I was enthralled and could hardly wait to start my studies.

In school I had taken German literature with the stern and reactionary principal of the Gymnasium. I disliked his politics but I loved his classes because he was so stimulating, and probably also because he said that I was a true writer. That surely was my ambition. Another class I chose voluntarily and with great interest was philosophy. I began to understand some of the relationships between religion and thought, and that really interested me.

The final examinations were exceedingly rigid. One was full of anxiety but as far as I remember, we all made it. The ending of school was always a large assembly in the "Aula." (assembly hall). Graduates had to come forward, make a deep curtsy, and receive the diploma. Whatever political "denomination" we belonged to, our class hated the authoritarian approach of the school. We swore to each other that none of us would curtsy. We were the first and only graduation class where each person took the diploma with head high and no bent knees!

And now, back again to earlier events. At around the age of twelve or thirteen, I spent one summer in East Prussia with Ruth and a young woman who helped in our store. She came from the country, one of the many poor peasant girls who came to Berlin to make a living. That summer she wanted to go back to her family because a younger brother was getting married. She wanted to take us along to show us her family and her home. There we were in a totally new environment: wide, endless meadows, the Baltic Sea, white sand dunes. Beautiful! The small farm house was full of people who lived there or came from neighboring places to attend the wedding. Having read much modern literature, I always thought of myself as very sophisticated. I already felt myself to be the champion of unmarried mothers, of subjugated people, but now I saw things I had only read about. The young peasant woman slept on the sofa with a man to whom she was not married. Oh, I understood love, but this seemed strange to me because she did not know him very well.

One of the fifteen-year-old neighbor boys came one evening to say that he wanted to go out. Suddenly his ear got boxed heavily by one of the older men right in front of all of us. I suffered with him and could feel how his pride was hurt. I learned that this man was his "master" to whom he was apprenticed. I knew that apprenticeship was a horrible exploitation. I knew this from reading, but I had not seen its reality right before my eyes.

Ruth wore a lovely pink dress with a large crocheted collar for the wedding. My mother, who could make something out of nothing, had made this from a few pieces of silk. Ruth looked lovely as a flower girl, walking ahead of the bride and groom together with another girl. I was very proud of her and described this experience in a detailed letter to my family. My beloved cousin, Annie, who was several years older than I, answered with a caustic letter saying how silly it was the blond Christian girl and dark-haired Jewish Ruth would walk together to the altar in a church! I was furious—there was nothing wrong with that!

Ruth and I were always very close and this summer brought us especially close together. She was my little sister whom I could protect, but with whom I could also talk about all the sadness that I had in me. I had read that Ernst Toller, my beloved writer, would soon be released from prison, and I had to talk with Ruth about that, and read Toller's "Song of the Swallow" to her.

At that time there were elections. We watched big landowners pick up farm workers on a wagon, plied them with beer, and deliver them drunk to the polling places. There, they made them put their cross on the ballot exactly where the landowners wanted it. We saw that, and we were appalled! That evening I went out into the meadow, threw myself on the ground, and cried and cried because the world was so bad and I could not do anything. I felt totally abandoned and desperate. Little Ruth came out to me, put her arms around me, and I, the "big sister," put my head into her lap. Ruth was the one who comforted me at that moment.

I had started to menstruate a short time before I went to East Prussia. I was very happy about that, because now I was a woman! Both Hanna and Mother had congratulated me when it happened and that made it very comforting to me. Now, in East Prussia, especially around the wedding time, I saw young men and women in tight embrace in the bushes. Obviously, I was a very impressionable child, and in spite of all that reading, I really didn't know how a child was conceived. I suddenly thought that I might be pregnant. It was a terrifying experience. I did not think there was anything wrong with having a child out of wedlock, but one had to be in love! Yet there was nobody. How had I become pregnant? I thought it may have happened because I was swimming with boys, and possibly one could be impregnated in the water. There simply was no other explanation. I did know that menstruation would cease when one became pregnant, and I did not menstruate at the time that I expected it. So, I assumed I was pregnant. I became very unhappy and anxious. There was nobody to whom to turn. We came back to Berlin. A few weeks passed, and I still did not menstruate. Mother sensed that there was something very wrong with me, and she asked gently, "What is it, child?" But I could not tell her. You cannot tell your mother! I asked Mother how children were born, and she told me; but she could not tell me how they were conceived, that was impossible to her. So I suffered until the period returned. I kept a diary at that time, which I do not have anymore, but I know that I wrote into the diary that never, ever would I allow young people to grow up without knowledge of their own sexuality and of sexual functions.

In the youth movement later, when I was a leader and finally had learned more about the "facts of life," I made it a point to discuss this with the younger girls. I remember that from that time on, all through my life, I have never understood why one should hold back and why this could not be discussed openly, letting young people know about their bodies, their own needs, their own responsibilities.

Chapter Three

Youth Movement

I was standing in the gym during a short intermission. A girl about one year older than I and one grade above me with long black braids, twinkling eyes, and a gentle face came to stand close to me. "I am Rose Ballin," she said, "and I would like to invite you to join the group to which I belong. We meet weekly, and we certainly go on hikes every Sunday." This invitation did not come as a surprise to me. Many young people belonged to youth movements.

I have to explain about the youth movements, because they are often totally misunderstood. They did not start with Hitler. The middle European youth movements, especially strong in Germany, Austria, England, in the Scandinavian countries, and somewhat in France, were protest movements starting around 1900. Their protest was against adults whom they saw as hypocritical. It was an anti-victorian, anti-authoritarian movement.

They wanted honesty in human relations. They fought confining artificial clothing. The symbols of that movement were the open-collar shirts for men and loose-hanging dresses for women. They rejected the confining corsets. They wore sandals in summer; their hair was not curled with curling irons but hung either loose or braided. The boys allowed their hair to grow longer than the usual custom. They hiked much, adored nature and poetry. They wanted to create a loving and natural world.

Sometime, I think it was 1902, a number of those "Wandervogel," as they were called, from various nations in Europe met on a mountain, the Hohe Meissner, near Kassel in Germany. They sang and danced (folk dancing, not ballroom dancing) and played guitars sitting round the fire. They ended their meeting with a pledge to be always truthful and to avoid any sham. I know this only from reading, since I was not yet born at that time.

The impact of the youth movement was somewhat lost during World War I, because it had been an international impetus, and during that war nationalism was high. After World War I, it not only grew but had a strong influence on many of the reform movements. In Germany after World War I, it split into a vast variety of groups with various ideological credos. Almost every political party had its own youth movement, so had every religious denomination. Their forms were quite similar—they hiked and sang and met usually several times in the week; but the content of meetings was not the same. Every Sunday, early in the morning, one could see small groups of young people at the train stations, each group in their particular clothing, often with a small flag of their own choosing, assembling to go out into the open country. The joining of such a group usually meant a commitment to its ideals and the work it was doing.

I was early attached to the idealism, the adventurous life and the marvelous development of friendship I saw in those groups. I did not know yet which one to choose. I knew that the group Rose belonged to was a Jewish group, but not a Zionist one. Many of my cousins belonged to Zionist youth groups which prepared them for a life in Palestine. The Kibbutzim in Israel grew out of youth movements. I had long talks with them. I visited their group several times in the evenings. I especially loved one cousin, Aharon, who belonged to one of those groups. Aharon and I were like brother and sister (we still feel that way), but I argued against his Zionism. He was a Socialist and a Zionist, saying that Jews needed their own country because nobody ever would let them live in peace in the Diaspora. I disagreed, saying that any creation of any new country would start new borders and therefore possibly start new wars. (I think my argument at the age of twelve was really not so bad.) I was at that time a very strict Pacifist. Rose's group seemed to come closer to my thinking, though I was not sure of that and told her so. Still, I went to visit one evening. How can one describe emotions? It was as if a flood of warmth, enthusiasm, excitement, all this came at me. I became very active in that group.

Soon I had my own small group, of which I was a leader. The girls were only a little younger than I, and Ruth was part of that group. We hiked in the woods near Berlin: we swam in the moonlight in the lakes: we read Martin Buber and Bellamy's "Utopia;" we discussed Socialism and Zionism and Marxism and Freudianism; we disagreed with and we loved each other! There are pictures of that period crowding my mind, but I cannot share all of them. I see us, for instance, in the Spreewald, a most unusual landscape, not too far from Berlin: woods, crisscrossed by channels, no roads, only water. The people who lived in them at that time were almost a separate tribe from anyone else known in Germany. They wore different clothes: they were heathens (we were told). They were supposed to worship wood nymphs. I don't know whether that was true, but they were different. We were very much attracted by the air of mystery surrounding that area. We sat in boats, sliding down those channels, always singing. Hilde, Rose and I were the leaders and very close friends. Both Hilde and Rose played the guitar and sang beautifully. I felt very inferior to them, because I could not do this, but the atmosphere of those groups never made for competitive feelings. They loved me for what I was. I remember an incredible experience of nature phenomena on that trip. It was moonlight. We had walked on the terrace of one of the youth hostels in which we stayed. Suddenly we saw that our shadows were thrown against the sky, not on the ground, and that they looked like huge giants in the air. We lifted our arms and saw those giants lift theirs, too.

We were only girls on that particular trip, but one boy, a cousin of mine, Luz, was with us. He played the guitar superbly, too. Almost all of us fell in love with him.

The moment school was out in summer, we disappeared for four weeks hiking across Germany. We slept in the open woods, in barns that farmers willingly opened for us, once in awhile in youth hostels (yet their inexpensive fee was often even too much for us), once in a convent; white sheets—unbelievable! We cooked out or ate what we found (or actually stole) in the fields or from the fruit trees.

Rose was the undisputed leader in a very gentle way. She was a person who had a quiet warmth with a somewhat remote gentleness. She seemed to have none of the anger in her that the rest of us had. Rose was wise beyond her years. Once when we talked about love, Rose said, "It is all right to love and to show love as long as one never plays with it or with another person. It must be honest!" Words I never forgot. (Rose became a well-known writer of child guidance work and lived in a Kibbutz in Israel.)

We called *Hilde* our "flag." She was beautiful, brimming with life! Hilde was always ahead of all of us when we were hiking. She could lead us with an enormous expanse of energy even when we were tired. Hilde had laughter and an enormous fire. While Rose was not in conflict with anyone, Hilde had early fights with her parents. She was supported in them by her older brother, and felt therefore, quite safe. I always admired her incredible equilibrium and strength. It was to Hilde's place I ran away one day when troubles at home became too hard. I stayed there a day and then returned.

Everybody fell in love with Hilde. Hilde is the only one with whom I have kept contact all through life, in so far as it has been possible. We separated when our whole movement fell apart and we did not see each other for years, yet after the rise of the Nazis and after I had been a short time in a concentration camp, on a rainy day, we met by accident in Berlin and fell into each others' arms. At that time Hilde's husband was in a Nazi prison (he later was killed there), and she prepared to leave Germany with her little son because her husband insisted on this. After this, we did not see or hear from each other for many years. Oddly, in the middle of World War II—I cannot remember how— we heard from each other again. Oddly, too, we both had chosen to become social workers, working with children who had difficulties. Hilde had been interned in England as "an enemy alien" but had come out of this. She later remarried and had a second son Martin, who became very close to Paul, my husband, and myself. When we visited, at his age of four, he asked whether we could be his chosen uncle and aunt; we loved being that. I still see the seven-year old Martin bringing me a huge bunch of flowers when I visited in London. At about that same age, he visited Paul and myself in Minnesota, and Paul taught him how to collect stamps and thus learn about the world. The teen-age Martin reminded me of the young Hilde, brimming with life and writing beautiful poetry. Years later it was the drugs that killed Martin. Hilde's and my life seemed to go in parallels. Three days after the sudden death of my own husband, I held a letter in my hands in which Hilde told me about her husband's death, almost as sudden as Paul's. We have stayed friends and she is one of the very few people from my youth whom I still see. Our feelings for each other have not changed. We often think of each other more like sisters than just friends.

Hertha: At that time she was my closest friend. We would walk and talk, then go home, and immediately write letters to each other. We did everything together. Hertha wore her hair cropped short and was considered a tomboy. She could run and run without getting tired. She could do cart-wheels down the hill without stopping. We always admired Hertha because she was the only one who always looked clean as a freshly peeled egg even after exertions like that. Hertha had no fear and unlimited energy. Once we took a boat on the Weser River in Germany. Hertha decided not to take the boat but to swim all that way, which was a considerable distance. There she was, with the bundle of her clothes bound on the top of her head and swimming vigorously. (It surely was good that our parents did not know what we were doing.) Hertha and I swore that our friendship would be eternal, that there would be nothing that would separate us, and yet Hertha and I are totally separated. She became a social worker for youth in Berlin and joined, as many others of our group, the Communist Youth for highly idealistic reasons. Hertha became very dogmatic about Marxism. I still see her before me, lying in bed and learning the "Communist Manifesto" by heart. I saw her a few years later after I had already been in Hamburg, approximately the year before the Nazis came to power. She talked to me, but mostly to try to convince me that I was wrong in not becoming a Communist. We walked through the streets of Berlin. In passing some unfinished buildings, she said, "Oh, those will not be ready before our great revolution will come." I said, "Well, Hertha, I'm afraid it will not be *your* great revolution—it will be the one of the Nazis." She only laughed. Her boy friend came to meet her and looked at me in anger because he did not want her to associate with anyone outside the party. Our goodbye was cool. I have never seen her again.

But we are still back at around the time that I am sixteen or seventeen years old and we are hiking across the country getting ready to meet some of the boys' groups and then to hike to the National Meeting of the group, this time in Nürnberg. The boys: They, too were very close friends. It is difficult to explain to Americans that I have never known "dating." We were in our group together. We talked with each other and loved each other, but we did not "date." The person I was deeply in love with was *Rudi*. It is hard to describe someone as sensitive, courageous, gentle and hard as Rudi was. He was in severe conflict with his father, a very traditional teacher. I remember coming back with Rudi from one of our Saturday/Sunday trips on which we discussed in great depth the question of Pacifism. Rudi insisted that at times violence was necessary to defeat tyranny. I insisted that killing was always wrong. We got so intense that I walked up with him to his apartment and we continued our discussion in his room. I sat on a chair and Rudi sat on the table and we debated and debated. Suddenly, the door to his room opened. His father furiously entered accusing us of all kinds of sexual misconduct and said that I had to leave immediately. Rudi was white in the face, but with his usual maturity, said to me quietly, "Leave now—I'll have to fight it out with him later." The next day Rudi's father wrote a letter to my father, telling him what a terrible daughter he had, spending hours and hours in his son's room behind closed doors. My father, who was not the calmest man, showed me the letter. I told him what really had happened, and he said quietly that he knew his daughter and believed me. In spite of all the conflicts I have had with my father, we trusted each other.

We had a saying among we young people about, "All those adults:"

"Dem Reinen ist alles rein—
Dem Schwein ist alles Schwein."

Translation:

"To the Pure, everything is pure—
To the Pig, everything is dirty."

We felt very pure, and we thought they were crazy to even assume all this nonsense.

Rudi was incredibly sensitive to everybody's hurts and concerns. When I had severe altercations with my father—and they became more frequent—Rudi somehow knew when to telephone, to meet me, and to strengthen me in my convictions. The most seri-

ous problem with my father arose when I refused to go to the synagogue during high holidays. My reason for this was that I could
not believe anymore in all the things that were taught, and I
would not ever lie. I also insisted that most people went to the
synagogue to show off their clothes, and that was absolutely
against my conviction. Father was horrified—he wanted to lock
me in. I said I would escape whenever I could, that he could not
"break" me. After several days my father finally decided to send
me to a reform rabbi; that means someone who was not as rigid as
the rabbi in my Hebrew school. I remember that interview
vividly. I talked about ethics and philosophy, but said that I
could not believe any more in a God who would give all these orders and especially a God who asked Jewish men to give thanks
for not being a woman!

"My father does that every morning," I said, "that is an insult to women."

The rabbi tried to explain it, but after some discussion with
me, he said, "Look, do you believe in an orderly cosmos and not
that the world is a wild chaos?"

I answered affirmatively.

"Well, then you believe in a God."

I answered, "I don't know. I don't like to call an apple a pear.
I can't simply say instead of cosmos, God."

The kind rabbi shook his head, but he told me that maybe I
might change my views with time and that he would tell my father not to lock me up. It gave me some confidence in some of
"those people in authority," of whom I had become very suspicious. And there was Rudi at the street corner waiting for me and
telling me how courageous I was.

I loved Rudi very much, but silently. I knew that he loved
Rose, and I would never, never interfere. I suffered silently, but it
never came into my head to compete, or to play up to someone
whom I knew was not in love with me. Today, I think that Rudi
perhaps knew my feelings, because he always showed great respect for me. At a later time, when all of us separated because of
political differences, and Rudi joined the Communist Youth, I was

told by someone that Rudi had said, "A lot of girls join the party of the person they love; the only one who will never do that is Gisa." Yes, he must have known.

I always somehow worried about what would happen to Rudi. In the days when we were still together, I looked at him reading a poem aloud as the shadow of a lamp crossed his face, and somehow I saw him in prison. Rudi, whom I never saw again after the age of seventeen or eighteen, was later a very courageous fighter against the Nazis. I have been told that he helped numerous people while he was in a concentration camp, and that he was, as always, a person who gave comfort and strength to others. He was tortured to death by the Nazis. I was right about his end in prison!

James: He was Rudi's best friend. The two seemed to be inseparable. James was very gentle, almost soft. He was a dreamer, reading, reading. As all of us, he was in conflict with his family; and he reacted with depression. He once painted the walls of his room black, to the terror of his family. James always seemed to belong to the "privileged classes." His parents, at least to my perception, had more money than anyone else, but he rejected their wealth. For awhile I was in love with James. I was attracted by his gentleness and his sadness. I wrote a poem about him when I was sixteen years old:

> Glutendes, Weiches, Schwellendes,
> Singen und Rauschen und Schwingen,
> Und ein Lächeln, ganz weich und fern und gross.
> Wie ein Meer, drin zu ruhn, zu schlafen,
> Schlafen und ganz versinken.
> Kein Laut, nur weiche, liebe Hände
> und grosse, schwingende Schönheit.

> Du grosses, schönes Lacheln Du!   1926

Translation:

A glowing, a softness, a growing, Singing and sounding and moving, and smile, so soft and far and great like the sea to rest in it and sleep, sleep and be totally immersed in it no sound, just soft, loving hands and great, moving beauty.

You great, beautiful smile, you!

I also thought that he liked me. Once, after we saw a movie about Ivan the Terrible, I commented on the relationship between one of the women and her beloved. James looked at me and said, "Ein Augenblick, gelebt im Paradise...." Translation: ("A moment lived in Paradise....") The next day he brought me lilies of the valley, my favorite flower. Yet, soon after this, I found out that James had become very close to one of the girls who had come from East Prussia. I liked the girl, and I liked James. I immediately withdrew.

Later, James also had horrible experiences during the Nazi period. He had actively stood up against them and then became a refugee in France. We had not seen each other for years. In those days, after the fall of France, when people came down the roads, running away from the advancing German armies, some of us in southern France stood at those roads to see whether we saw anyone we knew and whom we could help. At that time, I waited desperately for Paul. Suddenly, a voice said one day, "My God—Gisa." After all those years, it was James walking with bleeding feet. He had been separated from the woman he loved—she was in Paris, probably bearing his child. Weeks later, courageously, James went back through German lines to find her and brought her back—the child had been lost. Later, she also died.

Today James lives in the same city as I do. He is married, and has a beautiful family.

Heinz: We called him "Menne." I don't know why. He was a slim young man, with a most extraordinary face. He had no eyelids. In his childhood, another boy had played with a bee-bee gun, and his eyes had been mutilated; yet he could see very well. His body moved with an unusual grace. He had terrible fights with his family. Every day when he went out for dance lessons, they tried to lock him in; and every time when he came home late from his very intensive hard exercise, they shouted at him and demanded to know where had been. He lived at that time in Hannover. He wrote me long letters, telling me about all this. One day when the constant inquiries got too much for him, he told his parents that he spent every night with prostitutes. In his letter he wrote, "That shut them up. They were either too horrified or, they liked it better than my learning to dance."

Menne came to Berlin to the famous dance school of Rudolf Laban. He had no money. He lived in abject poverty and was always hungry. My mother felt sorry for that thin boy, and though she did not agree with many of the things I was doing, she always gave Menne a lot to eat. Whenever he had to leave us, she would put a big piece of chocolate in his pocket. Menne was in love with me, but I was not in love with him. That made for endless discussions in the back of our store, and a lot of trying to learn to distinguish between "liking," "appreciating" and "loving." Menne was wonderful with all of us. He taught us modern dance, the fluid beautiful movements of it. We did those dances in the woods near a lake, all naked. Nudity had no sexual meaning to us. It was just beautiful to feel our own bodies in the cool morning air or in the cold lake water. Later we did that kind of dancing, accompanying it by words, on the mountains. (I was quite amused to learn in 1980 that this was about to be a brand new art form.)

Awhile ago I left us on the road to Nürnberg. We had been hiking, and felt pretty dirty, but for the major meeting, we wanted to be clean and festively dressed. There was big scrubbing in the rivers. Our parents sent us our special holiday dresses by mail. Our dresses were black satin loose-hanging gowns, and the boys wore shirts of the same material with open collars. Those were symbols of our convictions. They represented the clothing of the revolutionary peasant movement in the Middle Ages, and we sang their songs. We met in Rothenburg, the beautiful small town completely preserved like in the Middle Ages. Menne stood there, playing the guitar, and we girls approached with Hilde in front of us, playing the guitar, too. How can one describe the sense of elation, excitement, significance that all of us felt! We loved Rothenburg. We saw every detail of the Riemenschneider Altar. All my life I have loved and admired Riemenschneider's marvelous work. He meant more to us than just being a great artist—it was his life story that influenced us: Riemenschneider had become a rich artist in his middle age in Würzburg after having created some of the greatest religious art of his time. He had been elected Mayor of this city. He could have lived a very comfortable life, but the peasant wars broke out and Riemenschneider sided with the peasants. They were defeated, and he was incarcerated and tortured. It was said that his hands were broken. (Many years later I learned that that version of the story may not have been totally true.) We had seen every Riemenschneider we could find, hiking through the Taubertal (the valley of the river Tauber). Years and years later, and every time when I come back to that area, I go especially to see the altar in Creglingen. To me, it is still one of the most beautiful pieces of art in the world. The gentle face of the Madonna is surrounded by the finest leaves cut from wood. The chapel is tiny. When the sunlight shines through the open church door, it is as if the Madonna lives and is just ascending to heaven.

I learned most about Romanesque and Gothic art in this time and this area from *Hans Litten*: Hans was a genius. There is a book written about him by his mother and about the horrible way in which he died under the Nazis. It is called, "Beyond Tears." Hans was one of the most tortured, then viciously revived, and tortured again Nazi victims. He was singled out for this by Hitler himself because, just before the ascent of the Nazis, he had been the lawyer in a trial in which he had called Hitler as a witness. Hans questioned him and Hitler was very uncomfortable. Never would that be forgiven. Hans, even in prison, continued studying Sanskrit and asked for a picture of a sculpture in the Naumberg Cathedral which had much meaning to him.

When we went to Nürnberg, some of us met Hans for the first time—a tall, pale young man, older than most of us, studying law, because his father had insisted on this, but knowing more about art, literature and architecture of the Middle Ages than anyone I have ever met. I see Hans explaining Gothic art to us: he held his hands like a Gothic arch, showing us that those arches were really praying hands and that they had to be huge and up-reaching because of their intense spiritual meaning. To Hans, the marvel of the Gothic times that was rarely an individual was named an architect. To him the Middle Ages were not the Dark Ages as they were presented in text books. They were times of great communal efforts, of individuals who were not eaten by ambition, but who wanted to serve a higher being.

To me, the Lorenz Church in Nürnberg will always be Hans' church. I know every corner of it through him. On the outside of that church hangs a Christ naked with sharply protruding breast bones. Hans took us there: "Look, feel it! This is suffering, but the breast bones also have the form of the arch. There is suffering and the spiritual intent." (Did he foresee his own future?) Years later, after the horrible times of the Nazis, when I went back to Germany under the auspices of the American government, I was also sent to Nürnberg. I immediately went to the Lorenz Church. The church had been destroyed by bombing, but the side walls stood, and there was still the Christ! I saw it in the evening glow with the red sun touching the suffering body. There, to me, was Hans again and all the many people who had died not only under the Nazis, but through the centuries as innocent victims.

Hans was the one who taught us chorus speaking, and he read aloud to us, especially Rilke and Stefan George. Hans was the closest friend of the then leader of our group, *Max Fürst*. Hans was in love with one of Max's sisters, Hanna, a tall blonde girl with long braids. She represented to Hans the Madonna ideal he had searched for all his life. I was Hanna's close friend, and for awhile she, too, became kind of my sister. That made Hans jealous of me. I saw him once in Berlin leaning against the window and staring down desperately where Hanna had just passed. I felt so much for him, I ached for him. I said softly, "Oh, Hans, I really can't help it if she does not like you as much as you love her." He did not answer, just looked at me with those big, sad eyes. All of us knew that Hans had serious conflicts in his family. His father had been a very respected prosecuting attorney in East Prussia. He was a Jew who converted to Christianity for the sake of making a career. Hans despised him. Hans' mother came from a Christian family that had connections in high places. Hans loved her and she understood her son. I do not really know why Hans followed his father's wishes to study law. For a long time he was so terrified of the examinations that he refused to take them. When he finally took them, he passed them with superior marks. He was brilliant.

There was another person who also made us love Nürnberg, *Korle*. Korle was a born Nürnberger—he loved the city, its environment, its culture. Korle was much older than most of us—he was not in school anymore. I think today, that to Korle, we, the Berliner girls, were something of a mystery. He loved us, I think, because we were so alive and so different from what he knew. Oh, how Korle could show us Nürnberg! With him, we saw the castles as if the knights were still walking around. In the Lorenz Church, it was not Hans Litten's Christ that had meaning to Korle. He showed us with great pride and love in his eyes a Madonna, inside the church. "Look at her," he said, "she smiles—she's a peasant girl—she just loves people. She is one of us, the Franken, and she smiles because she is in Nürnberg where people are good."

How I remember those words "Here in Nürnberg where people are good," when I think of Korle's end. Nürnberg was the capital of the Nazis and the home of Streicher, the most violent persecutor of the Jews. One morning, Korle was pulled out of the home which had belonged to his family for centuries. In the beloved meadow behind the Lorenz Church he stood with other Jews. They were ridiculed; they were beaten; and they were killed. The Christ on the outside wall may have seen all of it, and the Madonna inside of the church may not have smiled any more....

Long before this came to pass, all of us hiked together to a large meeting on one of the mountains in Bavaria. Besides the singing and the dancing (Horra is a Jewish folk dance and we danced it with wild abandon, arms around each other), we had very serious discussions of Judaism, of our attitudes toward other religious groups, of justice and of sexuality. I have to smile when in the early 1980's people thought that it was new to talk about sex. We discussed very serious problems: as, what did we think of prostitution? Some of the "older" young men thought that it was necessary because they could not always "wait" until they got married, and they certainly would not want to hurt us "nice girls." I can still see one of the young women as she got up to totally agree with them; in fact, she asked us to endorse prostitution as a significant protector of womankind. And then I hear some of us arguing intensely against this, saying that we have no right to consider ourselves better than any other women. I don't think we solved the issue, but it surely made us think. I struggled much with the whole question of thinking, feeling, of this whole purpose of life. I wrote in 1927:

Dome wachsen...
Weit hinten dämmert Neues, Ungeheures...
Erst langsam tasten—
Bis ich weiss.

Geist kann nicht Tat sein.
Tat will Körper, Hand,
Nicht schattenhaftes Denken, sich versenken.
Tat will Dich *ganz*.

Translation:

Cathedrals rise...
Far away the twilight of something new,
move slowly first...miraculous...
until I know.

Spirit alone cannot be action.
Action needs body, hand,
not a shadowy thinking, ingrown.
Action wants you—*totally*.

Those years gave me inner confidence. I was not anymore the
girl who was so completely unsure of herself and afraid of people
making fun of her. Hans Litten, without knowing it, had given my
self-confidence a real boost: We were once riding as usual in one of
the cattle cars. One could sit only on the floor, but these rides
were cheap. I had been very tired, and I was lying on the floor
with my eyes closed. Obviously, Hans thought that I was asleep.
He said to somebody, "Isn't she beautiful? Next to Hanna Fürst
she is the only other true Madonna we have." Hans, you never
knew how much you did for me!

Back at home, my parents had become very unhappy about
our behavior—*Max Fürst* was considered the Pied Piper who was
dragging the children away from their parents. Max had come
from East Prussia from a tight-knit warm family. He had learned
to be a carpenter. At that time many young Jewish men learned a
trade or agriculture to prove that Jews were not only intellectuals.
Max was a very gentle person, but of great inner strength, and
Hans' friendship supported him. When Max played the guitar
and sang, he could hold everybody in his hands. I never felt as
close to him as to some of the others, but I accepted his leadership role. Max very early fell in love with Margot one of the girls
in my group, wise beyond her years. The two married very young,
and had two children.

After having gone through some terrible experiences under
the Nazis and later having lived in Egypt and Israel, he and his
wife returned to Germany. Max died in 1980 after having published two books, telling about his life.

When I look back today I do understand the anxiety of the
parents. Here were their wonderful children traipsing around the
country, sleeping, God knows where and with whom, having all

kinds of radical ideas, looking so different from everyone they were used to by wearing those "natural" clothes, refusing absolutely to take even a drop of alcohol because they considered that the curse of civilization! We were a strange mixture of free spirits and strict monks. The parents organized—they met and discussed what to do with us. Max was called before them, but certainly he did not give in. Since I was the leader of one of the groups, I was also called before the parents. There I stood, all fired by my righteous convictions. I explained to them our ideals and the special importance of being totally honest. I concluded proudly with Martin Luther's words before the Congress of Worms, "Here I stand, I cannot help myself, God help me, Amen!" I had become very sure of myself, more sure than I ever would be later in my life. What could our poor parents say or do? The feud simply continued.

In the winter of 1927 when I was seventeen years old, I was asked by our group to go to East Prussia and visit the groups there. I was most excited about this! I told my parents that I wanted to do this over the Christmas holiday. They certainly were against it, but after all the meetings that had preceded this, my father said in resignation, "I won't forbid it, because if I do, you will do it anyhow." My mother hardly said anything. I was always angry that she was so submissive to my father.

East Prussia in winter! I had never experienced anything like this before. The train in which I sat rolled through huge tunnels of snow, endlessly. I cannot say how long the trip was, but I am sure that it was more than twenty-four hours. I sat at the window marveling at that wide expanse. All the passengers in the car were older than I, but for some reason I became their confidant and I listened to life stories I had never heard before. I travelled from the city of Königsberg all through the province of East Prussia up north to Gumbinnen. I had never seen thick ice on the lakes on which one could walk. I drank the icy air. This was the area where thousands of Russians had been killed and drowned during World War I and I almost saw in my mind the decaying bodies under the huge expanse of those lakes. It is a melancholic and beautiful landscape. Max, who loved this part of the country, as he had been born and raised there, had taught us the sad, haunting folk songs of that region. Now I sang them with the young members of the groups that I visited, looking at the dark sea and the ghostly dunes. I stayed in homes that were so cold that you could see your breath when you were speaking, but we were young, and we loved it. I knew that Königsberg was Käthe Kollwitz' original home, and I walked through its streets with reverence. I came back to Berlin somewhat more serene than I had left.

We felt very strongly that we who had grown up in the western part of Berlin had been very privileged and needed to know more about poverty, and should help others whenever we could. Now, I myself, was really more knowledgeable about poverty than the others. Many of my relatives lived on the north side of Berlin and were very poor. I wrote earlier about my Aunt Mindzia, who raised her four children during her husband's long imprisonment during the war and his later comparatively early death. She often made her living by doing piece work. The factories gave work for people to do, something like cottage industries. Whenever I came to visit that family—and I liked to visit my aunt who had a wonderful sense of humor—we always sat around the table doing piece work while we spoke.

I had another uncle and aunt in that same part of Berlin. They were the couple who had taken in my father after his mother died, and who had treated him so poorly and insensitively. I never liked that aunt. She was harsh with everybody, especially her children. That family had a bit more money because the uncle was a butcher, but the house smelled like poverty, and in the beds, for the first time in my life, I experienced bedbugs. I still remember my horror on seeing them and how my older cousin crushed them calmly with her fingernails and said that it was nothing.

That family had a very special meaning to me because even as a very young child, I observed the fate of the children very consciously and always with deep resentment towards their mother. There was the oldest, Henry. I knew as a nine-year-old that Henry was in love with a beautiful Christian woman whom I had met. She was loving and kind and very faithful to Henry; but the stern Jewish mother would not allow Henry to marry a Christian girl. So Henry married the daughter of one of the business associates of someone in the family. I was shocked! I considered him a coward for not standing up for his beloved. I never forgave him for that. He sometimes wanted to play with me, but I always refused. I never wanted to meet his new bride, though I certainly had to go to the wedding.

(Henry's first love never married and stood by him and his family when the Nazis came to power. I do not know what later happened to her. I do know that Henry immigrated under the Nazis with his wife and one child to England.)

One of the daughters was Lola, the only one in the family who dared to stand up for herself. She fell in love with a man who was a hunchback. Certainly the mother, who ruled the family with her iron hand, did not want her to marry him. I remember the two on some outings, laughing and running and shaking the branches of trees after a rain into each other's faces. They were young, loved each other, and that was that. Her mother had no power over Lola! Lola married her friend, and had two children, boys. Lola was the one, who, after I came out of the concentration camp, was willing to take me into her home in spite of the danger that that entailed. Lola was fearless and very kind. During the Nazi period, Lola escaped with her youngest son to England. Her oldest son went to Holland for preparation for immigration to Palestine. Her husband was supposed to follow her immediately, yet he was caught by the Nazis and put in a concentration camp where he died. And the same happened to her older son when the Nazis invaded Holland. Later, Lola immigrated with the younger son to the United States. She is one of my relatives I have seen more frequently over the years. She has visited my home, loved my husband. With practically no education, but knowing three languages fluently (Polish, German and English), Lola always made a living for herself and her boy.

When I write this, she is over 80 years old. When I telephone her, she is more concerned about me than about herself.

Minna: From the time I knew that family, I heard how stupid Minna was. Nobody took her seriously. Minna was pushed around, had to do all the heavy work. I never heard her mother say a friendly word to her. For some reason, at the age of seven, I began to like Minna. I saw her crying often, and certainly that moved me. Also, she was warm and cuddly, and I liked to sleep with her when I stayed over at that family. I remember vaguely a big wedding for Minna, as for all the others in the family, where she sat like a stone next to a man with a long beard whom none of us knew. Then Minna disappeared, and we were told that she lived in Poland. Only much later did I learn that Minna had become pregnant by somebody—I am sure the lonely girl needed some arms around her—and that the family quickly had found the poor Jewish "bocher" who got paid to marry her. I also learned that she had been very unhappy, lived in poverty, and had a still-born child. I don't know whether it is true, but I was told later that when the parents were deported under the Nazis, they first found shelter with Minna, who faithfully took care of them. Later, they all died together in the gas chambers. My uncle, whom I liked much better than his wife, at that time had become a solid rock to many others; he is one of those who calmly went to the gas chambers with the "Sch'ma Jisroel" on his lips. I am very angry when people consider it cowardice to have gone to death that way. I think it was great courage, because at that time, surrounded by weapons and inhuman men and dogs, there was nothing else to do but at least to die with dignity.

Malla: Malla was the second youngest in the family and courageous Lola had already paved the way for more independence. Nothing her mother said could deter Malla from doing what she wanted to do. I, whose life blood was the strict youth movement, considered Malla very frivolous. Imagine, she wore lipstick and powder! She danced and she went to the movies! In fact, Malla was the one who took me to the first movie in my life, when I was quite young. It was a movie of the "Golem," the artificial giant created by a rabbi. I was frightened to death of the giant and hid my head in Malla's lap. Frivolous Malla married George, who at the time when she married him was a Christian born of Jewish parents who had converted. Malla's parents were horrified at that, but they could not dissuade Malla. Gentle and intelligent George, very shortly after the rise of the Nazis, insisted on leaving for Palestine with Malla. They entered a Kibbutz at a time when work in a Kibbutz was hard, back-breaking; and there was the constant threat of the contraction of malaria. They never again were spoiled city children. Malla became the Metapalet for the whole Kibbutz for some years—that means the woman who worked with the children in the children's house. George, who had learned to speak perfect English when he served under the English during World War II, became the interpreter for important guests in the Kibbutz. I have a lovely photo of George walking the then-very-young Senator Edward Kennedy through the Israel landscape.

Well, how did I get to talk about that family? I was discussing the fact that I did know poverty and the stink of some of the ugly Berlin houses. I also have to say that I have never understood the animosity of German Jews against the Eastern Jews. I felt identified with both, since I knew them equally well; and I also appreciated my non-Jewish environment.

We young people wanted to do something about some of the poverty we knew about. There was an area in Berlin around the Mulack Street that was one of the poorest with the worst reputation. It was almost totally populated by prostitutes and their children. You should have seen the horrible courtyards! Four to five story buildings enclosed a tiny square. Practically no light fell into it. In that courtyard were two open toilets, available for a few hundred people who lived in that square. We decided that we had to, at least, bring some joy to the children there. I see myself, approximately seventeen years old, coming on a long street car ride from the tree-lined streets of West Berlin, entering the courtyard at the Mulackstrasse. There a pale child sat on one of the doorsteps. I sat next to her and asked her whether she

wanted to dance with me. We joined hands and, accompanied by
the children's song, "Schwesterlein, komm tanz mit mir, beide
Hände reich ich Dir." Translation: ("Little sister, come dance
with me, both my hands I reach out to thee.") Suddenly it was as
if children, like rats, came out of the holes. There came an endless number of them, and I was surrounded. Little arms reached
out: little faces pressed themselves against my skirt. For the first
time I saw faces where noses were eaten off by rats, whose little
bodies were devastated by illness. I wanted to cry, but I continued
dancing with the children and then I sat down and told them
fairy tales. Every week I and others would go to this or a similar
place because we could not let those children down. But surely
again, our parents were not allowed to know about this, since they
would have been afraid for our safety.

I learned something else in those horrible city streets—
namely, that there were good people, good mothers, even though
they were prostitutes, who cared about their children and worried about their health. In that environment I met *Hannchen*.
Among ourselves, the young people, we were sure that if there
was a saint walking around this world, it was Hannchen. She
lived with her five children in great poverty, but she never refused a person who needed a place to sleep overnight or a meal to
eat. Once when Hannchen was brought before the court because
she had allowed a run-away teen-ager to stay overnight in her
place, Hannchen said simply, "When Jesus said to let the children come to him, he did not ask for their age, did he?" That was
Hannchen—but there was much more to her: I do not know all her
story, but I know some.

She had come from a middle class family but had joined a
commune founded by a very strong and very authoritarian man.
Those of us who have heard of the Jones massacre may get a little
feeling of the atmosphere of that commune (nothing is new in the
world). The man was most intelligent and apparently most abusive. He based his convictions on Nietzsche and considered himself the superman. It was a privilege for any woman to sleep with
him and to produce his children. He beat women and children—

he made the children learn Nietzsche's Zaratustra by heart when they were still pre-school children, and beat them mercilessly when they did not succeed. Most of the women in this group submitted totally and let him do whatever he wanted. Hannchen was his favorite, and she bore him three children; two boys, Vertuemo, (virtue), Sagero (the sage), and one girl, Tamen (in spite of everything). It was no accident that the girl was named that way, because meanwhile, Hannchen had decided not to accept any more of his subjugation.

She fled secretly with those three children and two older ones from an earlier marriage. Hannchen radiated peace—it is almost inconceivable how a person with that history could be so all-encompassing with kindness and gentleness. She lived amidst the prostitutes, and she took care of them or their children when they were sick. I still see Hannchen before me with a small baby of one of these women in her arms, a child who already looked like a corpse, thin, and white with the bones sticking out. Hannchen walked and talked to the child and took her out for hours everyday into the sunshine when she went with her children, and she shared her milk with her. Only a few months later, this same child, now round and rosy-cheeked, cooed happily in Hannchen's arms. Hannchen knew some people in the north of Germany who had a farm. She sometimes went there with her children, but she always took an extra child along.

Once, when she was away, we decided to clean up her apartment. She had kept it as clean as she could, but because of the surroundings, it was totally bug infested. There we were, boys and girls, all dressed in long pants (by the way, that was very radical at that time for girls), long-sleeved shirts, towels wrapped around our heads to protect against the bugs. We took off every picture in the apartment. Exactly like a picture, crowded together behind them against the wall, were sitting those bugs. We killed them with brooms and the sprays that were available. We scrubbed the walls, the insides of every piece of furniture, the sinks, the floors with Lysol. We came back the next morning, and watched to see if a single bug was still running around. Then, when everything was clean, I think it was Max who took bright oil color and painted the walls, while we girls painted the floors. It was a beautiful place after that! What a satisfaction to have done such a job! (To be honest, I never was very neat at home.)

One summer Hannchen took me along to the Darss, the place where she went in the country with her children. I don't think the older girls were present. We picked blueberries all day, a rather back-breaking job, but we liked it, sitting in the woods with the sunlight breaking through. We ate blueberries all the time, drank milk, and sold blueberries to the vacationing city people, thus earning money for other food. Tamen, the little girl, was like a sunbeam—light, blonde, lovely. Vertuemo was a strong seven-year-old, his big dark eyes and a sunny smile. He was open with me and told me about the horrible days of his early childhood. Sagero, then about five years old, was my favorite. He was a sad child, sometimes crawling away and crying silently. We slept together on the floor, and I often woke up feeling the puddle of urine coming from Sagero. He was desperate about it, but he could not help himself. Both, Hannchen and I put our arms around him and told him that someday this would go away, and he should not be so ashamed of it. How often have I thought of this when I saw how cruel people are to young children.

Hannchen befriended a member of our youth group, I think his name was *Milt*. He was very poor, and had a horrible eczema on his face. Hannchen was like a mother to him, and he stayed often at her place. This is the period around 1928, at the height of Communist propaganda among working people and the youth of Germany. One must understand that they appealed to idealism, to a sense of international brotherhood, to a wish for equality and against a harsh class society. In Russia, the Communists had defeated the horrible tyranny of the Czar, and for many, they seemed to incorporate the hope for a better world. Milt had become a Communist, and in the beginning he encouraged Hannchen's children to join one of the children's groups in which there was much singing and hiking. But I remember the day when

Milt came to me and said, "I never knew that they would indoctrinate the children so much. It is horrible. They teach them to mouth slogans that they cannot understand. These children will never think—they'll just follow whatever they are told."

An international school (not Communist) had started in the west of Germany, and Hannchen's children later went there. Those schools were later moved to other countries after the rise of Hitler. But for awhile Hannchen's children remained at home. I know that it was her children who warned Milt when the Nazis came to arrest him. I do not know the details of their life. As far as I know, all three children are today teachers somewhere in Germany. And what about Milt? Hilde Monte (Hilde Meisel), wrote during the Nazi time when she was in England, a novel—but it is not a novel, it is reality. There she describes Milt's end:

He came back to the house. We never discovered why he did it. The police were still waiting for him and arrested him triumphantly. Bit by bit we learned the rest of the story. They found a paper on Milt from which they concluded that he had an appointment on Friday at 4:00 p.m. They wanted him to give particulars. He refused. The Nazis took shifts at cross-examining him throughout the night and the next day. By the second morning—that was Thursday—all his teeth had been knocked out, and he couldn't sit down or lie on his back, so badly had he been knocked about. On the floor and walls of the cellar in which the cross-examination was proceeding, his blood was mingled with that of earlier victims of the brown terrorists. He heard men scream with pain in neighboring rooms, and horribly distorted bodies were carried past him, twitching in the convulsions of agony or delivered from their sufferings by death. One more attempt was made to make Milt speak. They hung him up by his feet, and left him there, head downwards. They had to carry him into his cell afterwards, because he couldn't walk. But when he came to himself again, he still did not speak. They locked him in and left him alone. That evening and again the next morning, they gave him some food. And then they fetched him from the cell, and he was taken to the barber, who shaved him, and they gave him a clean shirt and his coat. They asked no more questions. But they ordered him to go and meet his friends at 4:00 p.m. at the appointed place. He was to go in his ordinary clothes, and without guard or shackles. He need not believe, however, that it would be of any use trying to run away. They would be there all the time, and keep an eye on him, and he would have to pay dearly for the attempt.

Milt went through the streets, very slowly, very conscious of the fact that he might never again walk as freely as this, and undecided still what to do to avoid betraying his comrades, but at the same time, if possible, to escape further torture. He knew that there was no way out for him. So when he got near the corner where his friends were waiting for him, he threw himself into the roadway in front of a fast-moving car. When he woke up he was in a hospital, with both his legs, his right arm and head heavily bandaged. His legs were broken, his arm and head were badly bruised. He was well treated in the hospital, and after two months' time he could walk again. Very soon they would throw him into prison again. He knew it, and was so terrified that he decided to put an end to his life rather than face a repetition of that dreadful experience. But it turned out otherwise. One day he was discharged. At first he did not understand what it all meant. Only gradually it dawned on him what was happening. Somebody else who also had a foreign-sounding name was due to be discharged. The nurses liked Milt, and they knew what was in store for him. So they just made a mistake and let him go.

We helped him to cross the frontier into Czechoslovakia the next day, and from there he made his way to Soviet Russia. In Soviet Russia he was shot three years later as an agent of the Gestapo and a saboteur of socialist construction.

(From *Where Freedom Perished*, A novel by Hilde Monte, published in London, 1947, Victor Gollancz Ltd. Pps. 19-21.)

Dictatorships from the right or left will always destroy, even the best.

Hannchen's death was just as ironic as Milt's. I do not know what she did during the Nazi period, but I am sure that she stood up straight against them and that she helped many who were persecuted. When the Russians invaded Berlin, they did not distinguish between Germans who had been Nazis and those who had not been Nazis. I was told that Hannchen was raped by Russian soldiers and killed by them. To me Hannchen's story is the story of a saint and a martyr.

Chapter Four

Political Affiliation

*B*ack again to 1927-1928 when we were still alive and full of hope for a better future. Our group had rented a small apartment in the north of Berlin which had become a "home away from home." There we had our meetings, there somebody could stay overnight if he felt he had to run away from those "awful" parents. And it was in this place that we sat around, night after night, debating politics. All of us felt that we had to be active in the political struggle that went on in the young republic. Reactionary forces began to be strong everywhere. But which party to join was the question. Several, especially Rudi, leaned towards the Communist Youth. This seemed to them the hope for the future, the party that stood for justice, and also for very humane reforms. The film, "The Way Into Life," done in Russia, was shown at that time. It presented a new and much more humane approach to the treatment of delinquents. It showed an attempt

to restore their self-respect. I myself and some others did not
want to join the Communist Youth. We did not like the dogma-
tism of their pronunciations, and I, for one, considered orthodox
Marxist theory rather stupid. I had studied Marx and Engel's
work just as intensely as everybody else. Yet I saw Historical
Determinism as unproven, and I could not understand how one
could expect the classless society to become an inevitable outcome
of history while at the same time ask for active involvement in a
revolution. I also abhorred violence and did not like its
glorification. I was not sure that I would want to join the Social
Democratic party to which my father belonged. It had become too
conservative for my thinking. The debates among us became sharp
and separation soon came. To me, to whom friendship had great
meaning, this was intolerable pain and despair. I wrote:

> Wir hielten fest die Hand, im Kreis gefügt,
> Und standen ineinander,
> Glieder einer Kette.
> Welt stand darum und lösen mussten wir.
> Der eine warf lachend kurz den Kopf
> und gab sich hin,
> Ein andrer aber riss und riss,
> Und eine blutend rote Wunde
> sprang dann auf,
> Als er die Kette riss, die uns verband;
> In grauer Arbeit schafft er hard,
> doch unaufhörlich rinnen rote Tropfen.

Translation:

> We held each other, a close circle,
> we stood linked to each other,
> part of a chain.
> The world was outside and we had to let go.
> Some laughed and shook their head
> and left with ease.

Yet another tore and tore,
a bleeding red wound
opened.
When he broke the chain, that held us;
He works hard in the grey day
and red drops don't cease to fall.

I was hurt so badly! And there was the inner obligation to find a
cause, a group, some organization that would carry on a good fight
for humanity, for the improvement of the lot of the poor and
those who were treated unjustly. The Communist Youth which
had attracted many of my friends because of its seeming concern
for the oppressed just was not for me.

What about the synagogue? I had rejected the childlike image of a father-God with a long beard, but there was Rainer
Marie Rilke and his deeply religious poetry that I loved. Well,
where did I belong? I had read about Bernard Shaw and the
Fabians, but this group existed mostly in England. One day,
someone, I don't remember who it was, said, "You know you
should talk with Maria Hodann. (Her former husband, Max
Hodann, a physician, had been an ideal for me in earlier years
because he helped young people to understand their sexuality in a
simple, forthright and unsensational way.) She belonged to an
organization called the ISK (Internationaler Sozialistischer
Kampfbund). They belonged to the Social Democrats, but they
have other theories and think much deeper." So—I went to the
apartment where Maria Hodann lived with her small daughter
and a few other members of that organization. I remember my
first impressions: Maria, rather cold and aloof, but not unfriendly. Hans, a young unemployed member of the household,
alive, warm, especially concerned with little Renate, Maria's
daughter. I had the feeling of intense purpose and also some sense
of community.

I liked the mixture of people I met in the ISK—workers and
intellectuals. And so I became more and more connected with that
group. It never had the impact the youth movement or the people

in it had on me. I found some of the thinking and organizational practices rather silly, but, with the intense background of the youth movement I could take them or leave them. The ISK had been founded by Leonard Nelson, a philosophy professor from Goettingen, a follower of Kant and Fliess. (Several of his writings exist in English translations.) He based his political practice on the concept of "duty," of obligation found in one's own conscience. I found this very compatible with my thinking. He considered democracy illogical because in it decisions were made by just counting votes. He maintained that majority was not always right. He drew the conclusion that society needs leadership. It should be leaders trained to consider the good for everybody, deeply imbued with a sense of justice and willing to sacrifice their own comfort for those ideals. He founded a school to develop such leadership which was later destroyed by the Nazis. Because leaders had to be totally selfless and dedicated, members of the ISK were supposed to be celibate. Because they should consider rights of all creatures they had to be vegetarians, as not to kill animals for their own pleasure. I personally took the demand for vegetarianism very seriously. I thought the celibacy rule quite silly but it did not bother me, I was not interested in anyone at that time.

I did not know Nelson personally. From what his followers told me, I always disliked him. He seemed to me an arrogant intellectual who loved the adoring bunch surrounding him—several of them were especially attractive young women—and he seemed to like his power. Yet I don't think that he misused it. He died early. I did like the contact with young men and women who worked in the factories, who knew a life different from mine and who earnestly worked in labor unions to improve not only their own lot but also that of others. They taught me a side of life I had not known in my environment. There was, for instance, terrible unemployment. "Go and see what days look like for people who have nothing to do. Sit in one of those movie houses near the Alexanderplatz, (a place in north Berlin) and you will see." I experienced it, sitting for hours in those places where hardly any-

one looked at the pictures, but where they slept in the dark for a
few pennies without being pulled out by the police. We watched
at night people going to the "Obdachlosenasyl," the asylum for
the dispossessed. We knew stories of the harsh and demeaning
discipline inside those places where everyone was regimented,
where they slept standing hanging over a rope that was taken off
to wake them up in the early morning. I met young couples hiding
in the bushes nearby, "Don't tell anyone we are here. We don't
want to go inside. They never let us be together." Love and despair in the streets. As in the youth movement, we had
overnights and hiking, but they were always accompanied by intensive learning about economics; for instance, this organization
believed strongly in rural reform with private property for small
farmers, contrary to the collectivism of the communist ideology.
We studied Franz Oppenheimer, who wrote about rural reform.

During one of those camping trips, I decided that I had to cut
off my long braids as a sign of emancipation. The girls who already wore short hair loved cutting off mine. I brought home my
long braids that day. My poor father—who had lived through
the haircutting before when Hanna had cut hers—only sighed
and then asked those braids to be wrapped in paper and saved.
(Later, when I helped my mother to leave the country, I threw
them away, but I suddenly understood my father's pain. His little girl had grown up.) My father and I grew farther apart. He
disagreed with my political affiliation. We could not talk to
each other. The only person who not only stayed close to me during this time in the family but with whom I became even closer,
was Ruth. She, too, suffered under the authoritarian atmosphere
in our home and school. She also had loved a boy in the youth
movement. He, later, joined a right-wing political movement and
that certainly broke the tie between them. Ruth was beautiful
and gifted in everything. She combined Hanna's gift for the
natural sciences with mine for literature and history. We were
sure she would be a great actress and writer...We were sisters in
the rare sense of the word. We discussed problems, intellectual
and emotional ones. We did not hide doubts, fear, or joy from each

other. She was four and a half years younger than I and therefore there were many things she was not allowed to do. Yet we always supported each other. I knew that I would want to leave home the moment school was out. The atmosphere at home was stifling, constantly filled with conflict and anger. I shared first with Ruth that I would have to leave. The nights we cried on each others' shoulders! "Ruth, I promise I will take you away from here the moment you have finished school." We clung to each other....

I had always earned the money for my clothing and trips since the age of 12, ever since I had entered the Gymnasium—as I had promised. I also saved money to leave after the "Abitur," the final examination. I had decided not to go to the university right away. I wanted to be independent from home and I also wanted to live like those for whom I fought, the workers in the factories. I decided to do this in Hamburg, a large city where I knew no one, and where I could start a new life. (I know this does not sound so different from the young people of the late 1960's. I did feel with them in those years when they were carried by a cause and not selfish motives—and, being then older, I also felt with the parents who were so bewildered by the young people's actions.) I had 90 marks and 2 dresses when I left Berlin for a new life.

Chapter Five

Factory Years

I was scared. I left everyone I knew, I left the environment I knew; home, friends, school, Berlin. I went into a life I had never experienced directly, a new city, Hamburg, new people, the life of an unemployed factory worker. I must have been very scared because, even today, I cannot remember a single goodbye from anyone, from family, friends, places. I only remember Ruth crying and our arms around each other, but nothing else, no packing, no thinking, nothing...memory surely can block out events that are too painful....

But I do remember the arrival in Hamburg. When the train stopped and I got off with my one suitcase a tall, young woman with copper-red hair and about my age came rushing to me: "Are you Gisa Peiper?" I nodded. In a brisk way she immediately took my suitcase, told me that I was expected by the people from the ISK, and that they even had found a little room for me. I was im-

pressed with her openness combined with a "no-nonsense" attitude. I later learned that she was studying to be a teacher. The
room she took me to was a tiny one in the home of a young woman
with a four-year-old girl. It looked out on a wall. I loved it, since
I had never lived in a room by myself. I was immediately thrown
into new experiences such as the endless blaring of the gramo-
phone, the nightly visits of a man to the young woman.

What really disturbed me were the sounds of fighting and
beating that went on day and night coming from the different
apartments. Wife beating was commonplace and completely accepted. The worst for me was to hear the beating of children,
their desperate crying, their helpless begging to stop. And I could
do nothing about that. The only one I could protect occasionally
was the little girl in the apartment where I lived. We became
close friends and she spent most of her time with me, my arms
around her, and my telling her stories. I could hardly stand her
crying when the adults, filled with beer, were beating her for
some childish thing she had done. (When some people say today
that there has been no progress in this world, I think of the fact
that we finally use the term "abuse" in such cases. To me that is
great progress.) I also remember the day when the woman where I
lived screamed in agony, and a neighbor came rushing to me saying, "Run quick to the nearest doctor—she has had an
'Umschlag.'" I had read a lot of literature, but I did not know the
word. It was a colloquial term for abortion.

"*What* should I say?"

"For God's sake—run—she's bleeding, it is an abortion." So I
ran to the nearest doctor and repeated the unknown word. He
hurried down the steps with me. The child was sitting in the
corner, trembling. I held her in my arms. Yes, I was discovering a
new life!

I had wanted to leave home: I had wanted independence; but
I would lie if I do not tell about my turning to the wall occasionally and crying my heart out with homesickness, questioning
whether I had done the right thing and whether I should not go
home again. But my pride would not allow that. One day when I

felt especially low, one of the young men who also belonged to the ISK, knocked at my door carrying a brown paper bag. He took out a cheap glass bowl in which he had arranged red tomatoes and green cucumbers. They made a beautiful picture.

He smiled and said, "It's tough to be all alone. Enjoy the pretty colors." I was very grateful.

It was 1929. There was much unemployment. I learned what it meant to stand in line in those ugly barrack buildings that were called employment offices. There were a few wooden benches against the wall, but most of us had to stand for hours. One waited for the official to come in with a sheet of paper and call out for a few job openings. I listened to those around me:

"You know what? I am twenty-one years old and that means I'm already too old to get a job. They have only jobs for the real young ones because they have to pay them less," or:

"Nothing left but to turn on the gas. We can't pay for that anyhow, but when the bill comes, at least we are dead." The horrible despair of not having work! (All my life I have feared unemployment as much as I have feared war and Fascism. It demeans people—it makes them hopeless.) Certainly I was still young, under twenty, and that made the situation a little better.

A call: "Young women under twenty, unskilled labor needed in a bottle factory."

I got the desired slip and went to the place of work to introduce myself. It was a dirty, dingy basement that stank of linseed oil combined with metal shavings and urine because of the open toilets. Women worked on long, rough wooden tables, quickly linking two pieces of metal into each other to make the closing for bottles. Their hands were filthy and torn from that metal. One or two men walked around being the supervisors. The work was "Ackordarbeit" (piece work). I was hired and started to work. I was appalled by the conditions—there was no union to help improve the lot of these women. Unionism to me was the heart and soul of the workers' movement, the only hope for people who were desperately exploited. I joined the Metal Workers' Union, then went to its office and asked what could be done about the situation in which I found myself and others.

"Well, you have to start organizing these women. If enough of them join, then we can do something. But it won't be easy."

I began talking unions in the factory. I found some women who, in spite of the danger that threatened us, were willing to join. (I have very little respect for intellectuals who call for radical action, but they themselves sit in comfortable offices, while others carry the load of losing jobs, and in some places, even their lives.) Those were still the days of the German Republic. Labor unions were legal, but it was easy for employers to dismiss the trouble makers, especially when they were women. Soon, the women who had joined the union and myself were called to the office and told that we were dismissed. We showed our records—we were especially good and fast workers. Nothing doing. They didn't need us. The union headquarters said they couldn't do much for us, because too few were organized in this place. I learned about bureaucracy even among those that I thought should have been of help.

Back to the unemployment lines. And then another job, again as an unskilled metal worker, in a somewhat larger factory where people were unionized. This time I worked on machines, every day for eight hours. I had to make the same hand movements, monotonous, tiring. Big drums were in the same building in which nails were coated. The noise was deafening. One could not talk with anyone. I could only live through all this by constantly singing to myself, reciting poetry or discussing philosophy with myself. Women did, again, the tedious and heavy work. Men were the supervisors, walking around, going out for a smoke whenever they felt like it, here and there adjusting our machines. They got much higher wages than we did.

One woman got almost as high wages as the men, but she did a back-breaking job. She loaded the heavy nails which had been thrown into baskets weighing at least 200 pounds into huge baskets and carried them to another place. She looked like a coal miner because her face was always streaked with dirt from the sweat and the metal dust running down her cheeks. Her hands were calloused. She was tough, talking and swearing like the men. She was the first one who talked to me at the lunch period. She looked at my hands and suddenly said, "Hey, fine lady, what are you doing here? Look at those hands! You are not one of us.

Oh, heaven, I knew that I must never admit that I had gone to school and had my Abitur. I said quietly, "I surely belong. I am a union member. My hands look like that because I have been at home for quite awhile, taking care of housework." I knew that was acceptable. Fortunately, she bought that. She even invited me once to her home, a desolate looking place where she lived with her man friend. The sink in the kitchen was used as a toilet. We talked, and the man's hands began to wander over my knees. I said I had to leave, but she had seen it: "Hey, you," pointing to her friend, "Don't you dare touch the fine lady." I was furious. The moment she called me a "fine lady," I knew she was very angry at me, yet I hadn't done anything wrong.

The next day on the job, she became even more abusive: "Look at that fine lady! You know what? She is even a Jew. My God, a Jew being a factory worker!"

That seemed to be unheard of, and I felt the hostility in the air, but Mina, one of the older women, shrugged her shoulders and said, "So, what, she's no different than others."

That is when I began to know Mina. She was rather quiet, was also a union member, but not very active. She asked me once to visit her. She lived in one of the worst areas of Hamburg, in a little room under a roof. There were holes in the roof big enough to stick a fist through them. She saw that I glanced at them, smiled and said, "This is very pretty at night—you can see the stars." I did not ask her what she did when it rained. Mina had a little boy born out of wedlock. She took care of him beautifully. Every morning she got up at four a.m., prepared a good breakfast, then dressed him carefully and took him to the day center. And every evening after work she picked him up, carrying him in loving arms.

And, like Mina, Lotte, another metal worker, also took good care of her five-year old daughter for whom she had to care all by herself. Lotte was very young. She was pretty, like a little Dresden China doll. One would never think that she could carry through a hard factory job and at the same time take care of her child. Yet, she did. Like Mina, her days were long. The child was always beautifully dressed, looking like a little princess. She once said to me, "Nobody will ever know who the father is, but I will make her the best child in the world."

One of the young women became my friend whom I felt I had to protect. Miele was the youngest of us, approximately fourteen years old. Her skin was so white, one felt one could almost look through it. She was thin, and had difficulties breathing. One day I asked her whether she had ever seen a doctor. No, there was no time and no money. She looked so sick. Something had to be done. I knew a physician who was dedicated to his work, did not look out for money and practiced in one of the slum areas of Hamburg. I said to her that I would take her to this doctor to see whether something could be done. We went together. I learned something that day that always has influenced my thinking. The physician acted so human and on the assumption of the totality of body and soul being one, and realized the significance of the environment.

Miele was very afraid. She had never before seen a doctor, not even as a child. He did not start with a physical examination. He simply sat down next to both of us and began talking with her casually, gently.

"How are things at home? How many brothers and sisters do you have? Is it easy to sleep when there are so many people? How many sleep in one bed? Do you like your work? What do you do when you come home?"

It was only then that I learned that little Miele, after a full day of hard work in the factory came home to pick up a large paper route, carrying the heavy bag full of newspapers, walking up and down the stairs of the apartment houses. She said that sometimes she was so tired that she could only crawl on all fours to make the last delivery. He also asked her what she ate. Nobody prepared meals for Miele. When she finally got home, she would grab whatever there was, but often she was too tired to eat. The doctor had given me a lesson that was better than all the books I had read. I do not know any more what he found or what he prescribed. I do know that he suggested to me to invite Miele for my morning swim. I swam every morning in the Alster, a river that flows through Hamburg.

"But that will make her day even longer", I protested.

He smiled. "Yes, but it will do her a lot of good, especially if you fix a nice breakfast for her before you go to work." What a beautiful man!

Next to my work in the factory, the most significant part of my life became my work in the ISK and the labor unions. There were meetings, things to read, the distribution of union materials and the Sunday hikes that were part of every youth movement.

Chapter Six

Meeting Paul

We either hiked or bicycled. One young man, an unemployed wood-worker, was often the leader. He had wavy blond hair, broad shoulders; he was slim and obviously very strong. I was sometimes angry with him, because I felt he was too domineering. On hikes, he always knew best where to go and which way to take, and unfortunately for me, he was always right. He was very serious, very efficient. Yet, once in a while, his bright blue eyes twinkled with merriment. Those moments were very rare. We had sharp differences when it came to discussions about people. I still see us on our bicycles, debating whether human beings were born good or bad. I argued that they were basically good and only circumstances destroyed that goodness. He argued that they were basically bad and that one has to "educate" them to become better. (Today, I would argue that we both were right, that we are born both, good and bad.) I knew that he had been for awhile in the leadership school that Leonard Nelson had started, and I was always suspicious of people who had gone to that school. Yet he did not talk much about it as others had done, and that pleased me. The person I am talking about is Paul; and from now on, this will hardly be the story of myself alone, but it will be the story of both of us, the life and love of both of us, that life we lived together for forty-three years, often separated, a life of much pain and incredible happiness, a real love. I am talking about a man who was my friend, lover, father, son and husband— all rolled into one. There will come the horrible Nazi years that separated us and made us sometimes think that the other one was dead, but there were also good years together. I wish Paul could be here to write this with me, but he is dead. Yet there are some of the things he wrote, and I will share those.

I did not know right away that Paul and I belonged to each other. I was much too involved in the causes and the issues that pervaded my life. But I remember my sister Ruth, once visiting me in Hamburg. I introduced her to my friends and colleagues. In the evening, in the sisterly intimacy that we shared, she suddenly said, "You know, that one with the long hair and the Siegfried body, you know that Erhardt (that was Paul's name originally), that's the one for you."

I said, "Oh, my God, no. We always find something to fight about."

But wise little Ruth laughed. "That's exactly why you belong together." How right she was.

Much later, after Paul's death, something strange happened: On a short visit coming from the U.S.A., I walked through the streets of Hamburg and saw the environment in which I had lived during those years. It had changed very much. Everywhere, huge apartment houses had been built. Yet, the house in which I had lived for awhile with several people from the ISK and where I had spent much time with Paul, that little house, stood there as always. There was also a small park still standing in which we had walked debating the problems of the world. Once he had said, "Oh, can we go arm in arm? I hate the wiggling next to each other." I was surprised because he was a very shy young man. I said, "Certainly." This was probably the first time we touched each other.

A second strange thing that happened in cleaning out a drawer, I found a notebook that we had bought when we were refugees in France. Throughout the years my gift to Paul for birthdays or wedding anniversaries or holidays had been some writing. I found what I had written into this notebook in those dark days when we lived in a stable of a farmhouse in southern France. It was written in German and was reminiscent of the beginning of our love. I translate:

> I think today of the story of our love—a long story, not always happy but so beautiful, so astonishingly beautiful! To tell this whole story would be too long, but I want to draw a few pictures. Difficult to make a selection—which one to draw, because I remember all of them. I had moved out of the apartment of friends because I earned very little and did not want to depend on their charity. I could make it alone, because I had learned to go hungry. In this picture: I live now in a little room near the university. I work quite well, but I am also very much alone. My friends did not understand my decision, and they are angry!!!
>
> Yet one person comes several times. He takes some lessons from me. He is very serious, very matter-of-fact. But he has never scolded me for having moved out. I feel in his silence a real understanding. He is without work for years. His shirt is frayed. I think, he, too, would like to wear something nice, but he never says a word about it. He, too, has the "pride of the poor." That is why he is perhaps the only one who understands that I had to do what I did. Today is a glowing summer day. My mother has sent me a lovely light dress. I wear it. My "pupil" arrives. Oh, for the first time I am distracted. What may he think of me? Does he think I'm dressed too fancy? He probably detests me. I see his worn collar and the poorly cut hair. I am very

inhibited. The lesson is finished. The "pupil" goes down the steps with me and outside he tells me something. I listen only partially. In me, a huge joy begins to sing and my embarrassment stops. While he speaks I see his—your—eyes, which smile friendly and quietly and look at me without any reproach. Much later you have told me that you found me very beautiful in that dress.

Another picture for you: After a long hike we went to sleep in the straw, but we were not tired. In a soft voice, so as not to disturb the others, you tell me for the first time about your home, your sad childhood. I want to stroke your brow, but I don't dare to do that. I just listen. Then I say, "I will make it up to you." We say goodnight, and then your voice says very shyly: "Am I allowed to turn around to you?" I smile and say, "Well, certainly." Your hands stroke softly over my face, and then suddenly pull back, almost frightened by this audacity. And we sleep quietly and calmly.

Another: This was a very special day. It was early Easter. There was still some snow in the woods. We had hiked vigorously—we were with several people. We had laughed, and picked up some twigs in the woods. At one time our hands had met, and we later often thought that this was the very moment when we knew for sure that we belonged together. In the evening, high on the mountain, villagers had laid an Easter fire. We gathered around it, singing. When the flame became low, young couples, hand in hand, jumped over the fire. By custom, this was a declaration of love. We did it, too, that night!

Another: You suggested we have a few days of vacation together. I work like crazy on some papers to have a good conscience so I could take some days off. I am a little scared. This will be the first time I take a trip with you alone. But I guess it will go all right. We leave Hamburg with a folding boat, running suits, a tent, a camera, a cooking pot. Not a single piece belongs to us, everything is borrowed. We are two laughing children. We are two have-nots who make a sea voyage!

There is Lübeck: How beautiful to go with you into the Gothic churches, how beautiful to admire together the gentle Madonna, how I loved to hear you talk about you four mischiefmakers, your brothers and sisters and you who once lived here in Lübeck. I can almost see you as children before me! And then we put our boat into the river and go down to the open sea.

It is a soft summer evening. The sea is very, very quiet. We had been swimming and had been lying in the sand and now we dance like children around each other, across each other, up and down. We are so light-footed in the soft air, barefoot. Later we go into the tent. Today your hands hold me tighter than usual, and I feel it that you want to kiss me. But I am afraid, afraid of something wild and unknown that may come after the tenderness. Somehow I'm not yet woman, and as shy as I have always been I ask you in a low voice: "Don't kiss, please. Don't be angry, but don't kiss."

Very gently, you put my head on the pillow and spread the blanket over us. Suddenly, I'm afraid. Did I hurt you? My hand searches for yours. Yours does not hide itself, it presses mine; a sign that you are not hurt. Suddenly, a deep confidence fills me. That you could do that! So quietly you respected my wishes and were not angry. I am so glad! Suddenly you move! Some animal had bit you in the finger. A snake? Suddenly I'm very afraid for you. I want to suck out the wound. You turn on the flashlight. We see the wound. Ha, it was a mouse! We laugh, very relieved and loud. All our shyness is gone—and you get the first kiss from me!

And another: It is Christmas Eve. I was invited to Ilse's home, but I look forward to coming home because you promised to come to me later that evening. A few days ago you had brought me your first gift: A marvelously worked sewing box. I am embarrassed and deeply moved. So much love was poured into that work. You also had cut my hair and suddenly you covered my whole face with kisses, you, this quiet, shy boy. All the time I saw something new, always something beautiful in you. Arm in arm we often went to our work, sometimes we wrote something together. It was wonderful to know that in the evening you would come.

And there you were. You brought flowers and a book that I had wanted for a long time. Together we read from it aloud. Then you left and I went to bed, being very happy. But suddenly the bell rings. Now, who comes so late? I open. There you stand in the night, so frightened, so unhappy.

"What is it?"

First, you don't want to speak. Slowly it comes, piece by piece: Your father had come home drunk again. First he did not want to let you in. And you had said, "O.K., I go." And then suddenly he followed you, crying, saying, "At least give me your hand so that I know that you forgive me." Full of disgust and yet somehow pressed by some pity, you had given him your hand and then you ran away. And now you accuse yourself because you have given your hand to the person who once beat your mother. I can only take your head in my hands and kiss your good sad eyes so that you may forget all this sorrow. We carry a bed into my room so that you can stay the night. We turn off the light, but I feel that you cannot sleep:

"Come, child, come to me."

You come to me. This is the first time our bodies lie close together, very happy and still very peaceful without desire. I am totally filled with a vast tenderness and a happiness to be allowed to protect and to be protected. We fall asleep in each other's arms.

And: it is a wet, cold February day. I take off my shoes. My feet are wet and frozen. You look at them: "Well, show me your shoes. My God, they are full of holes!"

I bite my lips.

"Why don't you bring them to the shoemaker?"

"I really have no money. The stipend will arrive only in Spring." I say that very hesitantly. I have an incorrigible resistance telling anybody about my problems with money.

"Now, that really is not right. Give me the shoes. I will repair them."

I break into tears. For the first time I feel the terror of this eternal poverty that seems to have no end.

But you smile: "Well, shouldn't we also share the worry about torn shoes with each other?"

"You are right."

I want to tell more about Paul's childhood as he had told me about it. Paul's father had been a very intelligent and capable man who had made his Master in woodwork. If he had not been drinking, the family could have been well off. Whatever drove him, I do not know. I met him when he was over 70 and was impressed by his intelligence. But in his drunkenness he was a cruel and unfeeling husband and father.

Paul's mother had come from Silesia from a very poverty-stricken family. Paul told me that she had grown up a Catholic, but when she was a small child there was no food in the house and she had gone out to steal some bread. As punishment, the priest had insisted on her doing the stations of the cross several times by crawling on her bare knees. She was then totally undernourished. She fainted several times and the pain was unbearable. Her knees bled. In addition to that, the bread was taken away from her. Paul loved his mother deeply and with a fierce protectiveness. This story made it impossible for him to ever go into a church. He felt her pain too much. Paul's mother herself never completely gave up her religion. I remember that she always lit a candle when she felt the need for some protection.

She was little, heavy and worn-out with an extended stomach. She had difficulty walking, because one of her feet had been severely cut in a factory accident and never completely healed. She loved her children fiercely, but definitely preferred the boys. She was very outspoken and claimed that women should not have children, that children were only born because of the pleasure of the man. But at the same time she was not a bitter person. She could laugh and sing. Paul told me that only thanks to her were they alive, and, as he sometimes said, "half-normal." She had worked in several factories to feed the children, since his father constantly abandoned his family. She worked for awhile in a Marzipan factory. She brought home rejected Marzipan, and the children practically lived on that. Paul, who was always very artistic, made sculptures out of the Marzipan dough.

Paul spoke with great unhappiness about the 1st World War years. His father was never around—his mother was incapable of feeding the four children, Paul, an older brother and two younger sisters. The children were distributed among relatives. Paul was sent to East Prussia to his uncle. He was so lonely! He felt that he was treated as an inferior. Yet human beings can somehow find solace in various ways. He loved animals. He gave names to his cows and treated them like people. One significant human contact came from some prisoners of war, a Frenchman and two Russians. At that time, prisoners of war were distributed among the farmers to help in the fields. Paul and those prisoners were assigned to sleep in the hay loft. He was supposed to be their guardian—he was then about fourteen years old. He loved it because they became close friends. Paul could play almost any instrument he put his hands on, though he never learned how to read music. At that time he had an accordion and a mouth organ. They found violins for the Russians and a flute for the Frenchman. Together they started an orchestra. They were so good that they were asked to play at weddings and funerals in the various villages. The prisoners cried when the war was over and they had to separate.

Paul's grandfather was very stern, but Paul learned much from him. Many, many years later, when I wondered how Paul knew how to lay a roof, he laughed and said, "Well, this is nothing. It was much more difficult to lay straw roofs with my grandfather."

Paul always felt closer to women than to men. He was much closer to his grandmother. He loved watching her bake bread and learned it from her. She was kinder to him than to the other children. I hear Paul say, almost with tears in his eyes, "She always kept some dough for me and let me have some sugar so that I could bake a special little cake for myself."

He rarely talked about any of the demeaning hurts that must have occurred, but I remember the bitterness with which he spoke about the day of his Confirmation when nobody came and nobody gave him anything, while there was much ado about his cousins. I got very angry when he told me about his experiences with the village schools. I knew from my reading about the cruelty and stupidity of village teachers in Germany, yet to listen to someone who had really lived through that was almost physical pain. These teachers called the students "idiots," while they themselves could hardly read. They beat the children violently. Once a teacher took off his wooden shoes and threw them at the heads of some boys, causing them to bleed. Then he took those same boys and beat them harshly. Paul and some others were so incensed about that that they snuck at night into the teacher's orchard and cut down all his fruit trees.

Paul, just like his older brother, became an apprentice in the same trade as his father. He was furious at the way Masters treated young people. He felt that after awhile he did not learn anything, that he was only used by them. He dared to contradict the Master, and this was considered a major crime. To get rid of him, the Master arranged to give him an especially difficult examination, both theoretically and practically. He passed it with flying colors, and therefore got his degree much earlier than originally planned.

Paul and his older brother joined the early youth movement of the Social Democratic Party. It was a youth movement just like many of the others I described earlier: hiking, concern with social movements and art. Paul, his brother and his brother's girlfriend, (later to become his wife and my good friend), did a great deal of hiking and bicycling together.

Back in Hamburg the shy boy still related more to nature and animals than to people. He felt close and protective of his mother. He had seen her so frequently abused by his father. He told me of an incident that was very decisive in his life: His father had been at home for awhile, and insisted that the growing boys must learn to be "men," which meant they had to learn how to drink beer. The youth movement was strictly against alcohol. There was a saying, "Drinking workers do not think, and thinking workers do not drink." Many of us, I included, had fights with our elders because we did not touch a drop of alcohol, even for religious purposes. Paul's brother refused to drink with his father. Paul was younger and curious about the world. He went with him. One day Paul came home dead drunk. In his stupor he saw his mother bedding him down, taking off his shoes, crying while she was doing this. He had seen her do this for his father all his life, and he felt deeply ashamed. When he woke up, he overheard his brother talking with his friends. One of them said, "Boy, your little brother is just getting to be like your old man, isn't he?" He saw the tear-stained face of his mother bending anxiously over him. From that day on, Paul never again touched a drop of alcohol.

Now, I have to go back to my own life. I had continued working in the factory. My life consisted of that and an active involvement in the labor movement. It meant long hours of studying economics and philosophy, of distributing reading material, of debating in meetings of various parties, of knocking on doors, walking up many flights of stairs. We tried to stem the reactionary forces which became stronger and stronger in the shaky German republic. When we distributed material in the high apartment buildings, we always worked two and two together, one person starting on the top floor, and one person starting on the bottom. Starting on the top floor was most difficult because one had to walk up in one swoop. I liked best working together with Paul. At that time, we were only working companions. Yet he was so considerate and gentle! Totally matter of fact, he would inquire whether I was menstruating, and when I was, he would insist on always going up those flights first and letting me do it the easy way. No other person ever thought of that.

Meanwhile I moved from my small room to a room in a house that occupied several of us from the labor movement. Today one would probably call it a commune. "Mother Mosch" was the oldest person in the house. All her life she had been a working woman, taking care of her son alone. She loved the work she did now, taking care of all we young people, including her son, cooking for all of us and distributing the chores. We loved Mother Mosch. Once in awhile she showed how amused she was about our utter seriousness in wanting to change the world, and I know that she secretly shook her head about our vows of celibacy. We strictly stuck to that. But Mother Mosch helped us to enjoy life once in a while. She was the one who encouraged some of the young men to use their musical talent. Some evenings they would play their instruments and the rest of us would dance. Paul and I began to get closer during this time. Once when he stood in the street looking up at the balcony of the house, another young women and I broke off a rose that was blooming in the flower box and threw it down to him. He blushed furiously and my girl friend teasingly called us, "Romeo and Juliet." Young people in this country have asked me how "dating" was in my younger days. But that is a custom we did not know. We fell in love, we hiked together, and even slept in straw and the woods together, as I have described earlier. But there was nothing like "dating." I remember, though, that our feelings for each other changed from just being "comrades." We discovered other mutual interests than only the political ones. I was enchanted to find out that one of Paul's favorite artists was Tilman Riemenschneider, the sculptor whose work I had seen in Rothenburg. I did not know at that time how gifted Paul was in wood sculpturing—I only marveled at his depth of understanding of Riemenschneider's work.

Another quality that endeared me to Paul was his gentle love and respect for children. Paul's mother had taken on a two-year-old foster child. She took in this child and later another one whom nobody wanted because they were not "pretty": they soiled themselves, and they were sickly. She treated them with loving care. Paul was very much part of this. I watched him playing with the little boy, letting the little fingers hold onto his strong fingers and pulling him up and down, laughing. With the child, this serious man became a child himself. When later they had a little older boy as a foster child, Paul talked with him, walked with him, cleaned him, always treating him as a reasonable human being, not as somebody "cute" or someone to talk down to.

I have photos of Paul playing with a group of children in one of the children's homes of the workers' welfare movement. There he is, this slim young man, holding a large round piece of cardboard in his hand while talking with them in a circle, and climbing trees. I asked him once what the cardboard was. He said, smilingly, "Well, that is the moon. I told the children a story about the moon having come down to earth, but now it wanted to go back; and we have to help him by putting him up in the tree." I was enchanted with his imagination!

At about that time I went to several institutes learning about the "Socratic method." Leonard Nelson rediscovered that method to induce people to learn to do their own thinking. Gustav Heckmann and Grete Herman who later became University professors, conducted most of those meetings. They were at that time teachers in the Walkemühle, which Nelson had founded. The most important leader in those seminars was Minna Specht. She was the head of the Walkemühle, a strong woman, beautiful, slim, with eyes that seemed to look through everybody. After the Nazis came to power, Minna Specht took the Walkemühle, which then served small children, to Denmark because the Nazis had destroyed it in Germany. Just before the fall of Denmark, she fled with the children to England. Later, after the war, she became one of the leading educators in UNESCO and also the head of one of the progressive schools in the Odenwald in Germany. Most of her students loved and adored her. I think, just as Nelson, she reveled in that adoration. That was the time when I knew her first. I felt that she was only relating well to those students who said "yes" to everything she suggested and looked at her with adoring eyes. Being quite an independent spirit, I kept away from her. Yet, I think her attitude must have changed in later years. My friend, Hilde, whom I knew from the early youth movement, met her and some of her followers later on the Isle of

Wright where the British had interned German refugees during
the war. Hilde told me that Minna got sometimes quite impatient
with that kind of unthinking adoration. When I was sent back to
Germany after the war by the American government, I met Minna
again. She seemed to me a very different person—kind, unassum-
ing and with a sense of humor. I think the war years had wiped
out some of the rigid facade she had to put on earlier. Paul, who
had as a young man been in the Walkemühle, had often told me
about the annoying arrogance of teachers and students who were
the "intellectual leaders," but he always said that Minna Specht
was the only one who seemed not to look down on him and the
gardener who came from the working class.

Chapter Seven

University Years

*I*t was Minna Specht who suggested that I should stop working in the factory and go back to my studies at the university. I was so imbued with the need to serve the "movement" that I first thought that was wrong. Yet, Minna convinced me that learning, becoming a teacher, would not prevent me from following my convictions. I am always grateful to her for doing this.

In 1976 I was asked by a German publisher, Felix Meiner Verlag, Hamburg to write a short autobiography in regard to my development of ideas in Social pedagogics, what we would call in the U.S. "group work." I am quoting from this report, because it tells the influences coming from the university.

> After the year in the factory, I attended the University of Hamburg to become a teacher. My wish was to become a teacher in a Volksschule, especially where there were children

from poverty, and then after a few years, I hoped to return to the university to study medicine. I wanted to combine those two professions. Already at that time, Karl Wilker and his extraordinary work with delinquents had become known to me, and his combination of medicine, psychiatry and pedagogics seemed ideal to me. In 1930, I entered the Hamburg University, which was one of the most exciting ones at that time in Germany. It was a new one, uncluttered by stodgy traditions and filled with the spirit of new ideas in education and psychology. It was the only university that allowed the "Arbeiterabitur" (Abitur for workers) as entrance to the university. It had a vigorous faculty and students. To me, getting into the university was pure heaven. There were *books!* And then the place was clean. I never realized until after I was back at the university, how much I had suffered under the ugliness and dirtiness of the factories. This is another reason why I have always been very conscious of physical environment at work, in children's institutions, in prisons, in schools and wherever my influence has extended.

What do I remember of my studies? It is not always clear. Some people stand out in my mind. William Stern was a superb professor in psychology. I still today remember his unusual combination of scholarship and human warmth. He had studied, for instance, language development in his own children, but had generalized and conceptualized it and taught us what language means to the small child. He also taught something of the questioning spirit in psychology, not a dogma. He was no Freudian, but he did know about Freud and taught us about him. He thought through the question of "Ganzheitstheorie" (holistic theory) and its consequences. I can still hear William Stern saying, "Intelligence quotients only mean a relationship between school knowledge and where the person is at a given time. You don't have a guarantee that you know an awful lot about the potential of the person." How much more cautious was he than his followers! Stern's co-worker was a young, Walkurean-like looking Martha Muchow. She taught us how to observe children, how to take careful notes, how not to make any judgment without careful observation. Stern's son-in-law, Dr. Werner, was the experimental psychologist, the one who worked with rats. I never agreed with him, nor did I enjoy his lectures, but I did learn about exact experimentation and I had respect for his intellectual integrity.

There was Ernst Cassirer who taught philosophy. I never exactly liked his way of presentation, but he was excited about Kant, and I did learn more about this philosopher than ever before. Kant influenced my thinking about ethics and Cassirer stimulated it. There was Deuchler in pedagogics. Students had to choose between Flitner or Deuchler as their major advisor. Practically all those who came from the Youth Movement or from the socialist movement, chose Flitner. Even years later when I went back to Germany, many of my friends could not understand why I chose Deuchler. I chose him because I liked his logical way of presenting his thoughts and his comparatively clear language. The very complicated "erziehungswissen-schaftliche" (scientific educational) language of Flitner did not attract me. Still today, I am teaching students that, "Anything of value that must be said, can be said in simple words." I never will believe that depth has to be disguised by an obscure language. I was also very interested in Deuchler's struggle with a concept of education for the individual's sake as well as for the sake of the community. Again I did not agree with everything that he said, but I was fascinated by the struggle in him. I know that Deuchler later became a Nazi member. It was a shock to me, especially since several of his younger assistants also went that way. I want to say here though that he offered me help when he realized that, because of the Nazis, I would never be able to enter the school service. (I never accepted this offer. One of my friends who unfortunately is no longer alive, Gottlieb Rahloff, who after the fall of the Nazis became the head of the Hamburger Jugendamt (Youth Authority), told me that Deuchler literally saved him from Nazi arrest by hiding him in his office.) I never saw Deuchler again after 1933. But I do think that he was like so many German professors, not courageous enough and not clear enough about his philosophy to withstand the Nazis, but not one of the monsters.

And there was Julius Gebhardt, one of the assistants to Dr. Flitner, who was one of the great human beings I encountered at the University. Julius Gebhardt had no face. He was one of the "Gueules cassés," whose face had been destroyed completely during World War I. He had one eye, a clamp instead of a nose, and a little hole that presented a mouth. But this man could speak about the beauty of art education. He influenced a whole movement of pedagogic in Hamburg, which worked with drawings to develop young children and adolescents who had difficulties expressing themselves in other ways. Gebhardt understood also the influence that people have on each other and he discussed "Sozialpädagogik" long before that word became fashionable. Gebhardt was the only one who dared to see me after the Nazis came to power and who was willing to take my thesis and submit it as a doctoral one because he thought it was so good. (This never happened because I was arrested. I had to get my doctorate much later in the U.S.A.) I did see Gebhardt frequently in the years after the Nazis were defeated and I returned to Germany, and was always deeply moved by the integrity of this man.

I did take some seminars with Flitner and especially with his assistant Geisler. I did not feel close to him but I enjoyed his sharp mind and the clear logic in which he presented his material.

And then there were those who came to visit and who were very special. The one who influenced me the most was Kurt Bondy. He was at that time the head of Hanöversand, the youth prison near Hamburg. He discussed the significance of human relations in helping others and the necessity for identification with someone one loves if one wants to change. Bondy's influence together with Karl Wilker (whom I knew at that time only from reading), the juvenile court judge, Paul Blumenthal in Hamburg, and Mack in Selent, were the strongest influences in relation to my work with delinquents. They proved that a human approach to young people in despair can help change them. I watched Blumenthal in his courtroom and saw him treating parents and so called delinquents with the same polite, warm courtesy that he would extend to anyone else. I saw him wear worn-out shoes because he gave his money away to the young people who had nothing. Many years later, when I interviewed Wilker, I felt the humanity of this giant who made out of one of the worst youth prisons in Berlin a place where young people met with joy and concern. After 1933, Blumenthal and Mack were killed by the Nazis. Bondy and Wilker had to go into exile. I was fortunate to meet the latter two again.

Kurt Bondy had immigrated to the United States during the Nazi period and I met him again after the war when he returned to Hamburg. Bondy and I discussed the use of social group work with delinquents, stressing its basic intent of helping the individual through group associations. Bondy, with his deep psychological insight, had begun to work on the whole question of motivating people while they are living in circumstances they did not choose. We both agreed that the major aim of treatment under those circumstances is to diminish the authoritarian impact of that kind of living situation, since it debilitates the human being and makes him or her doubly incapable of learning how to make decisions. We saw group work as a "freeing" method. I continued to develop the significance of a healthy environment as the major treatment tool. Both of us considered the beginning dogmatic use of peer pressure a real danger in treatment. What has later been developed in the United States as "Positive Peer Culture" has increased this danger. It allows those in power to use young people to pressurize their peers while the adults pretend that their hands are "clean." This group method teaches inmates to be followers. It does not help them to learn to make their own decisions. Social group work—"Sozialpädagogik"—under good leadership—would help people to learn how to help each other, how to create a supportive community, but it also makes demands on the individual to make his/her own decisions, not only follow pressure. The concepts of "counter measures against authoritarian determinism" and "supportive demand" became worked through in my discussions with Kurt Bondy.

Karl Wilker had influenced me greatly in my adolescence through his work in the delinquency institutions in Berlin. Much later, in the 1960's in the U.S.A., I worked on a historical view of the delinquency reforms of the 1920's in Germany to present them as a model for working with juvenile delinquents. I was then very fortunate to spend a whole weekend at Karl Wilker's home in Germany. I interviewed him about his life and work and thinking. The then over 80-year-old man was an inspiration. He, too, had to flee when the Nazis came to power and spent years in Africa with young Blacks in distress. Karl Wilker confirmed strongly my philosophy and the conviction that we can help young people to develop their potential and feel responsibility for others, but only if we are willing to let them meet adults who have no conceit, but are willing to listen and to think with them.

(End of excerpt from *Pädagogik in Selbstdarstellungen IV*, Editor Pongratz, Hamburg 1982.)

It was heaven to be back to be able to study and to think. I was very poor. Money came in only from lessons that I could give to various students. One of them was very special to me: Murki was a strong, tall fifteen-year-old who insisted on carrying my bicycle up and down the stairs of the apartment house and who would talk excitedly about his capacity in diving and swimming. All this would not be so unusual, but Murki was blind. He was a very gifted boy. When I read to him four pages of a history book, he gave them back to me, verbally. He never felt sorry for himself. Once when he overheard his father saying something about how sad it was that his son was blind, he confronted his father with, "Say, Dad, what can you see right now?" His father described the room in which they sat.

Murki: "That is all? Can you see the street?"

"No, we are in the room."

"Well, if you are *that* limited when you can see, I haven't lost very much, have I?"

I was his teacher, but he taught me much. And so did Yen Chen, another fifteen-year old, who had just come from China. I knew his sister, who had visited us in Berlin. They were young people, dedicated to a change in China's feudalistic system, but they did not want to be communists. Chen had to learn German to participate in his school class. I admired his patience and capacity. I still marvel at his learning German through the classics. I can never forget Schiller's beginning of "William Tell" as read by Chen, "Der Knabe schlief ein am grünen Gestade..." (The boy fell asleep in the green meadow...)

One day I saw that his face was swollen. First he did not tell me what had happened. Finally I found out. The boys in his class had been teasing him and made him jump into a shallow part of the swimming pool. Some of his teeth were knocked out. The power of race prejudice and the total disregard for another human being made me so furious that I wanted to go to the school to intervene. Chen prevented me from doing this. His quiet pride would not allow it. He did allow me to take him to a doctor and he said to me, "It doesn't matter. They are dumb."

I wore poor clothes. One person who offended me was an adult, well-to-do woman to whom I gave some lessons, I can't remember in what. Once when I came to her home, I wore a little scarf someone had given me. She said, "Well now, that is nice. I don't understand why you never wear something a little more pretty. You could make something out of yourself."

I bit my lips. She had no idea that I had not even ten cents in my pocket that day.

I usually lived on one free meal a day provided for underprivileged students by the university. Poor students got coupons and had that one meal. Once in a while I could afford a five-cent piece of cake. There was a little bakery in a basement, and every day it had this fabulous huge piece of cake for sale for very little money. Yet, I was quite happy because I was clean, I

was independent, and I could study! I loved my practical work in
schools and delinquency institutions.

And there was the marvelous increasing music of Paul's and
my love! To some people on the outside, especially to my family,
this was not an acceptable relationship. Marriage between a Jew
and a non-Jew was frowned upon by Orthodox Jews. There were
those who actually mourned their children as dead when they
went into such a marriage. My father, who had been once a revolutionary and had instilled into me a sense of equality of all people, had meanwhile turned to Jewish Orthodoxy and was very
unaccepting of a mixed marriage. In addition to that, Paul came
from a working class background, and in a class society, that, too,
was not very acceptable. I was very angry at the prejudice on the
side of the "minority," as well as the majority which also increasingly rejected marriage between Jews and non-Jews. (A short
time later, under the Nazis, this was made totally impossible
and was punishable by death or deportation.)

On Paul's side of the family, especially his mother, our love
was totally accepted. His mother only wondered why this
"intelligent teacher" would love her unemployed son, but I know
that secretly she was very proud of him. To both of us, our relationship deepened every day. I find it very amusing when some
people think that some forms and values of relationships between men and women were brand new in the 1960's: as, for instance, acceptance of equality, the idea that men and women
could share household chores, that one made decisions together
of where to live and whether one should have children. All this
applied to us as long as I can recall. For instance, from the beginning Paul could cook better than I and often he would prepare
dinner. I learned from him. We did our political work together,
agreeing or disagreeing. Paul taught me that one could do some
enjoyable things in life, even without money. I remember his
phone call one day, "Come on, there is a movie showing at the
Union Headquarters."

"I never go to the movies. I don't have money."

"Don't be silly. I don't have money either, but that showing is free."

I also remember the day he suggested our first vacation trip together that I described earlier in those memories I gave him. I thought it was impossible to do. He insisted that it could be done. Every piece of equipment, everything, was borrowed from somebody; but where did the train fare come from? Paul had been very mysterious about that. Only at the end of the trip did he confess that he had hocked his one precious possession, a gold watch from his grandfather. I still have that watch. I helped to get it back later. We always shared our money. It went into a common pot. Later, when we were married in the United States, we simply continued that habit. All through life, we felt like comrades, equals, husband and wife. Once during that early period in Hamburg I became very ill with a severe and painful ear infection. I had a high fever, and the pain was excruciating. Paul was sitting at my bed and I begged him to give me something to kill myself because the pain was so great.

I should explain that I usually can take much pain and take it quite stoically. Paul knew this, and later he told me that this was one of his worst experiences. In my feverish state, I considered it cruel that he did not follow my wishes. Suddenly he got up and disappeared for awhile. He returned, sat down quietly near my bed, and pulled out his mouth organ. Softly, he began to play; folk songs, Mozart, and our beloved song from Beethoven's Ninth Symphony. The pain seemed to dissolve. I fell asleep. I always will understand and empathize with the Bible story of Saul and David.

The time to write my final thesis came closer. I had always been interested in understanding the philosophical base for a non-authoritarian education. The most effective, and yet to my thinking, unacceptable authoritarian education existed within the Catholic Church. I therefore chose for my thesis to study the education done by the Jesuits, and then look at it critically. It was most exciting work! I still wonder today about the audacity of this twenty-one year old who knocked at the doors of one of the most famous Jesuit institutions in Berlin and asked to use its library. I was allowed to enter the cloister and study in that library. My advisor once asked me when he was reading my account, whether I was being converted. I was not. In fact, I did not agree with the kind of education that the Jesuits had developed, yet I felt it had to be presented as objectively as possible. At the same time I worked on my secondary thesis in my other field, history. There again, I was intrigued by the Middle Ages. We had always been taught that the Middle Ages were the Dark Ages where thinking was not allowed and science made no progress. Yet I began to read some of the Latin documents and found this false. Actually, it seemed to me that the Church had supported a great deal of scientific inquiry. I wrote this as my thesis and tried to prove this. (Many years later, when I was teaching at the University of Minnesota, I met a professor, Mark Graubard, whose field was the Philosophy of Natural Sciences, and he confirmed my thesis.) I loved working at night, thinking and writing. Paul often came over during the day, and I read to him parts I had written. I wanted to make sure that I wrote in an understandable language, not "gobbledygook." I was not writing in a field that Paul knew about, since his interest was more in the natural sciences. Yet, he, too, was interested in ethics and their application; his comments helped me to write so that it could be understood.

Both papers were due in the spring of 1933. I was always a person who liked to beat deadlines, perhaps because of some inner anxiety and pressure developed in early childhood. I had both theses ready in early summer of 1932. I went to the school authorities, which at that time were responsible for the acceptance of such work. The bureaucrat in charge threw one glance at it and said, sternly, "Get back and re-work this. If you are that early, it cannot be worth anything."

I was completely devastated. I went back with this verdict to my major advisor, Professor Deuchler. He laughed, shook his head and said, "Bureaucrats! O.K. put your work into the desk drawer just as it is and hand it in next March. That is all you have to do."

I could not believe my ears! How good that I had done it so early. The advent of the Nazis was in the air—the next months I could hardly think of any studies. It was not only the dark winter that came down on us, it was the darkness of total human destruction descending over Germany.

Chapter Eight

1933 The Nazis Come to Power

"Paul, did you hear it?"

"Yes, get away from the window, Gisa," the calm hand (the hand which steadied me often when it was necessary), Paul's hand, touched my shoulder softly, but urgently. It was a December evening in Hamburg, dark, wet. It was December, 1932, and the sounds I had heard were shots, rifle shots in the streets of a busy city! Terror had mounted in the last weeks. The Nazis were not yet in power, but the ascent was approaching fast. The shots and the sound of marching feet on the wet street pavement were the distinct signs.

"I must see what is happening, are 'they' out again?"

We went into the street: police were on the sidewalks. Around the corner came marching troops—the stormtroopers in brown shirts with spades carried over their shoulders like guns (the Versailles Treaty forbade weapons, but they began to train for them and carried some secretly)—their faces were brutal, their songs worse, "Wenn das Judenblut vom Messer spritzt..." ("When the blood of the Jews is on our knives") and "Heute gehört uns Deutschland, aber morgen die Welt," ("Today Germany belongs to us, tomorrow the world").

A policeman whispered to us, "Heaven help us, when they will rule."

At that moment hell broke loose. Someone must have said something against the brownshirts. Suddenly the spades flew on the necks and backs of bystanders. Police tried to break it up; shots again....The face next to me, the face of Paul looked grim.

"This is only a beginning. If we who are against them were not so divided...but this way they will defeat us."

Winter 1932. Unemployment was high; people could be bought for two marks to enter the ranks of the brownshirts: Two marks and promises, two marks and a uniform, which clothed the man and gave him the feeling he was "somebody." Two marks and stories how everything would be better for him when he drove out the *Jews* who had taken all the good jobs and the money, the *intellectuals* who had destroyed the good German working man, the *socialists*, who were international, and free himself of the "bondage" imposed by the "allies." All this allowed a man to throw this hate on someone outside of himself and of the situation in his own country, and blame someone else.

A sane force against all this was the free labor unions. But they were weakened by their "friends" on the left, the communists, who had started their own unions and who constantly told them that there was no danger of the Nazis winning or, "Anyhow," they said, "it must get worse before it gets better," so, "Let them get to power for awhile."

There were big rallies. I remember one where the communist speaker repeated a story about, "Letting the Nazis come to power to pave the way for the worker's paradise."

Some of us shouted, "There will be no such thing, we will all die in a mass grave."

They just laughed.

I was in the last months of my university study. It is good that this is a time of life when one apparently needs very little sleep. There were lectures to attend and work to prepare and examinations to pass, but daily we were outside, students and young workers, Jews and non-Jews, together, trying to convince people that a horrible danger was threatening Germany. Käthe Kollwitz signed a final call for the labor unions to unite against the disaster. Käthe Kollwitz was not only a great artist, but a symbol of courage. We fervently distributed Käthe Kollwitz' call, which she had signed together with other German writers and scientists.

It was five o'clock on a dark winter morning, before university lectures started, when we stood at the entrance of the Elbtunnel (the tunnel under the Elbe river) as workers streamed past to go to their work in the shipyards. I loved those workers at the harbor—they seemed strong and kind. They took our leaflets and read them carefully in the dim light of lanterns. Some saw us shiver.

"You must be cold, kid," one huge fatherly man said to me. He took my hands into his big, rough ones and rubbed them quickly. "Better? We'll not let those Nazis get here," and on he went.

In the evening, after work or classes, we were in that area again, this time visiting the dives where there was much drinking, but where most of the sailors congregated—they were important in this fight of life and death! We always teamed up, a young man and a young woman. Women could not enter those places alone. Yet sometimes we became separated if we got involved in heated discussions. In one such dive I lost my partner. Suddenly a huge sailor loomed large next to me, following me through the whole place.

"You're doing the right thing, so I'll watch that no harm comes to you," he said.

We would sometimes meet up with Nazis—they were not yet sure of their victory, so they did not always attack. Some tried to convince me to become a member of their party: "An active girl like you," they said. I usually discussed the issues with them for a long time. At the conclusion I would tell them that I was Jewish, and then secretly enjoy their bewilderment. (The Nazi propaganda said that one could "smell" a Jew.)

January, 1933: The old Hindenburg had named Hitler the Chancellor of the Reich. This had been preceded by the complete defeat of the Social Democratic Government of the largest state of Germany, Prussia. Many of us knew that this was the end of the German Republic and the beginning of the most horrible and inhuman terror system of modern times. In Berlin, Goering had started the "Reichstagsbrand" (the burning of the German Parliament). A poor feeble-minded Dutchman was blamed for it and put on trial. It was a sign and a pretext for arrests of people all over the country who were known to stand in the way of the Nazis: leading men in the labor unions, socialists, communists, outspoken churchmen and respected intellectuals and Jews. The raving and ranting of the "Fuehrer" became known to the whole world.

The arrests were always accompanied with the most degrading methods of treatment. In Hamburg—where I was—some of the leading citizens were forced to scrub the prison floors with tooth brushes. Horrible inhuman beating started. Some victims who were released did not dare to talk about them, but we saw the broken bones and, sometimes, the broken spirits.

Paul and I were sitting in my little rented room on a cold February night. I was trying to concentrate on studies since final examinations were coming up soon. Every knock at the door was frightening because we never knew who would be arrested. The knock this time was most frightening. It came late in the evening. Paul had come to repair my bicycle, our major mode of transportation. The man who entered was in civilian clothes, but he flashed his badge and said, "Police."

He asked Paul to leave, because he had come for me. This was to be my first interrogation under the Nazi system. The interrogation concerned my activities against the Nazis and I was repeatedly questioned about whom I was meeting with now, what their names were, and would they continue to fight the Nazis now that the Nazis had come to power. I cannot remember all the details, but I vividly remember the feeling I had. It had been agreed among us in the labor union, long before the Nazis had come to power, that under no circumstances would anyone ever reveal the name of any other person involved in anti-Nazi activity. Yet we had so little practice in this. Now here I sat for almost four hours, matching wits with a person who had much experience in questioning. I felt my inner spirit revolt against having to lie—because lying it was. Every time he asked for somebody, I would say that I didn't know where they were even if I did know it. He asked about Klara, one of our beloved teachers, a woman who should have been declared a saint. Only two days ago Klara had told me that she had to leave the country immediately, though this was the last thing she wanted to do. The Gestapo had already asked for her at her apartment. Many people thought her too valuable a person to simply die in the cellars of the Nazis. In spite of our agreement made many months ago to destroy every photo and every letter of anyone close to us who could possibly be arrested by the Nazis, I had kept one photo of Klara; it was dear to me. The policeman asked whether I had seen her recently and where she was. With the calm of a person who knew that Klara's life depended on being able to leave, I insisted that I had not seen her for many months and that I therefore had no idea where she might be—the picture and the lie both burning on my conscience.

Many of us who fought against the Nazis thought that one of the most horrible things they did to us was to force us to lie. I remember the words of Rudi, who later was killed by the Nazis, when I talked with him about this horrible situation which forced us to become liars; "As long as it hurts you to lie, it is all right. Just watch out that you never enjoy it and never use it in a decent society."

There was something incongruous about the policeman that evening. In spite of his obviously representing the new regime, he acted in an almost courteous manner. I suspect today that he was a man of the police force of the old German Republic who did this without really wanting to. At the end of the long, grueling interview, he got up, shook my hand and said, "I came here to arrest you, but I will not do it now. Please do not participate in anti-Nazi activities. I would hate to come for you another time."

When he walked out he met Paul, who had been waiting in another room. He could see that Paul was concerned about me. He said to him, "Now what would you say if I had taken her away? You know that's what I came for."

Again, the horrible truth that one could not trust anyone and that we had to be on guard all the time struck both of us. This man was the enemy and it was necessary to erase from his mind any relationship between two people as soon as possible so that never—if one should be arrested—would he remember to drag the other one in as well.

Paul smiling quickly said, "Well, if she has to go, she has to go."

The policeman looked at us and shook his head. I guess he must have felt that a force was growing against the Nazi terror.

Yet we were not "heroes." The realization of how our lives might completely change, our "youth lost," and our adulthood perhaps never to be achieved, began to take on real meaning.

At Easter, I visited my family at home in Berlin.

My sister, Hanna, then a medical student who had married a law student, was living nearby. I stayed in her apartment and heard her nightly desperate sobbing, saying that she did not want to leave a country in which she had grown up.

My younger sister, Ruth, was just finishing her "Gymnasium." All three of us had looked forward to the spring of 1933, when each one of us was to pass an examination: the older one in medicine, I in teaching, and the youngest the "Abitur" (entrance to the university). Now spring, 1933, would allow us to finish our studies, but would cut off any opportunity to continue in our chosen work because we were Jews. I was perhaps the calmest in the family because I did not consider myself only a *victim as a Jew*, but an *active adversary of the Nazi movement*, determined to oppose them together with other Jews and non-Jews who were carrying on the same fight.

I returned to Hamburg after the short Easter recess. Things were in a turmoil at the university. William Stern was told that he would have to leave immediately because he was a Jew. The same applied to his son-in-law. Suicide was around us everywhere. Many felt that there was no way out either for themselves, their country, and perhaps for all humanity.

In this atmosphere the days of my oral examinations approached. They had to be passed in pedagogics, psychology and history. The student body, too, was in turmoil. Several of the leading socialist students had been arrested or had fled the country. Many students had suddenly discovered that it was opportune to be a Nazi and wear the swastika. Many did it callously and others full of fear. I remember gentle, kind Herman who had been one of my friends, who had worked with me in one of the institutions for delinquents, and whose thinking seemed so similar to mine. He saw me one morning and said, "Last night the Nazis broke up every piece of furniture in the youth hostel where I am staying. They say youth must be educated differently." And then he added with a sad smile, "I have to make a living and maybe they are right?"

Fear, opportunism and the rationalizing of one's own cowardice were all rolled into one.

Jewish students were excluded from any future without question. Yet, Hamburg still allowed the students to take their examinations and finish their studies, and William Stern was allowed to give his last examinations. A Nazi representative would sit in on them. What a strange day this final examination day was to which I had looked forward for so many years. I literally had gone hungry for several years to be able to study; I had passed examinations every semester to keep my standings as a scholarship student. Now I knew that after this last effort there was no place for me in Germany to work with the children I loved.

The evening before my finals there had been a "Haussuchung" (search) of my apartment. The Nazis looked for "forbidden" books. They took a load of them including art books of modern paintings which they considered "degenerate art." I woke up in the morning in a ransacked room and with no hope for the future. It was a strange way to go into an examination. I took my bicycle and rode to the university. I seemed calm. Yet, before I went into the waiting room for the examination I had to go to the wash-room to throw up. In the waiting room were several of the students who had been my colleagues for three strenuous years. The girl next to me boasted that she had always been a Nazi long before they came to power. She said she was glad that the university would get rid of that dirty Jew, Professor Stern, who dared to discuss sex in his classes while decent Germanic women were listening. Jews were dirty, over-sexed and smelled. She could recognize any Jew simply by his smell.

She said to me, "I know you don't agree, but you will learn and become a party member, too."

I looked at her—holding on to a last thread of self-control—and said calmly, "You don't mean to say that you never smelled that I am a Jew?"

She turned white in the face, and said that it just wasn't true, that I was making fun of her and she would report me. Perhaps you cannot imagine the deathly calm anger can produce. Hardly ever in my life did I speak as calmly to anyone as when I said, "I am not only of Jewish parentage but my parents were born in Poland. Those are the 'worst' and the 'smelliest' Jews, aren't they?"

Other students, non-Jews, were hiding their heads in shame. Nobody said a word. It was on this note that I was called into the examination room, and faced the solemn examination procedures as only German universities can conduct them. And there, in this room, William Stern, who already knew that his career as a distinguished scholar had been ended in his own country and I, who had hoped to start a career, were discussing child psychology and its problems as if the world stood still. In fact, an inner elation came over me in thinking that knowledge was important and that our understanding of children must not be lost in spite of everything. My oral examination was followed by several others. When I returned to the examination room—after a short waiting period—I received the verdict that I had passed the written and oral examinations "with distinction" and passed with the highest grade in each subject. One of the professors followed me out of the room.

Turning to another one he introduced me by saying, "This is the coming genius of our public school system."

I said, "It is not. I will never be allowed to teach in a German public school because I am Jewish and also because I cannot teach Nazi philosophy."

A young instructor whom I had known well during my study time and whom I had known as a good democrat beckoned me into his office. Only then did I see the party member sign, the swastika, on his lapel.

He said, "This is terrible. I think we should have you in the schools. Maybe the government will become more reasonable after some time. But for God's sake, don't say anything like what you just said."

I only said, "How can you?" pointing at his emblem.

He shrugged his shoulders. "One has to make a living."

How often I heard this in the next weeks and years. The reality of "making a living" can be one of the most corrupting forces.

I said goodbye to Professor Deuchler who had been my advisor and mentor at the university. Only a few months before he had lent me the examination fee out of his own pocket. He had recommended me highly to the school authorities. He, too, beamed when I entered the office, congratulating me and himself to his prize pupil. Again I had to explain to him the situation.

He only stared at me and said, "Is there not some hole through which we can get you in?"

Again I had to explain to this man who had for years taught citizenship at the university the stern facts of the meaning of Nazism.

On the evening after my examination I met Paul. We walked along the dykes near Hamburg and we looked on the broad waters of the Elbe. I was in a strange mood, wavering between elation about the excellent result of the examination and deep depression. It seemed very futile to continue living. In the face of the enemy I could take a stand as I did that morning, but when evening neared, it seemed that there was no point to go on. The day had shown how far Nazi corruption had entered everywhere. Paul told me about a Jewish factory owner he had met during the day who had expounded on how good it was that the Nazis had come to power because now at least they could crack down on those disgusting labor unions. The man obviously had not yet seen the danger for himself. It was clear to us that Nazi persecution had to be seen as a persecution of *every freedom and decency* and not only as a persecution of Jews as Jews. That evening on the dykes of Hamburg, the sky had grown dark and the waves began to churn and they sounded like a call to me to end everything. I was bitter and said to Paul that it really would be better if I didn't exist. It wouldn't be only good for me, it would be good for him.

What was the use of his sticking to a Jewish girl whom he could not marry because he was a non-Jew, and the Nazi laws forbade such intermarriages. Paul taught me something that evening that in all my future work I have considered an important insight. He did not commiserate with me, as I probably expected. He simply got angry:

"Do you think that you are fighting this alone? Am I less attacked just because I don't happen to be Jewish? One doesn't solve problems by running away from them. If you and I don't do something, they'll reign to the end of the world. Stop pitying yourself. We are all in this together."

I was stunned by his anger, but he pulled me out of my despair by his stern demand for responsible action.

When we returned to my room there was a letter from Ruth. It was a desperate letter, showing the terrible loneliness and despair of a young person. Her poems spoke of it:

DIE 18 JÄHRIGEN

Sie haben uns alle zu Greisen gemacht
wir, die wir grad 18 Jahre alt waren.
Eben haben wir noch wie Kinder gelacht
Jetzt liegt über unseren Haaren
jenes leichte grau, das ein Herbsttag hat,
der feucht und mit Nebel beginnt,
irgendwann einen blassen Sonnenstrahl hat
und dann im Regen verrinnt.

Translation:

THE EIGHTEEN YEAR OLDS

They have made us into aged beings,
we, who are barely eighteen now.
A moment ago we laughed happily like children—
yet now lies on our hair
the light grey that you find in an autumn day,
that begins with the running mist,
shows here and there a weak ray of the sun
and then ends in the rain.

DER JUDE

6000 Jahre sieht ihn die Welt
6000 Jahre immer wieder auf die Erde gestellt;
6000 Jahre geht er schon.
6000 Jahre war er Vater, Mutter, Sohn.
6000 Jahre Weisheit, Leben, Tod,
6000 Jahre Dumpfheit, Elend, Not!

6000 Jahre trug er alle Qual.
6000 Jahre—seine Hände wurden schmal
6000 Jahre—Die Kraft ging dahin.
6000 Jahre, jetzt sucht er ihren Sinn;
6000 Jahre geliebt und geworben,
6000 Jahre gezeugt und gestorben,
6000 Jahre!! Er brüllt zum Himmel: "Du!"
6000 Jahre schweigen dazu.
6000 Jahre höhnen: "Der gute Gott ward alt."

Translation:

THE JEW

For 6000 years he has seen this world
For 6000 years have seen him placed upon this earth,
For 6000 years he walks and walks
For 6000 years he was Father, Mother, son.
For 6000 years he knows wisdom, life, death.
For 6000 years hopelessness, misery, despair!
For 6000 years he carried all this torture.
For 6000 years—his hands became thin.
For 6000 years—his strength vanished.
For 6000 years—and now he seeks for their meaning;
For 6000 years—loved and betrothed,
For 6000 years—being born and dying,
For 6000 years—he screams to Heaven, "You!"
For 6000 years—and no answer
For 6000 years mock him, "The good God grew old."

Those thoughts of a teenager...

Perhaps it was the mood of the day and the seriousness of the situation, but this was the evening when Paul and I became "betrothed" in the most old-fashioned sense of the word, "for better or for worse," regardless of whatever would happen to us and regardless of the man-made laws that prevented us from being married. (It was only in the U.S.A. that we were finally allowed to lead a truly married life.)

There was only occasional work for me, but I could make a living tutoring students who could not quite make the grade in school; teaching younger children English, especially children whose parents wanted to emigrate; working in a little bookstore; doing house cleaning for other people. Yet this was the least important work that was done. For a few months those of us who wanted to do anti-Nazi work "laid low," knowing that in every house there was a spy, that everybody was alerted to report the slightest signs of people meeting outside of the Nazi organization. Preventing communication between people is one of the most potent weapons of dictatorships. This way organized resistance cannot start. In those weeks those of us who were anti-Nazi had to observe who steadfastly refused to join the ranks of the Nazis and who wavered. It became obvious that former affiliations did not mean much.

There was, for instance, a man who had been a leader in the socialist Youth Hostel Movement. Nobody would ever have thought that he would become a Nazi. He held out for a little while, but then his wife began to nag him about what would become of her and his two young children if he would not join the Nazi movement. Very soon he not only allowed all youth hostels under his direction to become nazified, but he joined the party and kept his top position. We do not always know how much it costs a man to so completely repudiate his past. But in his case we know a little. His sister-in-law, who was one of our good friends, stayed at his house occasionally. She told about horrible nightmares which assailed her brother-in-law, how he cried out in his sleep, moaning that he was not a murderer. His wife—probably with a less sensitive conscience—took it much easier. While she at first admitted that they had to give in—"to make a living"— she soon told everybody that really Germany should become the strongest country and that it was right to raise her little boy in the Hitler youth, and let her little girl's hair grow so she looked like a "true German maiden" and not like those foreign girls. (In

1981 I heard again about this family. They were again "good social democrats." They denied that any of this ever happened.)

From my window, I could observe the formation of Nazi
youth. Every morning they gathered at the corner across the
street. They stood in line, tall boys in front and the small ones in
the back. When they marched, the little ones had to run. A big
boy with the voice of an army sergeant shouted orders for their
military drill. When some of the little ones did not quite know
what to do, they got their ears boxed by the big ones.

I had previously done some practice teaching in one of the
most progressive schools of Hamburg. I loved my class of ten-year
olds and I returned one day to pick up some of my belongings that
were still there. The kids clustered around me, happy, loving as
they always had been. Two of them, a boy and a girl, the most
intelligent children in that class, pulled me into a corner.

They pointed to one of the teachers, "Look at him," they said
to me, "he wears the SS uniform." (The SS wore a black uniform.
It was Hitler's most feared and most brutal stormtroop.) "Isn't it
disgusting? And before the Nazis came to power he preached
pacifism to us."

Here were little ten-year olds who were dragged into a desperate political fight, and they realized the cowardice of adults.
Bless you, Annemarie, and Klaus. Both of them were beheaded by
the Nazis in later years just because their young souls never accepted this kind of treason.

There was also Lottie, a delightful, active youngster whom I
later saw marching with the BDM (The Hitler Youth for Girls).
She met me alone after I had seen her and told me that she really
did not like all this Nazi stuff and all this "hating everybody,"
but it was so much fun to go on the outings and it was horrible to be
alone. How understandable!

Several of us in the labor movement felt that we hated to
wait much longer to do something active against the spreading
disease. But how to go about it, we did not know. Once in awhile
two or three of us would meet as if by accident and seriously discuss possibilities. All newspaper and radio was in the hands of

the Nazis and it was frightening to see how quickly this propaganda entered into the thinking of everybody. It was as if all contact with any outside information had been cut off.

Chapter Nine

Beginning Resistance

One morning there was a knock at my door. One of my neighbors who was a friend and whom I knew as a good anti-Nazi asked me to get dressed very quickly and to come over to her apartment. When I got there two or three others whom I knew were also there and, to my great astonishment, there was René, a union organizer from Switzerland, whom we had known in the days of the German Republic. He had come to talk with us about what could be done to organize some active resistance to the Nazis. This was a serious, soul-searching morning. We had to ask ourselves whether there was any sense in our doing anything actively against the regime or whether we were just foolishly delivering ourselves to death.

The penalty for any anti-Nazi activity was concentration camps, torture, jail, death—and we knew it. We had to decide what we could do, what we thought would be effective, and whether it was worth the sacrifice. We agreed that one of the most effective weapons against Nazism was to spread news inside of Germany about the fact that not all Germans were Nazis. We also thought it important to harass the Nazis themselves by letting them know that they had not yet the support of the total nation. Some argued that this would be wrong because a frightened dictator uses more terror. This view proved to be correct, yet that morning we thought it important to show our resistance. A third purpose of underground work was to keep an anti-Nazi spirit alive among all decent people regardless of religion or party affiliation. And, finally, there were practical tasks for an underground movement: the smuggling out of people in danger of being killed by the Nazis and the bringing of news to other countries regarding anti-Nazi movements so that they could in turn help to defeat this horrible system.

Who should participate and how should all this be accomplished? It had become clear that one could not trust anyone whom one did not know well. It therefore seemed impossible to recruit any new people to the underground work and that we had to rely on the ones we knew. It was also clear that one could only involve people who voluntarily participated and who were willing, not only to sacrifice their lives as one does in a war, but who were willing and hopefully able to withstand torture when they were alone in a Nazi prison. And something much more serious had to be asked of the active underground worker: He or she had to give up a hope for a "normal life"; one could not get married or have children. It was important to keep everyone separated from each other, because every single person was precious in the fight against the Nazis. Married people with young children could only be used with utmost caution or not at all. The reason for this was that underground activity had to be done with so much secrecy and it is difficult for parents to keep their activities secret from young children. Finally we decided that adolescents, whenever possible, should not be involved in this activity because of the horrible lying involved. We hated to teach young people to lie.

Those were some of the questions we discussed that morning. René was surprised that we were willing to do this dangerous work. He had brought the first underground newspaper, which was published regularly later on. It was printed on very fine paper so that each one could be rolled into a slim little tube and swallowed, if necessary. The news in this paper contained just what was necessary. It described anti-Nazi activities in other parts of Germany; it gave news of what happened in other countries which one could not find in German newspapers, and it called for the formation of small groups to keep alive the anti-Nazi spirit.

The first job was to get pamphlets to some of our friends and to ask them whether they wanted to participate in this work. Can you imagine going out with anti-Nazi pamphlets like that in your pocket, knowing that if just one was found on you it meant immediate arrest? If several were found on you it meant that you were a distributor and therefore the Gestapo would try to squeeze out of you the names of those you brought them to or the names of those who brought them to you. This would mean the torture of beatings, of hanging you by your thumbs, of letting the glaring lights shine into your eyes day and night.

I remember the first time I carried such a paper. It felt as if there was a hole in my pocket and everyone could see right through it. I visited several people. There was Georg, a shipyard worker who quietly looked at the paper and then without hesitation said, "This is what we need. I am with you." There was Anna, a young woman with a lovely madonna-like face, who worked in an office and who had always hoped to earn enough money to study. I did not think that she would want to participate, but she said, "It isn't worth living if one hasn't a good conscience," and she became one of us. I did not go to see Hans who, before the Nazis came to power, had been a leader in our little group of idealistic socialists. Someone else did. He slammed the door in the face of the caller, saying angrily, "I don't want to have anything to do with any of you." Only in times of stress will one ever know who has real courage, and who gained leadership only because he knew how to talk well when he was safe. Hans was a "liberal leader" only when it was fashionable and not dangerous.

The Nazis called for phony elections. No one who lives in a democratic country can understand how dictators know how to rig elections. The question asked in those elections was whether the German people agreed with Hitler or not. The ballots were marked "yes" or "no." Our little underground group distributed observers near all Hamburg election quarters. There were many where no pretense at secrecy was made. The curtain to the election booth was not drawn and ballots had to be marked in the open. But Hamburg was a city with a population not very friendly to the Nazis. This was known; therefore, in many districts the booths officially were secret. Yet, for instance, a slanted piece of cardboard was inserted into the ballot box, which made the ballots fall one on top of the other. When people entered the polling station they had to give their names. They were written down in order and therefore it was known who had voted "no."

In other places where this was not done the counting of the ballots was only a pretense. "No's" were thrown into the wastebasket and only the "Yes" votes were counted. When one of the election officers objected he was told to relax—but later in the evening he was found unconscious and bleeding in the street, beaten half to death on his way home. All this was known to us only because we organized observation and reporting. The news was secretly sent out of the country so that other nations would know about it and not fall for the Nazi propaganda that 99% had voted for them.

Another instance where the underground got active was when it was announced that Hitler would come to visit the shipyards in Hamburg. Frequently people have asked me why there were so few attempts to assassinate Hitler. There was much discussion among several of us about assassination and opinions were divided. Some thought it was important to kill Hitler because he was the mad man and the symbol. Others thoroughly opposed

any kind of assassination because of their principles of nonvio-
lence and also because they thought that Hitler alone did not
represent the system. Who was right, I cannot say even today. I
know, though, that before Hitler's visits to the shipyards several working men there were determined to kill him. They considered it an excellent opportunity. As one of them said, "You
need only to work up high on the ship's crane when he passes by
and accidentally drop a few bolts." I doubt that these specific
plans were known to the Gestapo but the hostility of the
Hamburg shipyard workers was known to them. Three days before Hitler's visit, the shipyard workers got four days off with
pay. Bloom and Voss shipyards were manned with SS and SA,
the Nazi troopers, disguised in workmen's clothes. When Hitler
went around smilingly shaking hands with the "Hamburg working man" and was photographed as such, he was actually shaking the hands of the storm troopers. Thus his life was safe. The
only thing the underground could do was to spread such news inside and outside of Germany hoping that this would be an encouragement to the anti-Nazi forces.

The distribution of the leaflets had to be worked out very
carefully. One could not always go to someone's home and bring
them there. Since the bicycle was the main mode of transportation, a number of leaflets were ingeniously packed into a lunch box
or a briefcase, then a few were slipped into the sleeve of the
blouse or shirt. At a specific time the carrier had to meet someone
else "accidentally." They would shake hands at the time of the
meeting and in this way the leaflets were distributed. It was
clear to us that split-second timing meant life or death. Nobody
could wait for another person. (I guess this has taught me all
through life how important it is to be punctual.) The meetings in
which such work was organized and discussed were held like
small harmless parties. Each time, at the beginning of the meeting, we discussed exactly what we would say if by any chance the
Gestapo would enter and ask us what we were doing there. It is
almost inconceivable how much time and effort had to go into
these precautionary measures.

Our meetings also had to serve one other specific purpose, and that was to prepare us for possible arrest and torture. One of the great gifts given to human beings is imagination. We had people who told us something about the methods the Nazis used to extract confessions. And with what we called "realistic imagination" we acted out possible similar situations to carefully prepare us to not denounce anyone.

Yet the longer the regime held, the more fear mounted. The uncertainty, the constant being on guard, began to wear people down. One evening one of the underground workers suddenly appeared in my room, though it had been agreed that he should never come there. With great agitation he told me that he was sure his landlady was a Nazi spy and knew all about him. I wondered whether he had any proof. With trembling hands and a flushed face he began to tell me about milk bottles being arranged in a certain way every time he left the house and the strange looks she was giving him. This story was interspersed with his sobbing and saying that he knew he could just never withstand Nazi questioning, that he couldn't go on living the way he lived, that he knew he did not want to denounce anyone but he would.

What I saw before me was the beginning of a mental breakdown, a most serious occurrence in such a situation, since the person not only suffered himself, but became a danger to everyone else. There was only one action to take and that was to stop him from further participation in the underground work. One could not tell him that, because his convictions were so great that it would hurt him. All I could do was to say to him that he should not participate for awhile so as to give his landlady no hold on him. After he left I immediately contacted others to tell them not to involve him in further underground work but continue to be friendly to him. Those were the heartbreaks of this work.

There was another evening when a sixteen-year-old girl I knew broke down in my room. Her parents were Quakers and conscientious objectors. Her father had been arrested by the Nazis. She told me about the sordid way in which she was treated at school. She had refused to say "Heil Hitler," the new greeting, which everybody had to use. Her teacher insisted that she pass by him and say "Heil Hitler" to him. She steadfastly refused. He made her pass by him over a hundred times, each time humiliating her and shouting at her before the entire class. He must have become tired of torturing her because he never got her to say "Heil Hitler." Here she was, crying, worn out and desperately pleading to be allowed to join any anti-Nazi movement I knew of, to do something against these people. How I wished at that moment to give this courageous youngster an outlet for her spirit. Yet I knew I could not do it because we had pledged ourselves not to involve teenagers. All I could do was strengthen her conviction by telling her that she was right in detesting the Nazis, that I knew there were people fighting them and that it was important she keep up her spirit, but that she must wait.

It was a bright winter day in 1935 when I came back from work and found on my table a strange document which had come in the mail. It said: "The President of the Police in Berlin" and it was directed to me.

> According to the document of April 19, 1921 1.5.P.61/20 you got your Prussian citizenship through naturalization and with that you had received your German nationality. According to Paragraph 1 of the Law regarding the withdrawal of naturaliza- tions and discontinuance of German nationality of July 14, 1933, (RGBL1 5.480) I herewith annul this citizenship.
>
> At the time of receipt of this document, you have lost your German nationality and you have ceased to be a German citizen. This withdrawal means also the loss of each citizenship of any other German land which you might have received.
>
> The withdrawal cannot be contested by any legal means.

I had expected this document. The law which made this possible was one which took away the citizenship of any Jewish person who had become a citizen through naturalization.

Actually I was born in Germany and had lived there all my life, but my parents had been Austrians and had been naturalized with their children in 1921. Now all of us lost our citizenship. The letter accompanying the document said that I had to appear at the Hamburg police which had to finalize this. I went to the police. The clerk took the document and looked at it. He then asked me for my other papers which included my university degree. He shook his head.

"Is this possible?" he asked. "You were born in this country and were one of the outstanding students."

He took all the papers and went into a back room. From where I stood I could see into this room. He called all of his colleagues together. Obviously the clerks in this office were not yet Nazis. I saw them shaking their heads in disagreement with this government action. It made me feel better. There was still hope.

The clerk returned and while he signed the paper he said, "Couldn't you just shake the dust of this 'beautiful country' off your shoes?"

I said, "Those of us who have no money cannot emigrate. And now, being a person without a country, you know that I have no passport and emigration is even less possible."

My own feelings that day while walking home were quite mixed. In a certain sense I was proud. I certainly did not think it was an honor to be a citizen of Hitler's country. Yet, I also knew that now it would be almost impossible for me to leave the country even if it became necessary. I knew from others about the fate of the "stateless." When I got home there was a note on the table. I had shown Paul the document before I left for the police, and here was the proof that love does not know any nationality or religion. Paul, who had to remain a German and could not marry me because, as he sometimes laughingly said, he was "just too Aryan," wanted me to be sure that I felt all his support. The note consisted mostly of a printed poem torn out of a book by Henrik Ibsen,

DANK

An meine Frau

Ihr Heim an dem Meere
Der Freiheit liegt,
Auf dem meine Fähre
Sich spiegelt and wiegt.

Ihr Höchstes ist, walten
Der Glut meiner Brust;—
Was stark mich erhalten,
Hat niemand gewusst.

Ibsen

Translation:

THANKS

To My Wife

Her home lies
on the sea of freedom,
on which my boat
sails and finds itself mirrored.

The most important to her is
to keep my strength going.—
What has kept me strong,
nobody has known.

Ibsen

Chapter Ten

Resistance and Family Destruction

$\mathcal{F}$or my father, the whole situation had become intolerable. Everything he had worked for and hoped for was destroyed. My oldest sister and her husband had immigrated to Palestine. My younger sister had been able to get permission to enter England to become a nurse. Father suddenly suffered a stroke. I was called from Hamburg to his bedside in the hospital. The doctor told me that this hospital, a Jewish one, was full of men of his age (about 50 years old) who just could not take the destruction of all their hopes. Father could speak very little to me, but when he spoke, he asked fondly for Paul.

In the early days of the advent of the Nazis, Father had visited Hamburg and had spent almost a full day with Paul, who showed him the city. I think it was through this contact that my father realized that the fight against the Nazis was carried on by any decent person regardless, of whether they were Jews or non-Jews; in fact he learned painfully that there were many Jews who would be Nazis if the Nazis had not persecuted them as Jews. Paul's clear and unwavering attitude toward human rights for everybody made a great impression on my father. In those last days of my father's life the closeness with him I had known as a child was revived.

When I fed him, he smiled and said, "You know, I once did this for you. Now you are doing it for me." I felt the horrible pain of seeing a strong person die without hope.

I had to return to Hamburg before we knew the final outcome of his sickness; I was called back again after he had died. I saw him in the open coffin-box and I will never forget the expression on his face that did not look peaceful, as they say the dead should look. He wore the expression of disappointment and pain and accusation. It is a face that has haunted me for a long time...Mother stayed alone in Berlin.

My hard life of an underground worker in Hamburg continued, but the situation became more serious because all the time people were being arrested. We were aware of the fact that usually the life of an underground worker lasted only about three years. At that time he or she would either be arrested or, if warned in time, had to be helped to leave the country. We had developed many ways of warning devices to know when the Nazis were approaching. One never would enter the dwelling of an underground worker without looking for such signs. In the place where I lived, for instance, the windows faced the street. It was agreed that my curtains were drawn in a certain way when everything was clear; in the case of the Gestapo being in my apartment, I should draw the curtains quickly in a different way. It was most difficult to invent such warning devices for people who lived in apartment houses where windows did not face the street. In some places it was impossible to install anything.

I had worked closely for instance, with a very intelligent young woman who had two small children. We could easily arrange for meetings because I gave English lessons to her children.When some of our acquaintances were arrested, she found it necessary to take the children outside of the country so that they would not be caught if she were arrested. (Her husband had died when the children were young.) Those were the heartbreaking decisions underground workers had to make. For a mother to send away her children is difficult under any circumstances, and to have to do it when you do not know if you will ever see them again, is especially hard.

She felt her obligation to fight the Nazis very strongly and took the sacrifice of separation from her children without complaint, though she suffered greatly. One day shortly after the children had left, I went to see her. Going up the stairs that led to her apartment, I saw three milk bottles in front of the door. We were used to watching very carefully for any unusual sign. This was a danger signal. If she had been home, she would have picked up the milk every morning. Three milk bottles meant that for three mornings she had not picked up the milk. There was only one explanation for this: the Gestapo had taken her away. I quickly left the building. Through contact with others who had worked with her, we found out that she had been arrested two days previous to my visit. The Gestapo waited in her apartment for over a week, arresting everybody who entered it....

There had been an agreement that anyone who carried anti-Nazi leaflets on his bicycle must carry them in front of him so as to never lose sight of them. It was in the beginning of 1936 that one of the younger underground workers disregarded this rule and put the leaflets in a small bag in the back of his bicycle. The worst happened. While he was bicycling the bag fell off and was lost with the leaflets—his name was inscribed on the bag. He knew that with this disregard of the rule he had not only endangered himself but everyone else, and he became panicky. He ran into the house of one of the other underground workers and confessed, begging him to help get him out of the country immediately. This seemed actually the best way out and the young man was brought over the Danish border.

One must understand how terrifying such an experience is to a young person. From one minute to another he had lost every familiar contact and was not able to say goodbye to anyone. Intellectually every underground worker was prepared for this situation, and it was discussed over and over that no love relationship should ever seduce anyone to return when he had to leave. Yet human needs are strong and our young friend must have felt desperate and lost in the strange new country. Nobody knows exactly how it happened; yet he returned to Germany and was immediately arrested. We are sure that guilt and fear must have been very strong in him. At any rate he was the first among the group who gave the Gestapo a large number of names of people who were part of the underground.

Because of the many arrests, most of us were far more cautious in meeting each other. Paul and I met only when there was great need to do some work together. At the time, for instance, when the Nazi launched their armament program, we distributed leaflets which used Goering's words, "Cannons instead of butter." We would walk through darkened streets and push those leaflets under closed doors.

Hamburg welcomed many foreign guests for the Olympic games held in Berlin. We were anxious to let those people know that Germany was not the wonderful place that they saw on the surface. Paul and a friend worked at night on a device which made invisible letters that became visible only in daylight. They glued those letters to the bottom of a suitcase and walked with this suitcase from the railroad station to the main thoroughfare, looking like people who had to set down their heavy suitcase from time to time. Each time they put the suitcase down, it left the imprint saying: "Germany's calm is the calm of a graveyard." In the morning, this slogan blazed forth announcing to all visitors that there were people in Germany who did not agree with the Nazi regime. The printing fluid was so strong that it could not be erased and therefore workmen had to chisel it away from the pavement. This made the Nazis furious and they searched intensely for those who had done this.

Workers were forced at all times to attend Nazi rallies and listen to the Fuehrer rant, though they did not agree with him.

Before such rallies, leaflets were printed by us to ask them to show some open resistance. We rode up on an elevator to the roof of one of the houses, placed the leaflets near the edge of the roof and calmly rode down. The wind then did the job of distribution for us. There were also little stickers which we pasted into office buildings. This could be done by the use of the "Pater Nosters" (these are open elevators in large office buildings which ride slowly up and down.) We held the stickers hidden in the palm of our hands and in passing by pasted them on the partitions between the "Pater Nosters." All this does not sound very exciting in a free country where one can get news in every paper, but it was very effective work. It spread news and it gave those who were not Nazis the feeling that they were not alone. The call to resistance against the large Nazi rallies paid off.

An example was one of those first May rallies where workers were forced to meet at their factories and then march to the meadow where Hitler was announced to speak. On the way one worker after another left the marching columns so that they had already thinned out considerably when they arrived at the fields. The Nazi guards, feeling the resistance, formed a large human cordon around the field to prevent anybody from leaving it before the Fuehrer had spoken. Yet a number of workers approached this wall of Nazi guards, joined their hands and then imitating the movements of a huge machine broke in rhythmic intervals the human chain built by the Nazi guards. This in itself was success.

It was important to send out eye witness reports of this to the underground newspapers so that in other parts of the country one would know of Hamburg's open resistance. It had helped in Hamburg, for instance, that we could publish reports of resistance at the opening of the Autobahn near Frankfurt. One of the engineers had secretly connected a record to the loudspeaker through which Hitler would speak at the opening of the Autobahn. When Hitler started to speak, he was drowned out by a record accusing him and his henchmen of the murder committed against many Germans. Fortunately the engineer was never found.

Chapter Eleven

Arrests. Paul's Escape

*I*t was spring of 1936. When I came to eat at a certain restaurant which belonged to underground workers, one of the waiters, also one of us, handed me the menu with a note folded in it. The note said, "C. talked. Paul and Kurt must leave the country immediately. Gestapo waiting in their rooms. Try to catch Paul on his way home from work. Meet us at the cemetery to discuss what to do. Bring flowers to grave X."

The letters of the note swam before my eyes. This was the end. Paul was in great danger and after this we would never see each other again, I thought. Yet the most urgent thing to do at this moment was to find some way to meet him after work. It was impossible to go directly to the place of his work because I would be recognized and the Nazis always had people posted at the working place as well as the living place of someone they wanted to arrest. The only hope was to reach him on the way. Fortunately I knew the route he took with his bicycle. I stood at the corner of the Gänsemarkt, a place full of traffic, watching every bicycle approaching. He was late and every second I thought that I had been too late. Finally, there he was and the package on the back of his bicycle indicated that the delay was only caused by his having picked up his laundry. He jumped off the bicycle when he saw me, we smiled at each other as if we were two happy people just meeting as acquaintances. And as he smiled, I gave him the horrible news that the Gestapo knew about his activities. I told him that they were waiting in his apartment for him and that he had to leave the country immediately, but to first meet me at the cemetery. A short hour after this Paul and the others met with flowers, as if we were mourners, at one of the graves. Whoever lies under that grave should still be thanked today because he saved the lives of several people. In the short time we had at that grave, Hans and Erna, who were in charge of the arrangement to get people out of the country, explained to Paul and Kurt how they could bicycle over the Dutch border, and how they should proceed from there to France. The route to Holland was chosen because we were sure that the Gestapo would first look for them at the Danish border, which is the closest to Hamburg and over which most of the underground workers of this region disappeared.

(Does anyone who lives in a large country such as the United States where one can travel for miles and miles without having to use a passport know what a "border" means? Even an American traveling today in Europe does not realize how much horror can lie in the word "border." As Americans we travel with a passport that opens the doors to almost every country. All we have to do is show it, let somebody look into our suitcase and we are on our way into the next country. But it is different when borders are closely guarded because an authoritarian state does not want its citizens to escape torture and death. Borders become the walls that seem almost unsurmountable and which require not only ingenuity but courage and luck to be able to cross.)

A man in a Gestapo prison had succumbed to the horrible pressures put upon him and now others were endangered. How could we help them escape? There were people in the labor unions in Holland and Belgium who would help those fleeing because they had fought for freedom. But one had to reach them first. It was decided among us as we sat around the unknown grave that Paul and Kurt, the two in immediate danger, should leave on their bicycles but stay in the vicinity of Hamburg for two days because by then the Gestapo would get confused, not having encountered them immediately at one of the borders. This would also give those of us who had to stay behind an opportunity to contact the underground workers near the Dutch border. A place near the Elbe was decided upon where we would meet Paul in two days to make the final arrangements. Meanwhile they would have to pretend that they were on a vacation tour and bicycle around and sleep a few nights in the woods.

And what about the families of these two? Neither lived at home, but both visited their families regularly at least twice a week. What could we tell their families? It was tragic how one had to hurt people one loved. Paul was very close to his mother and to think that he had to disappear without giving her any warning, to put her through the agony of not knowing whether her son was alive or dead, was a horrible decision to make. I wondered whether I should go and tell her about the decision since I, too, loved her and felt like a daughter to her. But this was impossible. The only safety for Paul, for myself, and for others involved in this work now lay in the fact that not one single person more than necessary knew anything about Paul's and Kurt's whereabouts. Both men themselves made the decision; "We have to let our mothers find their way through this alone. We know their strength. These will be desperate days for them, but say nothing." There was only one request made and accepted, namely that at the end of about two weeks, when and if they were safe, we could let their mothers know that this was so. The news about their having crossed the border would reach us through one of the Dutch underground workers.

And then came the hardest moment. "What about you, Gisa?" Erna, who had to make the arrangements, knew of Paul's and my closeness. "Are you willing to stay?" Actually there was no question about this. When we had decided that it was important to actively fight the Nazis we knew that this would entail separation and death and little personal happiness. But, 0 God, I was just 25 years old! The decision seemed to mean the final parting for Paul and me. We were sure that we would never see each other again. Yet, I said, "If I stay, can I be sure to continue the fight or must I be 'put on ice'?"—as we called it when someone had to stay clear of active work because his presence was too dangerous. The answer was not too reassuring. Yes, it was hoped and wished that I would stay to continue in the underground work, but for a few weeks at least I could not have the satisfaction of active participation because first we had to see how much Paul's and my relationship was known to the Gestapo. This would mean many empty days, full of anxiety for Paul's safety, without the relief of fighting the common enemy, without the relief of knowing that the sacrifice of separation was worthwhile.

Erna said gently, probably feeling strongly with me, "You can do a last thing for him. You will be the messenger to bring the money and directions to Paul and Kurt so that they can get away. You are the best one to do it. If the Gestapo knows your relationship and you are caught, then at least nobody else is involved." And with the odd gentleness of our sense of horror she added: "In that case at least both of you know that you died together."

(It is in such moments that the young feel very old. To feel death so close and to accept it gives one an amazing feeling of calm.) The following two nights were nightmares. My troubled sleep was populated with dreams of Paul being caught and tortured. It was a relief that sleep actually was not too frequent and though my waking mind was a troubled one, too, I at least found myself thinking of possible solutions to the situation.

It was a raw spring morning. The Hamburg fog lay over the city and from the harbor came the sound of the tugboats. By afternoon I would be at Hanna's apartment, another underground worker, a gentle mature woman who loved her children and her home. Yet both she and her husband had begun to think of the necessity of sending the children away into another country because they were becoming dangerous to the parents' underground work. The little one, for instance, had recently pointed to a rolled stocking and wondered why dad kept a paper in it (these were illegal leaflets). The older girl was outspokenly anti-Nazi and therefore presented a danger to the family. Also both Hanna and her husband were afraid that the children would slowly soak up too much of the atmosphere of a Nazi Germany. They could not believe in doing what some other parents did, namely to detest the Nazis but—because of fear—let their children enter the Hitler Youth and become—what they considered—criminals. Here was a happy home full of warmth and gentleness that was beginning to be destroyed because there was no freedom to continue it.

At the appointed time I arrived at Hanna's apartment. She gave me the money for the escape, the exact directions and the name of the person to contact. During those 48 hours I had not shed a single tear but my face was obviously white and stony. Hanna looked at me and with her warm motherly instinct felt my despair. She gave me her house-key and said, "You will have to come back here to report whether everything went well. If you are not back by midnight, we know that all three of you are arrested. Take my key, and if you want to, spend the night at our place." And shaking her head, she said: "You are much too young to have to give up life like that."

The commuter train takes one to Blankenese from Hamburg. It is a place where one goes to spend a pleasant day or afternoon sipping coffee or walking along the lovely broad river. At a given place, as was decided, I would meet Erna again, as if we were two friends just having our coffee and then she would observe my meeting Paul. Such precautions were always built in because it was important when somebody was leaving the country to know whether things worked out. If, for instance, Erna observed our being caught by the Gestapo, she could immediately spread the news to others so they would be warned of the new danger ahead. With every arrest the danger increased of someone talking.

Erna and I met. She, too, had the same information that I was supposed to give Paul and we repeated it to each other. Even the most complicated directions had to be learned by heart and could not be written down. I then said goodbye to her and walked along the boardwalk. I saw Paul approaching on the bicycle and wanted to start toward him when I realized that his eyes stared straight ahead and that he pretended not to know me. We had learned to observe such signs and always to approach each other cautiously. I saw him bicycling straight past me without giving the slightest sign of recognition. This meant that he knew the Gestapo was following him, and I could not reach him at this moment. I panicked for a moment, but then the discipline of the underground worker returned to me.

"He is passing by to let me know that he expects me to meet him somehow, but I cannot meet him near this open expanse close to the river where he must have seen people observing him and Kurt." Kurt was nowhere in sight. I decided to simply move back into the shadows of the trees away from the waterfront, and sit down as if I was tired. Soon Paul passed by again without a sign of recognition but his bicycle speed was slowing down. I interpreted this to mean that I should follow him. I walked slowly after the bicycle. We were entering the woods where it would be harder for us to observe whether anyone was observing us from behind the trees, but on the other hand, we would see if anyone was following.

Finally Paul stopped, put down his bicycle, and pulled out a piece of bread as if he were going to eat. I walked slowly past him, and then I heard the familiar warm voice, "It's all right now. Nobody is behind us." I sat down beside him. He told me that he had observed several men following him closely during the morning. He had bicycled enough to confuse them and he had lost them, since they were on foot. This was our last chance to be together. I rapidly gave him the directions for his escape and he repeated them several times—names of places, routes to follow, people to contact. I also gave him the money. Then I pulled out two things that I thought would perhaps be the last gifts I could ever give him—a dark pullover I had knitted, and a copy of DaCosta's "Till Ulenspeegel." In all the wandering that we had to do later, with all the prisons that followed, this copy of Da Costa is still in our library today. At the time it was a symbolic book to us. It was a book of people who fought for freedom against tyranny. To me the important person was Till himself, the "laughing fighter," a person who fought and yet could laugh at a joke, and who loved people. He was a person with a fearless courage and yet not brooding about it. This was Paul. And to Paul (we had read the book together) Till's love, Nele, was akin to me, a woman who faithfully waited for her man to come back from the battle. When things went badly for Till, somehow Nele would appear as if by a miracle. We both felt that Till's song was our song:

> Leben schrieb ich auf meine Fahne
> Im Lichte leben, allzumal.
> Meine erste Haut, die ist aus Leder.
> Meine zweite aber ist aus Stahl.

Translation:

> Life I wrote on my banner
> To live in the light.
> My first skin is made out of leather
> But my second is made out of steel.

Paul carefully hid the money. He placed the book and the sweater in the back of his bicycle with the little food he had. We embraced quickly, said, "bon courage," (another very personal greeting we had "taken" from Rilke's letters), and—Paul was gone. This was the first time I was really alone. Now the relief came and the pain. I walked through the woods crying as I have never cried in my life before and only once more later, after Paul's death. There was no one to whom I had to show a courageous or happy face. I could just be who I was, a little girl for whom the world had come to an end. I walked and cried, and cried and walked. When I came out of the woods, I would have to cease my crying. In Nazi Germany crying would only have been cause for suspicion.

(Years later when Paul left for service in the American Army, I brought him to the station. In the midst of all the other wives and sweethearts, I stood next to "my man" in uniform, thinking that I might never see him again. Yet a very different feeling surrounded us, not at all the same despair as at that first parting. When we kissed goodbye, we both said in wonder, "Think of it. We can kiss in public. We can even cry in public.")

I had the key in my hand, and I opened the door to Hanna's apartment. She had waited up for me. I told her that I did not want to stay the night, although I knew how kindly she had offered it. I wanted to be alone. She said softly, "Gisa, why don't you cry?"

"It's all right, Hanna. I did cry. It is over now."

Have you ever walked through streets on which you once walked with someone you loved which are familiar because of the many things you have done together? If she or he has died you must have had that experience. But this was worse. The streets not only brought those happy memories, but they constantly evoked the vision of a beloved face with blood running down and a familiar voice crying in agony. The long trek across a hostile country, once their homeland lay before Paul and Kurt, and it would take several days before I could know whether they had reached their destination.

At this time I was living in a rented room in the apartment of a family with two teen-age daughters. When I came home from this exhausting experience I found them in the living room glued to the radio and looking glum. I was too occupied with my own concern to ask about theirs. Yet before I could get to my room, they called me back asking me to stay with them because of the very important news that was to come. This was the day of King

Edward the VIII's abdication. It seemed to me almost incongruous that while we were in a country where people were dying under the hands of cruel sadists, the event that really shook the world was a king's abdication for the love for a woman.

The following days dragged on in agony. Once Paul's sister came asking me to tell her and her mother what happened to Paul. He had disappeared. I had to tell her that I didn't know, and her friendly compassionate face told me that she understood why I couldn't tell. I also had to ask her not to see me again, because it was quite possible that the Gestapo was following her. We agreed that another underground worker would bring fresh eggs to sell to the family when we received news of Paul, and through this ruse enter their home to give them information.

The second week after Paul's disappearance I got the message to go to a certain movie theater. An underground worker would also be there and after the performance he would meet me "accidentally." No news could be expected before that time. I sat in the darkened theater, forced to sit through a picture that I will never forget because it probably was the most inappropriate one for me to see at that time. It was "Peter Ibbetson," the story of a man captured and thrown into a dungeon. After all those years I can still vividly recall some of the movie: Peter Ibbetson, handcuffed to the wall and writhing in pain, and then sleeping, dreaming where he and his love would meet. During the film, Peter Ibbetson's face seemed to change to Paul's, and I sat through a few hours of nightmare.

After the performance, in the midst of the jostling around, I "accidentally" met my friend. He greeted me heartily, talked about the movie, and then suddenly whispered by putting his hand on my shoulder, "They are all right. They are now in Holland," and we continued to discuss the picture. The day after this meeting I sent word to Paul's mother that Paul had to leave the country and was safe. Soon the Gestapo was haunting Paul's mother. Not once in all these years did she yield to Gestapo threats. They came to her frequently insisting that she tell them where he was. One day they told her that they had arrested him, and now she should tell them what she knew of his activities. With her innate intelligence and sense of humor, she pretended to be delighted to hear that they found him and said: "That boy! I'm sure glad you found him. Now, please, take me immediately to him so I can give him a piece of my mind." They had a hard time wiggling out of that! Another time the interrogators threatened to take her to Gestapo headquarters and torture the knowledge of her son out of her.

She said, "Just take me along. This is fine. But you know that I cannot walk. (She had a lame leg.) Take me along in the fancy car you always come in. I have never had such a nice automobile ride. Don't think that I will step into the 'Grüne Minna' (the name for the paddy wagon.) I am a mother who has raised four children and I won't be degraded like that, but I'll gladly go with you, and the state can take care of my children."

She baffled the Gestapo, but they did not let up and she had to put up with them for several years. They only stopped coming to see her when they came to believe that she was slightly deranged. In one incident, they asked her where Paul was. She smiled mysteriously at them and said that she knew at last and could tell them now. She then sat in front of a mirror, where she took out a deck of cards and began to lay them out on the table. She said the cards would tell her where her son was, and that they could then see for themselves. On top she laid a king, so clearly he must be in a country where there is a king. That surely could not be Germany, could it? Hitler is no king, is he?" In the mirror she observed as the men looked at each other and made a gesture indicating that she was crazy. She never gave them the satisfaction when they asked about her son's girl friend. She said she did not know. "He perhaps had several—as all young men."

For myself the knowledge that Paul was safe was a relief, but otherwise it was a hard time. I continued to work in a little bookstore while waiting to be called back to "active duty" with the underground. This store was run by a Jewish woman who had been a Montessori teacher but was not allowed to continue her teaching under the Nazis. I learned a great deal about the Montessori method from her.

The artist Fritz Husmann came to visit frequently. I was deeply impressed with his work, and he gave me one of his pictures. (In 1981 when I visited Hamburg, I found much of his work in the "Kunsthalle," the Hamburg Art Museum, and found out that he, who was by then around 90 years of age, was still alive. Only after the Nazis had been defeated, did he get recognition in Germany.) During my free time, like everybody else, I read or went boating on the Alster with friends. For those of us who were Jewish, attendance at theaters was forbidden. We had to find our cultural outlets mostly in our own homes. Once in awhile a Jewish theater group was allowed to put on a special play, only for Jews. Many young Jewish people emigrated. All around us were sham marriages of such young people because it was easier for two to receive permission to leave the country. Only those of us who felt a responsibility beyond the confines of the Jewish community and who were convinced that the Nazi ideology was totally unacceptable, felt that our place remained in Germany where we could fight the Nazis best.

During this time the situation for our group of anti-Nazi fighters became worse. One of the underground workers had been able to see in court the young man who had given the names of some of the underground workers. He was struck by the young man's strange appearance and the glazed look in his eyes. We suspected that he was drugged. He had completely broken down and had informed the Nazis about many of our activities. Several people whom he knew by name had been arrested, others, like Paul and Kurt, were helped to get out of the country in a hurry. It was around such escapes that I could finally be helpful again. I had contacts with a photographer who was willing to make passport photos which could be used for freedom fighters. He willingly risked his life. Thanks to him, a young woman with whom I shared room and work for awhile, is alive today in Australia. And he probably helped many others of whose fate I do not know.

Chapter Twelve

My Arrest

It was winter 1936, one of the rainy cold Hamburg winters. The Nazis became more strict in their methods of suppressing every anti-Nazi movement. One reason for this, obviously, was their feeling of power and their intention to conquer other countries. They did not yet openly discuss this, but there were heavy restrictions on consumer goods while war industry was pushed. Especially alarming to many of us in the Hamburg area was that the Nazis began to build secret underground factories which produced poison gas. This had first become known following an explosion in the Hamburg area. We felt it was important to let the free countries know about this and give them information on where these underground factories were so that in case of war they could act to put them out of business. We bicycled into this area looking like innocent Sunday riders and "by accident" got into an area we thought was used for such installations. At times we found the proof: suddenly, in the middle of the woods there would be barbed wire and a sign forbidding entrance. We smuggled out maps showing the locations.

The tightening up of Nazi surveillance meant increased Nazi terror and arrests. We often had to change leadership in the underground movement because an important person would be arrested. That meant that more people knew of dangerous information as, for instance, names and addresses of underground workers. Yet it had to be done. It also meant that the circle of trusted underground workers became smaller. In a dictatorship, one of the most terrible things that happens is that one cannot trust one unless one has known that person for years. It is therefore almost impossible to recruit new workers for the underground. After Hans and Erna, who had been leaders of the movement in Hamburg, had to leave the country, much of the vital information and the decisions to be made came to rest in my hands. I felt it was important to share this information very soon. Since I was Jewish and the Nazi anti-Semitic propaganda increased daily, I felt an increasing risk of my being arrested even if I had not been connected with anti-Nazi activities.

In the beginning of December, another Rudi, also Jewish, pressed me about wanting to be more intensely involved in anti-Nazi activities. He felt that life was not worth living unless one had a real cause to work for. It was late in the evening when I went to see him. I gave him a great amount of vital information, including addresses of people who could take refugees over the border, if necessary. I painstakingly taught him our secret code, a way of writing designated in such a way that one could even smuggle information out from prison or concentration camp as long as one was permitted to send any innocent letter. We both heaved a sigh of relief when I said, "It is time to go home and if anything happens to me, at least I know that you know how to carry on." He offered to take me home. Walking through the silent winter night, we told each other the oddly bitter jokes that flourish under suppression and which give some sense of relief. I remember most vividly the one he told me shortly before I entered the house: "One man said to another, 'You know Fühlsbüttel is really a very tough prison and concentration camp. It has such huge walls and there are SS guards (the blackshirts, Hitler's most brutal troop) everywhere and there are men with cannons and other weapons.' The other answered, 'Oh, if I want to get in, I get in.'" (I remember it so well because I got there the next day.)

I went to bed around midnight using the careful routine of every underground worker: next to my bed were the most important addresses which I could not keep in my head, written on very thin paper. At about 2:00 a.m. the doorbell rang sharply and awakened me out of a deep sleep. When the doorbell rings at night, someone had said jokingly: "You know it is not the milkman." When this bell rang at 2:00 a.m., I did not feel like laughing. I instantly awoke, and immediately knew that this was the moment I had expected all these years. It is odd how quickly and clearly one can think under such circumstances. I knew that it would take but a very short time before they entered my apartment. I felt sorry for the poor innocent landlady who would be dragged into the hall, but I was glad that I had never told her a word about my activities. That way no information could be pressed out of her. I had perhaps three minutes before they would reach my door. My hand shot out to the paper with the addresses on it and I quickly swallowed the material. It was good that I had practiced paper swallowing for a long time. It went down very quickly. I settled back, pretending to be fast asleep. At the next sharp ringing of the bell I opened my eyes, but I knew I must not get up. I knew I must look as unconcerned about this as possible. I heard Mrs. S. open the building door and ask, "Who is there?"

The heavy boots of the Nazi Gestapo immediately entered and I heard them ask for me. Already the landlady was crying, telling them that there was nothing wrong with the nice girl who lived in her place. But the Nazis tore open the door to my room and three young Gestapo men stood in front of my bed, shouting at me to get up. I pretended to wake up, and asked what they wanted from me. Then the abuse began.

"Don't be stupid, you damn Jewish bastard. You know what you are. Get up."

I asked whether I could get dressed while they waited outside. There was laughter. There is no point in expecting even the slightest feeling of decency. Two men watched with the greedy cruel eyes of sadists while I got dressed. It took all the self-discipline acquired in years of preparation for this moment for me to take off my nightgown and put on one piece of clothing after another while they leered at me. The third man was already ransacking my little room. Every piece of clothing was taken out of the closet and ripped apart to see if anything was hidden in it. My books (my beloved books!) were thrown on the floor, covers ripped off. They found a photo album full of photos of my little nephew, born in Israel to my older sister, a boy I had never seen, but whom I loved with the fierce love of someone who knows that not many of the family will survive. They questioned me especially as to who this child was. I gave them the information, but somehow they didn't believe me. For some reason that at first I did not understand, the whereabouts of this child seemed to become exceedingly important to them. When the questioning about him became insistent and cruel, I suddenly realized what it was all about: in the distorted stereotyped mind of a Nazi, a Jewish child must have a hooked nose and black hair. To them this was a child who looks very "Aryan" with his blond hair and his lovely round face. These idiots actually thought that I had hidden an "Aryan" child, and they believed that each child like that must be available for the "Fatherland," for Hitler's war machinery.

There was intense questioning about my whereabouts the evening before. (Did they observe me when I met Rudi? Should I tell them? But there was a rule among underground workers that one should never, ever admit connections even if one thought they knew, because there was always the chance that they did not know about it. And one must never drag in anyone.) So I told them a story about where I had been. I struggled with my innate horror of being forced to lie. Something inside me moaned. "What will become of humanity when the spoken word has no meaning?" And at the same time I thought, "The only way to prevent them from getting someone else is to lie."

(As you read this you might think that such philosophical considerations are only now in my mind but could not have been there then at that moment. I can only assure you that this struggle was so painful, more painful than their ugly voices, that I remember it not only vividly, but with great pain.)

The room looked like a shambles. I was dressed. One of the Gestapo men said: "Get your coat, you are going with us."

I objected, saying I didn't see why they were going to take me when there had been nothing incriminating against me. I also begged to write a little note to my mother who was alone in Berlin and who would be frightened to death if she never heard from me again. They only laughed. My landlady stood by trembling and crying. I gave her the little money that I possessed and said that she should save it or—if I did not come back—keep the rent and send the rest to my mother. One of the Nazis wanted to take the money away from her. Oddly enough, another one shouted at his colleague to let her have it. This was the same man who had searched the room but had not watched me get dressed. Looking back over the years I sometimes wonder whether the way he was ripping the books was not only his anger at me but perhaps at beginning disgust with his job?

We were no heroes and we were afraid. But perhaps this moment, when the final blow fell, had a calming effect. Suddenly everything I feared had occurred. Much terror still lay ahead of me. I was so sure, though, that I would die the next day that this gave me a certain strength and calm. I comforted the landlady and asked her to write to my mother and tell her that I did not feel too badly about being arrested; somehow everything would come out all right. Walking between two Gestapo men and with one following us, I went down the stairs to the waiting Gestapo car. As we stepped into the car, one of them said curtly to the driver, "We have her. Now to the next one."

That was the worst news. I realized then that others would be taken prisoner that same night. We drove silently through the dark. When they stopped I recognized the place. Lieschen lived there, another young union worker who belonged to our underground movement. "Oh, God, how will she be when they bring her down?" The driver sat silently watching me while the three men entered the house. After a long time she appeared in the same way that I had been brought down between the two burly Gestapo men. What should I do? Should I pretend not to know her? I decided to follow her clue. The moment she entered the car, she turned to me and said: "They told me you were here. It is certainly different from the time I helped you on the vacation trip with your school class." This gave me an indication of how she had explained our relationship.

Lieschen was really the hero that evening. Her presence of mind was extraordinary. She also gave me another clue as to what role she was going to play. She was going to be the cute little girl, innocent and kittenish. She could do that. She was not Jewish, and therefore this could be more easily expected of her. She also was not an "intellectual" as I was. She was a working girl and could play the role of someone who knew little of the world and its events. Besides that, she was younger than I and a pretty, sparkling young girl. While we were riding through the night, she turned around to me and held out a cookie. Laughingly she said, "My God, the way they treat us. I'm hungry. And here's a cookie for you." Flirtatiously she turned to one of the Gestapo men and said with a bright smile, "How about you, Mister, you must get hungry on the night shift?" One of the men growled, "Stupid goose". One could almost feel how her act worked.

The ill-famed police station loomed before us in the dark. We knew of the cellar downstairs and we knew of the inhuman beatings which occurred there. I was silent. But when we entered the place a cat came meowing down the corridor. Lieschen turned to the cat and said, "Mooshy, mooshy, mooshy, come here." One of the Gestapo men pushed her away and muttered under his breath, "Scatterbrain." No one could have applauded Lieschen better.

My first encounter with the Gestapo was a routine police one. But then the typical Gestapo methods started. We had to stand with our faces against the wall without touching the wall. Behind us other prisoners were brought in and at times I heard them being slapped and kicked. If I made the slightest move, as for instance, I wanted to turn my head, or if my head started to nod because I was tired, I got a swift kick or slap in the face. More and more people were brought in. To my horror I recognized the voices of two other friends involved in our movement. They made us turn around and look at each other almost every time when new people were brought in. In this case both Lieschen and I looked as blank as we had looked when others we did not know were brought in. They too responded that way. This gave us a clue never to admit that we had known each other.

Morning came, but we had no notion of time under the electric lights of the Gestapo cellar. I only realized it was late morning when we were brought to the first floor for photographing and fingerprinting. Suddenly the sun flooded through the windows and I saw the slow movements of a window washer on the ledge. I remember thinking, "He is free. He can move about the way he wants to. He can go home tonight."

After the fingerprinting came the first interrogation. The interrogator was a young man in SS uniform. Never before in my life had I heard such language as he used when he spoke to me. His were the worst gutter expressions the German language knew. "You dirty whore, look at me." Similar expressions were constantly hurled at me. He shouted, threatened, and wanted to make me feel like the last piece of dirt. All during this time I couldn't take my eyes off this man. What did he think or feel while he was doing this? An odd detached sensation of curiosity arose in me. It seemed almost unbelievable that a young person would want to treat another one like this. His insults were constantly interspersed with reference to my being Jewish. "Jewish pig" was one of his favorite expressions. Once in a while I thought, "How strange. I feel as though I'm wearing a raincoat. The flood is just sliding off of me. This kind of person cannot really insult me."

After this, several of us were brought to the Gestapo cellar, the sub-basement. I and some others were each put into a separate wooden contraption, something like a standing coffin. One could not sit down or turn around, just stand straight. It had no window, was completely dark and was locked. Psychologically, it was a horrible torture tool. After a night of questioning and of threats, of having heard others being beaten and chained, to be put into a completely locked box in a torturous position, was pure hell. At first I had the sensation of choking and every muscle hurt because I could not move. My feet hurt because I had stood for long hours and continued to stand. In my mind swirled desperate thoughts. What do they know of us? Whom have they arrested? What will happen to my mother? And: Paul, oh, Paul! The physical pain of my cramped muscles increased. I knew I had to do something so as not to break down. I decided sleep would be a benefit at this moment. And in the complete darkness, with every muscle screaming with pain, I closed my eyes, told myself that I was lying on a comfortable bed, that there was soft music in the air and I just wasn't where I was. I was in a sun-flooded meadow. It worked! The cramped muscles relaxed and I began to fall into a light sleep.

(Several times later in my experience in concentration camps I learned how beneficial daydreaming can be. The capacity to remove oneself from a situation at will is a great gift given to the human being.)

My slight sleep was interrupted by the wild screams of a man in the "coffin" next to mine. I heard him shaking this box and his cries, "Let me out. Let me go. Yes, I will tell you anything you want to hear. Yes, I did listen to the French radio. Let me out. Let me out. Let me out. Let me out!" Before my eyes was an image of the man I had seen earlier the cellar, an older person with a deeply lined face of a working man. Here he was, already broken by the cruel loneliness and the horror of the living coffin.

All sense of time passed. I don't know how long I was in the coffin. I heard the key and then the door opened and, stiff as I was, I almost fell into the arms of the old guard who had opened the cell. It was a man with a grey beard and tired blue eyes and a faded prison guard uniform. He muttered to himself, "I won't keep her in here any longer. This is inhuman. This is terrible." I don't think he knew that he said it so that I heard it. To me this old bearded man redeemed humanity at that moment. He felt with the victims.

He lined us up in a row, apparently the way he had learned it when there was a "normal prison." He asked in a loud voice what time we had been arrested. Only then did we realize that it was the late afternoon of the next day and we had been in the Gestapo hands for almost 24 hours. He asked whether we had eaten and we said we had not. Again he shook his head mournfully. He called for a helper and soon some huge pots of soup were brought in. Each prisoner got a bowl full of soup. Most of us had a hard time holding the bowl because our hands were so cramped, but it was a relief to get something warm to eat. Lieschen was standing next to me. The last 24 hours had done something to the courageous sparkling girl. She looked harassed and her eyes were filled with tears though she tried hard to hide them. Her hands seemed so weak that she could not hold her bowl at all. (Many years later we learned that Lieschen already at that time had a heart condition.) The old guard saw her discomfort. He supported her and held her hand with the spoon for a moment until it steadied. (I will never know what happened to this guard. I am sure he has been dead for a long time. But once in a while I think that maybe angels wear beards and look like an old prison guard in a Gestapo cellar.)

After the meal he was replaced by SS guards. They put handcuffs on us. Always two prisoners were handcuffed to each other. We then marched upstairs to be put into a patrol wagon which would bring us to a concentration camp. It seemed incongruous to see a group of citizens, obviously not violent criminals, and a majority women, being treated like dangerous criminals. The handcuffs served mostly to let us know that we were criminals and should feel as such. I was especially surprised to see several older women. I couldn't imagine what they had done to bring the wrath of the Gestapo upon them. It was only later that I learned that most of them were Jehovah's Witnesses. They belonged to a religion which refused to say "Heil Hitler," the required greeting instituted by the Nazi regime. They believed that one should say "Hail" only to God. They were strict in their beliefs and did not compromise. They were cruelly persecuted by the Nazis for this audacity.

When we entered the police wagon there were other prisoners on the benches, mostly men. They wore prison garb which meant they had already been in the concentration camp. For the first time I saw with my own eyes the real concentration camp inmate: the men were all haggard and pale, wearing thin clothing in the cold winter weather. The worst of it was that they all wore marks of recent beatings, fresh gashes in their faces, on their necks and on their hands. Eyes looked bloodshot and distant. They sat close to one another and I could see that some were kept upright only because they were in that position. In the wagon was a separate compartment, like a small cell with heavy meshed wire and bars in front of it. First my eyes could not distinguish anything behind those bars. But finally I recognized a human figure and even a face. It looked like a wild animal caged in there and crouched on the floor. It was a long ride to "Fuhlsbüttel" and I could not take my eyes off the human being held prisoner in this isolation cage. The face moved closer to the meshed wire. It was a face with blood streaming all over it, drying on the cheeks and over the eyebrows, yet the eyes were alive and they looked at me steadily with none of the greed of the Gestapo eyes but with the steady sad eyes of a martyr. It was the face of the suffering Christ reborn after centuries....

Chapter Thirteen

Concentration Camp

*I*mmediately after our arrival in Fuhlsbüttel we new women were brought upstairs to be put into our cells. Again we had to wait facing the wall. At this time something occurred which changed my mood of grief, unhappiness, worry and despair into a feeling of fierce anger and at the same time almost triumphant exhilaration. What occurred was that the SS man in charge of the entire concentration camp appeared and screamed in rage, "What shall we do with all these new people? There are too many. The place is getting overcrowded."

He did not know it, but he could not have given me more encouragement than to tell me that obviously the resistance against the Nazis was large enough to overcrowd the prisons. He made me turn around and then spat in my face. He was an absurdly ugly-looking man, a degenerate. He had a thin birdlike head on a long neck with cruel piercing eyes, long ears and claw-like hands. He was known to personally abuse prisoners and to enjoy torturing them.

He treated one of the older women, a Jehovah's Witness, especially cruelly. While standing in the corridor, he insisted that she say "Heil Hitler" to him. Calmly the woman refused. He kicked her with his heavy boots. She faltered but still did not raise her arm in the fashion of a "Hitler greeting." He screamed at her, hit her, pushed her, almost wrenched her arm out of its socket, but the woman never flinched for a moment. While he did this, one could see that his mood of sadistic lust increased. I did not see the end of this treatment because I was led into a cell, although I can still hear in my ears the moaning of this woman.

The heavy door behind me clanked and I was for the first time alone, in solitary confinement. It was good that I was filled with the fierceness of anger, because the first object that I saw in the room was a sharp knife lying on the table. While in every other prison great care is taken that prisoners should not harm themselves, obviously the Nazis hoped that the persons brought in the first day would commit suicide. This would make one opponent less. Oddly enough the knife spelled out another message to me, namely that they really didn't know too much about my activities and did not consider me so important that they wanted to save me for any important information regarding the underground. Otherwise they would not have wanted a suicide. For the first time I smiled to myself rather grimly, "I certainly will not give you the satisfaction of committing suicide. You will just have to do the dirty work yourself, if that is what you want. I will stay alive as long as I can. Only when I feel that I cannot stand torture any longer and that I might denounce others, I might commit suicide." This was my pledge and I pushed the knife away.

Solitary confinement combined with no permission to do anything, to read, write, or sew, is torture in itself. The lack of human communication adds terror to it. This is a method used to make people so desperate that they begin to talk just to see someone. For days I was treated as if I did not exist. No one interrogated me; no one spoke to me. The empty wall gave no response and my hands that were used to doing things had nothing to do. A dry piece of bread and something black called coffee was brought in the morning, and soup in the evening. I learned what it meant under such circumstances to hear the clanging of a door at the far end of the corridor and that food was arriving. I felt reduced to the level of an animal in the zoo. Have you ever observed how they get up shortly before meal time and start to walk up and down in the cage? It suddenly occurred to me that I was doing the very same thing. I was not only hungry, but the opening of the door was my only contact with the outside world. The women who brought the food in were prisoners themselves and were not allowed to speak to us. Yet even under the surveillance of the Gestapo they somehow managed to bring a spark of humanity to us. I will never forget the young woman who put the soup bowl into my hand and without hardly moving her lips said, "Chin up."

By the commotion outside of my cell I learned a little about the situation on the women's floor. I soon realized that apparently most women were not in isolation as I was, but were in a larger room together. Isolation was a special form of punishment. Women guards were on duty. Once I heard one of them call Lieschen's name and I realized that she had gained the privileged position of someone allowed to work. Doubts assailed me. Had she started to talk? Was this the reason she walked around the corridors? I suddenly realized that it was rather unusual for the guards to call someone by name. It became clear to me that this was done purposely so that I might get suspicious of Lieschen and speak against her.

What does one do when the days are desperately long and one wants to be sure to keep one's sanity and one's alertness? We had discussed this possibility in our small underground groups and we had prepared ourselves for it. I knew that idleness was very hard for me to take. I therefore decided that I had to arrange my day like a "working day." Yet there was no sense of time, nothing but the two meals and the early "lights out" to in-

terrupt the day. I was called to get up by about six o'clock in the
morning and then I had the whole day to spend doing nothing. I
was not allowed to sit down on the bed in the cell. I, therefore,
arranged my day in the following way: after I got up I did sitting-
up exercises, more than I had ever done in my life before (or
since). After that I decided to go on a good long morning walk. My
walk consisted of walking three steps forward and three steps
back—the length of the cell. While I did this, I would sing hiking songs, as if I were hiking in the woods. In spite of my poor
voice I knew hundreds of songs, and it gave me a lot of satisfaction
to finish 20 or 30 songs in a day with several verses. Once the
woman guard looked in and shook her head. She obviously
thought I had gone insane, walking up and down and singing, for
instance,

> "Wer recht in Freuden wandern will,
> Der geh der Sonn entgegen...

Translation:

> "Who wants to hike in joy
> Must rise early, meeting the sun...

After this it was about time for "breakfast."
    After breakfast I introduced my class lessons. I sat down at
the table and began to repeat Latin and French vocabulary. I kept
that up for a while and then gave myself arithmetic problems. I
had no pencil and no paper, so it all had to be done in my head,
but at least it was some method of using time in a disciplined
way. After this, time became long and heavy and I found myself
very frequently day-dreaming. It helped me. There were hours
when I just wasn't where I was. I climbed mountains, swam in the
lake, sat in meadows, and especially met Paul and some of our
friends. Those were also very painful hours, because I woke out of
those daydreams thinking that I would never again see those
people whom I loved. The worst was to remember how my friends

must feel right now and how anxious they must be. I had to force myself not to think of these things, telling myself that I could not do anything about it.

The evening meal, a horrible mush, was still a welcome interruption, and then came the long evening. It was dark early in December. A small lightbulb glared down at me. With nothing to do and not being allowed to lie down I found it hard to stay awake. My hours were filled with torturous thoughts until I discovered a very helpful device. They had left me a handkerchief. In my hair was a bobby pin. I now used the long evening hours to pull out the threads in my handkerchief, making various patterns. I was not allowed to do this either, but I did it by keeping my back turned against the little spy hole through which the guard could observe me from time to time. I became so proficient in the use of the bobby pin that I could even use the pulled out threads to do a kind of sewing with them.

There was also a faucet in my cell. After a few days I was permitted to write to my landlady and ask for my toothbrush and comb. She sent the toothbrush in a plastic container which had a tiny hole in the bottom. I used my evenings making experiments with water and this plastic container to find out how long it would hold water, how hard I would have to squeeze to make it drop out, and tried to investigate all kinds of laws of physics. This way of passing time proved an important sanity saver. I also discovered that I carried with me a marvelous treasure I had never estimated highly enough until that time: I knew hundreds and hundreds of poems by heart. I loved poetry and I could take hours of "reading" by just standing in my cell and reciting poetry. Poetry also helped in the moments of terrible stress when I was finally called before the Gestapo for further interrogation. One of my favorite poems was Rilke's "Mount of Olives."

Der Ölbaumgarten

Er ging hinauf unter dem grauen Laub
ganz grau und aufgelöst im Ölgelände

und legte seine Stirne voller Staub
tief in das Staubigsein der heissen Hände.

Nach allem dies. Und dieses war der Schluss.
Jetzt soll ich gehen, während ich erblinde,
und warum willst Du, dass ich sagen muss,
Du seist, wenn ich Dich selber nicht mehr finde.

Ich finde Dich nicht mehr. Nicht in mir, nein.
Nicht in den andern. Nicht in diesem Stein.
Ich finde Dich nicht mehr. Ich bin allein.

Ich bin allein mit aller Menschen Gram,
den ich durch Dich zu lindern unternahm,
der Du nicht bist. 0 namenlose Scham...

Später erzählte man: ein Engel kam—,

Warum ein Engel? Ach, es kam die Nacht
und blätterte gleichgültig in den Bäumen.
Die Jünger rührten sich in ihren Träumen,
Warum ein Engel? Ach, es kam die Nacht.

Die Nacht, die kam, war keine ungemeine;
so gehen hunderte vorbei.
Da schlafen Hunde, und da liegen Steine,
Ach, eine traurige, ach, irgendeine,
die wartet, bis es wieder Morgen sei.

Denn Engel kommen nicht zu solchen Betern,
und Nächte werden nicht um solche gross.
Die Sich-Verlierenden lässt alles los.
und sie sind preisgegeben von den Vätern
und ausgeschlossen aus der Mutter Schoss.

Rilke, Ranier Marie, *Ausgewählte Gedichte*, Leipzig, InselVerlag, p.l8.

Translation:

The Mount of Olives

He ascended under the gray foliage
quite gray himself and merged with the olive-landscape
and he laid his forehead which was full of dust
deep into the dustiness of his hot hands.

After everything—now this. And this was the end.
Now I am to go, while going blind
and why is it The will that I must say
that Thou are, while I myself find Thee no more.

I do not find Thee anymore. Not within me, no.
Nor in the others. Nor within this stone.
I do not find Thee anymore. I am alone.

I am alone with all of mankind's grief
which I had undertaken to sooth through Thee,
and Thou art not, 0 shame unnamed.

Later, they told: "An angel came..."

Why an angel? Woe, it was the night which came
and leafed indifferently through the trees.
The disciples were moving in their dreams.
Why an angel? Woe, it was the night which came.

The night which fell was not an uncommon one;
Hundreds of those are passing thus—
When dogs are sleeping, and when stones are lying.
Woe, a sad night, woe, just any night

which waits until the morning should return.

For angels do not come to such in prayer
and nights do not become great for their sake.
Everything lets go of the self-abandoned,
and they get deserted by their fathers,
and they are banned from every mother's womb.

I said it especially fervently when I was called before the
Gestapo. The dreary days—always filled with suspense because
one did not know what might occur—were suddenly interrupted
by being told to get ready to be brought for questioning before the
Gestapo. One never knew what would happen to one. I had heard
of their ferocious beating, of the many cruel ways in which the
Gestapo could elicit information and I had had a taste of it when
I was first brought in. What would happen now? I looked at the
little piece of sky that I could see through the prison window.
Perhaps never again in my life would I think such beautiful
thoughts! Somehow I reviewed to myself all the important reasons for having given up so much joy in life and I found my solace
in a deep conviction of the need to fight evil and of the joy of
having done this together with the man I loved.

I "wrote" poems by singing them to myself. I wrote one down
later:

Song in the Concentration Camp

Ich weiss nicht, soll ich denn hier trauern,
Die Wände stehen fest und dicht.
Ich weiss nur, über diesen Mauern
Wölbt sich ein Himmel, klar und licht.

Ich weiss nur, über mir gehn Schritte,
Die rastlos wandern, her und hin.
Ich weiss in dieses Hauses Mitte,
dass nicht allein im Leid ich bin.

Ich weiss nicht, soll ich Dich denn hassen,
Der mich verriet und brachte her,
Ich weiss nur, Deine Hände fassen
Auch Mauern, kalt und liebeleer.

Ich weiss nicht, soll die Sehnsucht fliegen,
Hin zu den Menschen, die mir lieb,
Ich weiss nur, einmal muss doch siegen
Der Wille, der unbeugsam blieb.

Ich weiss nur, draussen gibt es Bäume
und frischen, hellen, klaren Wind.
Ich weiss, es sind doch keine Träume,
Dass überall doch Brüder sind.

Translation:

I don't know whether I should cry here
The walls stand tightly closed.
I only know that beyond these walls
arches a sky, clear and full of light.

I only know that above me sound steps,
that wander restlessly back and forth.
I know that in this fortress
I am not suffering alone.

I don't know whether I should hate you,
you who were the traitor and got me here,
I know only that your hands too
touch the cold and loveless walls.

I don't know whether my longing should fly
to those I love
I only know that some day must be victorious

the will that could not be bent.

I only know that outside are trees
and fresh, clear wind.
I know that it is not a dream
that everywhere are brothers.

The police wagon took us handcuffed into town for inquiry. Through a little hole in the car I could see the roads. It is strange to look, as a prisoner, at free people, or at least at people who can move freely. I wanted to shout at every man on a bicycle, at every woman walking down the road, "Do you know that there are people in this car who cannot see the sun, who cannot move freely, only because they believe that terror should not reign in this world?"

The questioning began by the interviewer offering me a cigarette. I refused because I did not smoke. I recalled that this "friendly" gesture was quite commonly used because many prisoners who were avid smokers would be willing to give away all they knew, even the names of their dearest friends, to get a smoke if they had been deprived of one for a long time. The torture of a person smoking in front of them while they had the craving for a cigarette was often too much for them. It became a rule for underground workers to learn to stop smoking so that they could not be tempted by the Gestapo.

The interview started friendly enough in great contrast to the earlier treatment I had received. The interviewer made constant reference to the way some of our underground "leaders" (as the Gestapo men called them) would leave the country while letting a young girl such as myself, "hold the bag." This again was an attempt to gain information. The Nazis had learned the method of "divide and conquer." When this did not work, another attempt was made. The Nazis brought out information in regard to our underground work including leaflets that they had confiscated, and names of real people involved in underground work, thus trying to convince me that there was no point in denial and in fact, that I would be better off in telling the truth.

When all of this did not work, the discussion became threatening. The Gestapo interviewer pointed to a sign over his desk which said something about Hitler's regime being the Thousand-year Reich. He glared at me and said, "You are the most stubborn person we have met, but we have much time. You must enjoy solitary. You can enjoy it for many years to come." I was angrily dismissed and put against the wall. I heard the voice of a man who was brought in and whom I did not know. While I was standing facing the wall, the man was first cruelly made fun of in words, and then severely beaten while I was not allowed to turn around. I was not touched and not interviewed again but simply sent on my way back to the concentration camp to solitary confinement

I returned in a turbulent state of mind. The calm of the past few days had disappeared. My mind was turning around and around in a torturous way. Had I done everything right? Had I given them any clues? Was it right that I had denied everything? What happened to others? Paul's name had appeared in the list of the known anti-Nazis. Was he really safe outside the country? Why did they have the leaflets? Were they out of the package that the young man had lost on his bicycle, or had they found more? What would Paul say when he found out that I was in a concentration camp? What would my mother say? What would they do? The nice calm that had told me that I couldn't do anything anyhow and I shouldn't bother about things I couldn't do anything about, all this was completely gone. I had no sleep at night. My tortured thoughts returned and returned and body and soul cried for human assistance and love. My fears mounted: what would happen if a war broke out right then and there when we were locked up? We would burn alive. For the first time the locked room almost suffocated me. Hate suddenly flooded me.

I had fought the Nazis out of a deep sense of revulsion against their terrorism, and my feeling for humanity. I had hated what they did, but I had not hated as personally, as deeply and as horribly as at that moment. I was far away from

Rilke's acceptance of pain or my beautiful morning songs! I hated, I feared, I doubted.

About two days after such horrible nights, I was allowed for the first time to go to the basement to take a shower. Silently I had to fall in with a group of women who marched downstairs to take this shower. The young woman walking in front of me looked like a 15-year old. I could not see her face, but I was struck by the odd position of her hands and the slowness with which she moved. I began to concentrate on those hands and, in the dimness of the walk towards the shower, I realized that both hands were broken, dangling down in an odd angle. I almost cried out when I realized in what horrible pain the woman must be who walked in front of me. Yet no sound came from her lips, and though she walked slowly, she walked steadily. (Later when I was out of the camp, I learned the story of this woman. She, too, had been a member of the underground and had been caught with anti-Nazi publications in her hands. For this they had broken her hands in the first interview. She too was kept in solitary all the time, but, worse than I, was handcuffed to her bed every night so that she could not move. I cannot say whatever became of her; perhaps, in these short words, I can set a monument for a courageous woman.)

Before we returned to our cells we were each asked to fill a large pail of water and carry it back to our cells for cleaning. The young woman with the broken hands also had to take the pail and with a painfully jerking movement lifted the heavy load from the floor. I think at this moment hate and rage prevented me from feeling fear. I simply turned around, grabbed her pail and said, "I'll carry that." For a fleeting moment I saw the sweet face of a young woman, a little frightened and yet with incredible surprised relief. The attendant, a woman, turned sharply and bellowed that speaking was not allowed. Then the guard's eyes met mine and I suddenly recognized even in this woman's face a moment of compassion. She said gruffly, "No talking, but you can carry her pail." Still today, I know that the long way from the shower to the upper floor of the jail with the two heavy water pails was one of the most beautiful, most rewarding moments of my life. To be allowed in this cold and lonely and frightening place to do something for another person was the most wonderful experience that I could have had; to be lifted away from one's own worries and fears.

I slept better the following night. There were some humane gestures that I found in the concentration camp, along with the cruel ones. There was the morning when the woman guard woke us and entering my cell said softly, "If you prefer it, I don't have to turn on the electric light. The sun is coming up so beautifully and you can see a little of it if I do not turn on the light." And so I witnessed in the small square of a window the eternal beauty of the rising sun.

Another time, when again we were brought to the car for further questioning, I witnessed one of the women shivering and crying. She obviously had a fever but there she stood in the cold winter morning in her prison clothes. A young SS man whom I had not seen before suddenly said to the driver, "For heaven's sake, let her have her coat." He himself went back to the cell and threw the coat around the shoulders of the woman. Somehow with this one small gesture he became human.

I was allowed, finally, to go for the short 15-minute walk in the prison yard which was permitted to most prisoners. We walked silently around and around in a large circle in single file. SS guards were stationed at intervals. They made cruel jokes about the older women who could hardly move their swollen legs and they loudly and crudely told each other sex jokes about the younger women passing by. Yet, to me, it meant a little change from the dull loneliness; it meant air, and the feel of earth under my feet. It is odd how one can remember small incidents, as for instance, a pebble lying on the ground and I playfully pushing it ahead while walking like a child playing in the street. Or, I looked up at the tower where the machine guns and other SS guards were stationed and almost chuckled to myself remembering the joke I heard the evening before I was arrested.

Yet there was no walk on Sundays. On Sundays all prisoners were inside. One Sunday I was sitting on my little stool in the cell thinking my own thoughts when I suddenly heard commotion in the prison yard. There were the heavy sounds made by the crushing boots of the SS guards. This was unusual for a Sunday. I could not see because the small prison window was too high, but I could hear. Suddenly sharp orders were rapped out. I heard the barking voices of two Gestapo men. The whole thing was ominous and frightening. I pushed my small chair into the corner of the room where I hoped I could not be seen through the spy hole by a guard. I climbed on it to see what was going on. Everything I had ever been told about concentration camps and the cruel tortures perpetrated was displayed right in front of my eyes on a cold December Sunday. In the courtyard was one gaunt prisoner in the thin brown prison garb given to the men. And while I watched with horror, *he was literally hunted to death.* He was made to run as fast as he could, to throw himself on the wet, stony ground, and to jump up again to the orders barked by two men alternately because one alone was not able to do it quickly enough. This continued for hours until the prisoner began to bleed out of mouth and ears. Then the orders were given faster and faster and the slowing body was prodded with butts of the gun. This ended when life finally ceased and with a dull thud the body fell. Blood spurted from the mouth. The hands looked like the claws of a bird lifted up against the sky. Then everything was quiet. I felt as if there was no world around me. I felt as if I saw in every window a person like myself looking at the dead man who had been crucified in the 20th Century....

My witnessing this murder did the same thing to me as the encounter with the knife when I entered the concentration camp. Defiance increased and the cold feeling that I was dealing with beasts, not with human beings. It became easier to lie to the Gestapo.

One of my fingers became infected during this time. I said nothing about it, thinking that nothing could be done about it anyway. The finger swelled up angrily and caused a great deal of pain. One of the women guards, the same who had let me look at the early morning sky, saw it when she came on duty. She exclaimed over it and insisted that something be done about it. Since it was evening, no health officer was on duty, but she brought hot water and soap so that I could bathe my finger. She came into my cell, shook her head and said, "I'm not supposed to talk to you, but I can't stand it. Such poor young things. Sometimes I can hardly stand it."

She wanted to know why I was there and all the time in solitary. Again it struck me what horrible things this whole system did. I really felt that this woman was sympathetic and I had proof that she had made life a bit more bearable for me, and yet to save anyone else I could not trust her. All I could say to her was that I did not know. I saw the shadow cross her face, and I realized how it hurt her to feel the distrust.

The next day she insisted that I be seen by one of the medical attendants. Before I was brought there she came into my cell and brought needle and thread, an unheard-of luxury. All of us had been put into prison garb the first day we entered the concentration camp. Prison garb for women was a shapeless sack of a dress in the ugly brown color of the Nazi movement. There was no collar on the dress and it had long sleeves. The dress I wore was torn in several places. It was covered by another piece of sack cloth serving as an apron. The woman guard said, "It's a shame to let a young girl be seen by a man this way. Come on, sew up the dress." It was one of the most enjoyable half hours. I had been yearning to do something with my hands and this was an opportunity. I am sure that the guard purposely "forgot" to ask me for the return of the needle. For the next few weeks I had one of the most precious tools, a sewing needle! Now I could pull out the threads of my handkerchief in a much better way. I could thread the needle with the pulled-out threads and do some fancy embroidery on the old hankies. (In all the years of wandering that followed, these handkerchiefs went with me, and I still have them.)

In the dispensary my finger was treated on the insistence of the woman guard. The medical attendant had no intention at first of even looking at it. For some reason the guard dared to speak sharply with the young man, and she insisted that he do something. He opened up the infected wound and sent me back. In the afternoon she smuggled two magazines into my cell saying that she would be off duty in about two hours and that I could do a little reading until then. I was absolutely elated to see some printed pages. I placed one of the magazines on my desk like a picture because there was a photo of some trees. After about an hour the guard came into my cell. She snatched the magazine off the table and threw it under the bed. Then she said to me, "You dope, you don't know a thing about prisons. I could have come in here with someone else and you know you are not allowed to read, so hide the stuff when you hear a key." The next two hours were pure joy. I wanted to be sure that I kept something of this enjoyment, and I learned by heart a 12-verse poem by Gottfried Keller that I found in the magazine.

Again later, I learned that this guard did similar things for other prisoners. Lieschen told me later that she had been hiding some part of her bread and used it to make sculptures out of it. The guard had found them, but had only said that she felt sorry that she had to use bread for this, but had never reported it. She had given her other little privileges. After the fall of the Nazis when Hamburg came under Allied occupation this guard as well as many others were put on trial because of their participation in concentration camps. Lieschen herself, who was in Hamburg, testified for her and told me that quite a number of political prisoners came forward to do this. Because of this she was shown leniency.

Christmas Eve in the concentration camp: the day before Christmas we got a piece of newspaper to clean our windows in the cells, carefully cut out, so that nothing about the daily news could be read. But I hid a very precious piece of this newspaper— a small map of the world used to indicate the weather. The whole evening I dreamt of this map; there and there and there and there were my friends, who had fought together with me against the Nazis, before they came to power and afterwards. I saw their faces, I heard them speak, I dreamt about the day when we would all be together in a free country, perhaps a free world....

It was Christmas Eve in this barren concentration camp. It was bleak, no steeple or tower with a clock to watch. Gongs shrilly rang the orders to the prisoners. The gongs clanked, and I had to lie down on my cot in the darkness. Still my head was full of good thoughts, but suddenly I heard the drunken voices of the guards, I heard them running up and down. There was shrill laughter and drinking. The SS were celebrating Christmas, with shouts of ribaldry in a silent house full of men and women torn from their homes and families, lying restlessly on their iron cots.

The SS's drunken voices grew louder and louder, as they yelled the Horst Wessel Lied and "Heute gehört uns Deutschland, morgen die ganze Welt." I shivered. I knew what it meant when the SS reached such a state of hysteria. Abruptly, there was a clatter of keys, a slamming of doors, a heavy thud and the horrible inhuman cry of a man, only interrupted by the scornful laughter of the SS. The cry faded away in a low awful moaning. The SS had their victim and their Christmas joy.... Behind barred doors we hundreds and hundreds were lying with fists clenched, bodies taut and hearts heavy with frustration.

The next morning I heard the man above my cell wandering up and down, up and down. I did not know who he was, but I had learned to know by his steps, what he thought. This day they said the same that my steps would say to those under my cell: how long still? How long still have we to bear them?

Wandering up and down I stared at the bare walls—walls I had looked at for weeks until I knew every crack—and then for the first time I discovered in the pale light of the snowy winter day, some scratches in the wall. I went nearer and saw first a word written with a fine needle in the paint. I studied patiently and for a long time, until I discovered the whole sentence, the encouraging message a woman had written: "You who are after me amid these walls, do not despair. Also for us the sun will shine once more. Think of all those who died for the cause of freedom. Do not despair."

I had not heard a kind spoken word for weeks—only the Gestapo questioning: "Whom did I know? Why did I go there? Whom did I go with?" Now the wall had spoken. I heard the voices of thousands who did not live any more, or who were tortured, or who lived behind stone walls, or who lived insulted and despised in their own homes, or in far-off exile. It was the voices of those who "did not despair." It was like a miracle, and I felt I had to give something to the next one to come. The precious needle was in my hand, and I scratched into the wall also a message of hope, "In spite of everything, humanity will live."

After the horror of the Christmas Eve night and the elation of Christmas day followed one of the most severe tests. While my doors were locked I heard the voices of Lieschen and some of the guards frequently. She was called to perform tasks which are usually rewards for "very acceptable behavior," which in a concentration camp for political prisoners usually means that they have finally told what the Gestapo wants to know. I could hear how she was addressed in a friendly manner by men and women guards alike, how she was sent on errands which allowed her to get off the floor, etc. I knew that I would be called for more interrogation. What had Lieschen told them? It would be terrible if she had admitted much and involved others and I continued to insist that I knew nothing. There is nothing worse than doubting friends. I caught myself saying aloud, "Maybe they just do this to make me feel she has told everything. Why would they so frequently address her just in front of my cell?" I could tell this to myself, but it was not always easy to believe it. One day the woman guard who was more lenient, opened the door and Lieschen followed her with a dish of water which I was supposed to use for cleaning. This was the first time I saw her since the night we were arrested. She looked healthy and her usual old self. The guard was constantly close to her when she put the water on my table. Lieschen turned and followed the guard. When the door closed, I suddenly heard a little sound and saw a piece of paper pushed under the door. I grabbed it and hid it under my pillow. Almost immediately the door opened and the guard looked around angrily, "Was there something you two were up to?" and then slammed the door shut again. Again I wondered whether she just gave lip service to what she was supposed to do because she did not search the room. Courageous Lieschen had really stuck out her head this time. She had actually, (as I found out later) stolen a pencil from one of the guard's desks, since she too was not allowed to have any writing equipment. On this piece of paper she had given me the most precious news, namely, identifying exactly what she had admitted and what she had denied in those interrogations. I was ashamed of my doubts about her, and I was much better prepared for future hearings. As usual, I swallowed the paper.

One morning the woman guard came into my room with a large box containing my civilian clothes and said, "Get dressed quickly, you are going out." What did this mean? Transfer to another concentration camp? A mock trial and then a prison? Death? Release?? But the latter was impossible. Only two days before this I had been interrogated again and this time the Gestapo man had shouted at me furiously, screaming that I was the most stubborn person he had ever talked to and I could just as well count on being with them for the rest of my life.

Chapter Fourteen

Release

*T*hat morning I was again asked to stand before the door of my cell, facing the wall and waiting. Then one of the most incredible, most beautiful things happened: the door to the women's dormitory, where a large number of women lived together, was opened. I had never met those women personally, had only seen them at the shower or walking on the grounds. They knew that I was the only one totally isolated. They, too, must have felt the suspense, not knowing what would happen to me. And suddenly, in spite of the guards, the women pushed the door wide open, ran out and I was embraced by women with the faces of strangers, but with the eyes of sisters, eyes with tears and eyes trying to give me courage. They threw their arms around me and they shouted, "Good luck to you, and don't come back here again." The guards were stunned for a moment shouting that they should get back to their room. One of the women said softly, "There is nothing wrong with a kiss, is there?" and then they moved away. All these women were political prisoners and Jehovah's Witnesses and among them one or two prostitutes, but to me still today, whoever they were and whatever their belief, they *are* sisters and they taught me that one never should generalize about any nation. In spite of solitary confinement I learned again in the concentration camp that there were decent people even among the Germans.

When I entered the police wagon I immediately saw Lieschen. She, too, was in civilian clothes which meant she too, was leaving. She pressed close to me in the crowded wagon and spelled into my hand the news that she knew she was being released. I spelled back that I did not know yet what would happen. Lieschen, just as I, must have thought that I would be sent to another concentration camp, because she pressed a little gift into my hand, her only handkerchief.

In the Gestapo cellar we were separated. I was again called into the room where my "inquisitor" was sitting. He smiled, "Looking nicer today, aren't you?" I didn't answer. "Don't be so gloomy," he said, "you are going home. There are just a few little formalities." I still did not say anything, I just didn't believe it. He pushed in front of me the familiar pledge that one should not tell anybody about anything that had happened in the concentration camp or what one had seen there. I was to sign this. He impressed on me that if I would ever tell, it would mean return to the concentration camp. I really began to believe that I was being released. My fingerprints were taken. When I washed my hands, I saw myself for the first time in a mirror, and—at 25 one is still very young—I was so excited that I made faces at myself and laughed. But reality cut in crudely. The Gestapo man questioned me, "To whom are you making signs? Should we keep you here?" I did not realize that I could see in the mirror another prisoner being questioned by the Gestapo. I quickly realized that being released into a Nazi world did not mean being free and that I had no right to be a prankful youngster. The same Gestapo man who had constantly interviewed me brought me to the exit.

"You can leave now," he said, "Auf Wiedersehen." I could not help it, I had to answer, "No, not 'Auf Wiedersehn' to you, good-bye." The heavy door of the police station closed behind me and I stood in the streets of Hamburg. All this had come so unexpectedly that I could not believe it. It was clear to me that I was not released out of view of the Gestapo. I had heard about such releases. They meant that you were now used as bait and that the Gestapo watched whom you contacted and where you were and I was quite sure that they were watching me. But I was outside. I could walk, and not only three steps! I could see a whole sky and not just a little piece! I could turn around a corner, I could run! I could see other people, I could hear them talk! Every step was a new discovery. Does anyone who has not been in prison know what it means to see the bark on a tree, to see a train passing by and people waving, to just feel your body moving freely? Every step was elation, but every moment, too, I felt as if a hand would grab my collar and pull me back.

The landlady looked as though I had arisen from the grave when I arrived home. I had to be careful not to visit anyone who was actually involved in underground work so as not to endanger them. On the other hand, as quickly as possible, I had to notify someone about what I had learned of the knowledge the Gestapo had of underground activities. I had to constantly remind myself that it was possible the Gestapo would rearrest me immediately and I had to use the few hours of freedom to warn my friends. It was possible to reach Rudi without having to telephone him. He was a friend of my landlady's daughter and therefore could come to the house without being suspected of coming to see me. One of the girls asked him to come. We fell into each other's arms. At times like that the bond was so close! I told Rudi as quickly as possible everything I had experienced. While I talked I learned how closely body and soul work together. Nobody could see it, but I felt that constant trembling of my legs while I pretended to talk quietly. I tried to control this trembling but there was no use. Only when I told him about some of the beatings I had observed and that these people were still in the hands of the Gestapo I began to cry. It was the first time I had cried since my arrest. It was a strange feeling of guilt that I was no longer in the midst of those horrors, that I was free while others still suffered.

Rudi told me how he had continued our work and had arranged for news to get to my Mother. Mother later told me how kind he had been, and how he had sent her flowers for the New Year in my name. Mother, unknown to me, with the courage so special to her, had actually written to the Hamburg Gestapo and had gone into the offices of the Gestapo in Berlin, pleading to release her daughter, in this way exposing herself in a most dangerous way. Rudi also told me that news had gone to Paul about my arrest but unfortunately he could not tell me much more about him. (Later I heard how terribly that news had affected Paul. He lived, at this time, under most poverty stricken and degrading circumstances as a refugee in Paris. The French government gave no permission to work, perhaps the worst that one could do to an active man such as Paul. When he heard the news of my being arrested he wanted to return to Germany to do something drastic, either to actively try to liberate me or to be put on some special dangerous assignment in the underground. The terrible inactivity of the immigrant was suffocating. He who had always been a very stable person went into a state of shock. When he didn't appear at some meetings for several days someone went to look for him in his room. There was Paul lying on the bed staring into space and not saying a word, even when people talked to him. He was in this state for several days. Somehow he recovered.)

It was important for me to leave Hamburg immediately to try to get mother out of the country and then to find a way of leaving it myself. I had become worthless for underground activities in Hamburg; in fact I was dangerous to everybody. I knew when I left Hamburg that I would not return but at the same time it had to look as if I was just going to visit my mother. This meant leaving behind me all the things I loved and was attached to, my books, my pictures, the beautiful bookcase Paul had made for me, the photos, my little flower vases and, especially, it meant to leave behind so many people I loved without being able to tell them that I would be away for always—as I thought.

Among others it was hardest to leave Aaron. Aaron was a young Jewish student who had studied literature and art and who was a sensitive artistic kind of personality. When the Nazis had come to power Aaron had at first not understood the impact. He had tried to continue living in his world of beauty. His odd detachment from the reality around him showed a complete disregard for his own health and for the way in which he was living. We discovered that one day, when he came for a visit with the daughters of my landlady and suddenly fainted. We realized that he ate irregularly. After the fainting he refused to go back to his room, showing signs of great anxiety. At the time we two young women accompanied him to his room. The picture that we saw was something awful: obviously nobody had cleaned his place for a long time. It was not only totally messed up, it was covered with dust and dirt. While Aaron was still studying, life outside of his studies had become a nightmare. My landlady suggested that Aaron stay at her apartment for awhile to be with other people. Meanwhile I could use my great talent: house cleaning. After a few days when Aaron returned to his room, he gasped. The room was sparkling clean and a shining blue vase with bright yellow flowers was standing on his desk. From then on all of us had made a concerted effort to bring Aaron out of his dream world. One of the professors at the University declared himself willing to give Aaron his final examination (this was still possible, though only in Hamburg). Aaron wanted it, but feared it. I see before me the thin, white face with the lovely brown eyes of a poet when he said, "You have to stay with me the morning before the examination. I can't go through with it." That morning I walked with Aaron back and forth in the botanical garden in Hamburg, listened with him to the birds and told him jokingly that they were all saying, "Good luck, we know you will pass your examinations." And Aaron went into the examinations and passed them!

Poem for Aaron

Sieh, einmal werden auch die Strassen schön,
Die dunklen Strassen, die Dich so bedrückt.
Einmal hebt all der dunkle Druck sich auf,
Der wie ein Alp in Deiner Seele lag.
Einmal, da dehnt sich frei der Atem, und beglückt
Sehn Deine Augen weit gespannt den Himmel.
Und hell befreit liegt vor Dir nun der Tag.

Translation:

See, once again the streets will be beautiful,
The dark streets that oppressed you so.
Once the dark pressure will lift,
that lay like a nightmare on your soul.
Once breath will come freely again, and happily
your eyes will see the open sky
and free and light the day now lies before you.

The friendship with Aaron was such an incongruous lyric interlude while at the time I was actively concerned with smuggling
papers with anti-Nazi news to other people and went through
the uncertainty of Paul's safety. (All this was before my arrest.)
The day I had to leave Hamburg for Berlin, Aaron was sick in
bed. I said goodbye. He smiled a sad smile and said, "You came
back from the dead, but I will never see you again." Aaron's
faithful girl friend who had lived through the anxious times
with him was sitting next to him and looked at me sadly. I could
not tell them the truth, but I kissed them goodbye.

It is true, I never did see either of them again. Both were
killed by the Nazis and both are in some mass grave; we don't
know where.

Chapter Fifteen
Immigration to Czechoslovakia

*I*t is strange how certain memories stand out and how others completely vanish. I cannot remember anything about my arrival in Berlin and reunion with mother. It must have been too painful. I begin to remember again only the nights that followed with mother begging me to sleep with her, this strong independent woman now fearful and dependent. I remember the nights when I told her about the concentration camp, leaving out the worst. I told her that this may not be the end of the suffering, that I just could not sit still when barbarians were trying to rule the world and spout race superiority. I do remember mother's quiet nod. I was amazed at her understanding.

My sister who had immigrated to Israel (then Palestine) had sent mother the papers which permitted her to immigrate. Mother did not want to leave as long as I was still in Germany, the last of the family, but I persuaded her to leave as fast as possible, since I had no idea how and when I could leave the country. I had decided that I would only leave "legally"; that means not by a secret passage over the border because this would increase the hostility of the Nazis against those who were still in the concentration camps and prisons and would point toward a well-organized group. The next weeks were filled with trying to sell our little grocery store and arranging for mother's emigration. This involved frequent visits to the offices of the Nazi authorities. Only I knew that I was filled with panic each time I entered such an office and discussed business with men wearing the swastika. At the nearby police station were still some old police officers who had known our family for many years, long before the Nazis came to power. One of the officers almost cried when he heard that mother was leaving the country. He had known my parents since they had married. They had always lived in the same place. Father had been respected in the neighborhood and mother was loved since she was gentle and helped many when their children got sick or when they were worried about something. This man almost tried to persuade me to keep mother in Germany because, as he said, "It won't always be as it is today."

One day mother called me to say that someone was asking for me. In our little store stood "Herman," (as we called him then), one of the leading personalities in the underground movement. Herman was a rare person. He originally came from German nobility but had early cast his lot with those who were deprived, and had become an idealistic socialist. He was an outstanding economist. He had taught at universities, but when the Nazis came to power had immediately participated in underground work. He was one of the most hunted men in the "Third Reich." There were rewards on his head. He never stayed in one place for more than a few nights. I was so elated to see him, to know that he was alive, and to feel again the contact with the movement that was my life blood, that I flew into his arms. He was usually a rather cold and forbidding man, but he was most human at this moment.

He had come to find out more about my experiences in the concentration camp. He had also come for something very difficult: he wanted me to take several articles of the underground newspaper to a certain place where they would be printed, wait until this was done, and then deliver this package to another place. This kind of activity was something I had done frequently before, but now, I was deathly afraid, more than ever. Somehow I had found peace with my decision that I was out of underground work. Without knowing it, I had felt relieved of the responsibility. I saw before me what would happen to me if I were caught a second time. I said to Herman that I just couldn't do it.

"I can't take it going to the camp a second time. They have treated me like an outcast the first time. If they catch me now, it will be worse. I am living at the house of my mother. What will they do to her? I just can't do it."

Herman listened patiently. He finally said, "If you don't do it today, there is no one else. The information we have in this paper will make it possible for three people to sabotage an important Nazi meeting and many will be encouraged to know that there is resistance. One of the items will also warn some of our friends whom we cannot reach in any other way. It might save their lives."

What could I do? I accepted the assignment. I was so afraid that even today I cannot remember much of the day. I only remember the person to whom I brought the package of material because I saw him many years later in London and he reminded me of it. I do remember that we pinned the material to my underwear when I left the place but I have no recollection of the content of it, of the streets I walked, or the people I met.

I still had no direct communications from Paul. I had some tenuous indirect ones. My younger sister, Ruth, who was a nurse in England, was in contact with him, and her letters told me about him without mentioning his name. We called him "Nunx" in our letters and pretended to talk about one of her colleagues. This way I learned a bit about what he was doing. On my birthday my sister sent some money saying that this was money that "Nunx" wanted me to have to buy red roses (thus telling me of his continuing love for me). Mother looked around the torn-up place (we had begun to pack), shook her head sadly, and said, "Roses don't fit in here. But some day you will have them again." The "some day" did not come so soon, but it came (Paul never forgot red roses on my birthday). Mother had a terrible time separating herself from anything that had accumulated in the many years of living in one place and raising a family. It was heartbreaking to see her trying to discard something and then again asking for it to be packed, to be shipped; shipped to her new place of life.

Finally the movers came. I was to take mother to Leipzig, where we were to meet a young couple who were also immigrating to Israel. They had decided to drive south to Italy and then take a boat across to Israel. They had agreed to take mother as a passenger. This made the trip cheaper. Mother, who seldom traveled, was afraid and trembled like a small child. It seemed incongruous to me that such a beautiful voyage of which one would dream and for which one would save in Europe for half a lifetime should be made under such sad circumstances. Again I can remember nothing about Leipzig but the little dark hotel room where we stayed overnight, and my waving goodbye to the car which took my mother away—thinking that I would never see her again. I have not even the faintest recollection of the train trip back or forth. As a good-bye I gave mother two poems:

Mutter

Ich war in Dir
Als keiner mich gekannt.
Ich lag bei Dir
Als keiner mich genannt.

Du gutes, liebes Sorgenangesicht
Ja, Du verstehst mich
und verdammst mich nicht.

Die ganze Last der Erde
Muss ich tragen.
Du, Mutter, wirst nicht
Wie, warum nur fragen.

Du glaubst an mich,
Wenn noch so fern ich bliebe.
Oh, Mutter, hätten alle Menschen
Doch *die* Liebe

Translation:

Mother

I was in you
when no one knew me
I lay next to you
when none yet could name me.
Your loving, sweet face
full of sorrow,
yes, you do understand me
and you will never condemn me.
The burden of the Earth
is laid upon me
yet, mother, you will not ask
why or wherefore.
You believe in me
even if I am far away
oh mother, if only all human beings
had that love

And

Dort ist das Ziel
Und zagend stockt der Fuss
So weit der Weg

Und überall sind Steine,
Und hinter uns die Last der langen Jahre
Und hinter uns das Leid, das wir gelitten...

Und in uns—
Gram und Kummer, Sorge?
Wir horchen still hinein
und staunend fühlen wir:
All dieses trostlos Dumpfe
Hat sich nun verwandelt,

Und ist zerglüht in einer grossen Liebe,
Die jeden fasst,
der einmal ging gebeugt,
und jeden, der nach einer Hand verlangte,
die nicht mehr da ist....

Und diese Liebe trägt den Fuss
Und gibt die Kraft, ans Ziel doch zu gelangen,
Und unsre Hände
werden stark und—sanft,
Und tragen mit und stützen, streicheln
Und weit nun öffnet sich das Tor des neuen Lebens.

Translation:

There is the goal—
yet one hesitates.
So far the way
and everywhere are stones.
Behind us lies the burden of long years
behind us all the sorrow we have suffered...

And in us—
despair and suffering, unhappiness?
We listen quietly to ourselves

and feel with surprise:
all this desperate dullness
has changed,—

It is forged into a great love
that embraces everyone,
who once was bent
And everyone who hungers for a hand
that is no more...

And this love carries us
and gives us strength to reach our goal,
and our hands
become strong and—soft,
and help, support, caress—
Before us the door of a new life opens widely.

I remember reentering the now empty apartment in Berlin. All I had to do was to give the key to the caretaker. A courageous cousin of mine, Lola, and her family had offered to have me stay with them until I knew if I would return to Hamburg or what would happen to me. I stood in the middle of a room in which we had all grown up. I can still see vividly before me some of the remnants the movers had left. Mechanically I took a broom and swept them into the middle of the floor. I stared at those broken pieces and felt myself becoming panicky with loneliness, with fear, with the feeling of complete helplessness in the face of all this. A friend of mine had seen me only two days before and had reported that the Gestapo had asked for me in my room in Hamburg. I had not told mother about this. Now I was all alone. What would happen to me? That evening young Hilde Meisel, who later died of a Nazi bullet, spent an hour with me, arms around each other.

Lola and her family were a blessing for me. They had two little boys, one 8 and one 10 years old. They were a warm and giving family, but I saw with terror what persecution and isola-

tion did to these children. The older one had lengthy serious discussions with me far beyond his years. He questioned what it
meant to be a Jew, why people thought they were different from
other people. The younger one did not discuss this, but the
shadow fell over his young life. One day he was in the street
playing with a ball. Suddenly the doorbell rang and two policemen stood in the doorway with the frightened little 7-year-old
between them. Everybody in the house held his breath. Police
entering a Jewish home in 1937 could mean the worst. The policeman said that the boy had played carelessly with the ball
and that it was disturbing a neighbor by whizzing past his head.
The child wanted to speak up, but Lola immediately interfered,
apologizing profusely for his behavior and saying that he would
not be allowed to play ball downstairs again. When the policemen left she screamed at the child that he should know better
than to bring disaster on his family. The bewildered child
crawled into a corner. The overwrought mother sobbed in the
other room. The innocent play of a 7-year-old was turned into a
nightmare and the education for hate and cowardice had started.
Only in my poetry could I allow myself to express my feelings.
Outwardly I had to be strong.

For Paul:

Da draussen hängt so weich die Sommernacht,
Und tiefer Duft von Maien füllt den Raum,
Du solltest bei mir sein und leise, sacht,
mich streicheln wie ein guter, ferner Traum.

Ich möchte bei Dir liegen, nur ganz still...
und Deinen Arm sollst Du nun um mich tun
und alles, alles, was der Tag sonst will
Das soll versinken und auch einmal ruhn.

Ich bin allein und Du bist fern von mir,
Doch fühl ich heut so stark wohl Deine Nähe

Dass mir so ist, als stündest Du bei mir
Und nur des Windes Atem leise uns umwehe.

Translation:

Outside hangs so soft the summer night
and the roses' perfume fills the room.
You should be with me and so softly
touch me as a good, far away dream.

I want to lie near you—oh, so quietly...
your arm should be around me
and all this that the day demands
should sink away and rest for once.

I am alone and you are far away
Yet I feel today so strongly your nearness
that it is as if you stood closely to me
and only the wind's breath caresses us softly.

To Paul:

Wenn wir weinen—sind wir doch allein,
Und die müde Nacht umfasst uns bang.
Ach, wir gingen ja so gerne ihn zu zwein
Diesen Weg, den schweren, steil und lang.

Bangend tasten unsre leeren Hände,
und wir wissen: fern von hier ist einer,
der, wenn er sie in den seinen fände,
Stiller würde, grösser, heller, reiner.

Doch gehören wir noch zu den Reichen,
In uns lebt ein Wille, gut und klar,
Und wir weinen nicht mehr—sondern streichen
leise einen Wunden über Stirn und Haar.

Translation:

> When we cry—we are so alone
> And only the tired night is around us.
> Yet, oh we would want to go together
> this way, the difficult steep and long way.
>
> Our empty hands reach out fearfully,
> And yet we know: far from here is someone
> who, if he could hold them in his own
> would become calm and great and free and pure.
>
> And yet we do belong to the rich of the earth,
> In us lives a will, good and clear.
> We do not cry any more—yet we stroke
> softly the brow and hair of another who was hurt.

Now I had to work on my leaving Germany. I had contact with one person in the underground who kept me informed about the efforts my friends made in other countries to get me out. This person was Julius. Julius had been a Jewish high school teacher, intelligent and gifted. I think his field of teaching was mathematics, but when Julius pulled out his violin one knew that he was also a musician. He belonged to our political group. He was an idealist but seemed cold in his relation to individuals. In fact, at times I did not want to work with him because I disliked his rigidity. After the advent of the Nazis he had given himself body and soul to the underground movement; he, as was Herman, was hunted by the Gestapo and led the nerve-racking life of an underground worker who had to sleep in a different place every night.

When I met Julius at this time in Berlin, he was a very changed person. He was warm, outgoing, gentle. I asked him what had happened to him. He smiled and said, "In the years before the underground work I thought I did my *duty* working in such movements as the labor unions, and I decided to keep all my human warmth and love for people outside of this, for my students, my family and friends. I thought I had to make a sharp distinction between those in political work and my friends. Now I have learned that one cannot do this. The people to whom I am closest are those who do the same work as I do against the monsters who rule Germany. What else can one give but love?" And then as if ashamed of such a confession, he quickly changed the subject. "And you? We must find a way to get you out soon. You won't help anyone if you are dead."

My passport was practically worthless. It said "Stateless" and this was sufficient to close every door. My sister in England tried desperately to get a permission of entry for me, but at that time the English government wanted to keep peace with Nazi Germany and very few visas were given to refugees. France let some refugees enter illegally and then usually refused them a permit to work. The same applied to many other countries surrounding Germany. I tried one embassy after another and constantly got refusals. Time seemed to run out. Again the alarming news came that the Gestapo had asked where I was. They obviously were still content to know that I had a legal address in Berlin and could be reached anytime. Julius who was my contact with our underground organization, pressed me to leave illegally but I still refused, hoping for some other way out. One day I accidentally met a young Jewish woman whom I knew only slightly. She looked healthy and sun-tanned, and I asked her where she had spent her vacation. She told me that she had been in Czechoslovakia in one of the famous health resorts which had special springs. She mentioned also that she was stateless but that it was possible to get permission of the German government to go there if one had the recommendation of a doctor certifying a medical need. I almost jumped but held back and asked cautiously whether this had to be signed by some official medical authority. She said that a doctor at the Czechoslovakian Embassy had to give the certificate.

That same day I entered the Czechoslovakian Embassy asking for the physician in charge. An older physician looking tired and kind was sitting behind the desk asking me if he could help me. I told him that I needed to go to Karlsbad and needed to go immediately for health reasons. Could he give me a certificate? I needed this because I was stateless. He looked at me seriously, "What kind of sickness do you have?"

"Oh, I feel very run down and irritable, I badly need some rest." This was the truth.

Again the same direct look, "But for this, one does not need Karlsbad. You can rest here in Germany."

I thought desperately, "What sickness does one need to have to go to Karlsbad?" I suddenly remembered that the water of the famous Karlsbad Springs was supposed to heal kidney diseases. I said, "I think I have a kidney ailment. They do not function right."

The doctor took out his stethoscope. He did not even ask me to open my heavy winter coat. The listening to my heart beat was an obvious pretense, but we both went through the motions. "You feel you must leave to regain your health, don't you?" The face before me was grave, no smile. I nodded. He quickly wrote out and handed me a certificate. On it he had noted that he had examined me, that I had a severe gall bladder and kidney ailment and needed absolutely the benefit of those waters at Karlsbad. I had difficulty reading this because suddenly tears blurred my vision. The kind voice said, "The German government gives some special permission to take out of the country 500 marks if you are sick. You can get this at any bank with this certificate." I could only stammer a thank you. His eyes looked sad and comprehending. "It is all right, I wish you the best for your health." Not a single word about my true plight was exchanged between this stranger and myself. I have never seen him again. I only hope that he, too, found someone to help him get out of the hands of the persecutors when the time came for him.

The next day I had my permission to take out 500 extra marks. This was not a large sum but it was sufficient to live on for a short time. Anyhow, it was an unusual situation to leave Germany with a legal permission to take out money. But then came a horrible blow. The Czechoslovakian government gave the visa to enter its country, but I was informed that the German police had to give an exit visa, and that the only place that could give it were the police in Hamburg, as I still legally belonged to Hamburg. What now? Nobody could go there for me. It meant that I would have to go to the same police station in Hamburg to which I had been brought that fateful night when the Gestapo entered my room. Julius again was the one with whom I could talk this over. First he suggested I give up the whole idea of leaving legally and to accept the services of a guide across the mountains into Czechoslovakia. Again I refused this. We then decided together that the only way that was open to me was to go back to Hamburg for a day and take the chance. I had all the legal documents. If the Gestapo did not get hold of me that moment I might get the exit permit. I should immediately take the next train back to Berlin, take my suitcase and leave the same day.

I felt cold, desperate fear when I entered the police station in Hamburg and knocked at the door of the office which issued visas. It was next to the room where the Gestapo had taken me that night! I said to myself goodbye to freedom, to any hope of escape. It took all the will power and training of years to enter this room, to calmly hand the policeman at the desk my passport and to say that I wanted the exit visa on grounds of the medical certificate and the visa issued by Czechoslovakia. The man pulled out my card which existed at every German police station giving my status and whereabouts. The odd trembling of my leg muscles started again, but I held on to the counter. He glanced at me, said, "Well, you look as if you need it." He stamped the passport and I was free to leave with the exit visa in my pocket.

People have often asked, "How did you ever get out?" This is by no means the end of my story of "getting out," but one of my answers has always been, "Dictatorships are not perfect and thank God that they make mistakes."

I went back to Berlin. The train to Czechoslovakia would leave in a few hours. I had said goodbye to my relatives and the children. Julius had arranged to come to the apartment to give me either last minute instructions or get some from me. He was there on the dot. He, who led such a sad, hunted life, was filled with happiness because one more victim would escape the Gestapo. I said that I wished he could leave, too. He shook his head, "I can still do work here, and I am needed, Gisa." And then the usually reserved and cold-seeming Julius embraced me with all the warmth and strength of someone who knows that it is probably the last time. We knew that he could not come to the train with me, but he could go part of the way with me. At the Potsdamer Platz stood the flower women with small bunches of violets. Julius grabbed a whole bunch of a dozen of them and put it into my arms.

"In all this horror, we must not forget beauty, Gisa." I could not speak.

Those were the last words I ever heard of Julius. Some time later he was arrested with several other anti-Nazi fighters. He was part of one of the show trials the Nazis staged from time to time. Julius was condemned to life. His behavior before the Courts was that of one of the great heroes of the century. He died in prison—how, we don't know. But we have one of his last letters he wrote to his parents. In it he wrote to them that they should forgive him for the suffering he brought upon them. He said that he had done it because he loved humanity and this was the only way to stand up for humane ideals, but he could understand that it was hard for his parents. He said that they shouldn't think that he is unhappy. He ended with a beautiful poem by Rabindranath Tagore, which went about like this (I quote from memory:)

> I wanted to live with joy—
> I found out life was duty.
> I worked, and see,
> Duty was joy.

I was on the train, riding toward an unknown country and an unknown world. I knew that at some time in Czechoslovakia someone would contact me to help me find my way but where, I did not know. I was going east when my heart wanted to go west because Paul was in France and my sister, Ruth, was in England. Julius had told me that the underground movement considered my services too valuable to just dispose of them. There was some hope that I could continue this work against Nazi tyranny in Czechoslovakia or in Austria. Both countries were rightfully considered dangerously prone to fall for Nazi propaganda. This did not apply to all of Czechoslovakia but to the Sudetenland, the German part of Czechoslovakia; it was flooded by Nazi propaganda. The beautiful Bohemian mountains came in sight when the train approached the border. I should have felt elated, finally escaping the Nazi nightmare, but I did not. I was going into a completely unknown future separated from every single person I knew. In my pocket I had two addresses, one of some person my mother had known whose daughter now resided in Czechoslovakia and the other an address written in code, a journalist, who was in contact with the labor union underground.

There was no delay when I showed my passport at the border since it had all the legal visas.

In Karlsbad I took a room in a cheap hotel. Since I did not know how long I would have to live on the little money available, I ate only one meal a day. The rest of the time I filled my stomach with the hot water from the springs which one could drink without having to pay. My first contact was with Oscar Klein, the journalist. I found him and his very kind wife in their friendly home. It was as if I was entering a world I had not known for years. It seemed too peaceful and normal. Klein's intelligent fatherly face was framed by white hair. He was a man of great culture and deep feeling. He spoke with great concern about the situation in the Sudetenland. Nazi ideology was penetrating fast. He was outspoken against the Nazis, writing about them in daily papers and in many journals. Several times he was threatened by Nazis. He knew that he would be one of the first to be arrested and tortured if they ever came to power. Terror already had begun. Several times windows were broken in his house and property destroyed. Klein was identified deeply with the Czechoslovakian Republic. In my few contacts with him I acquired my knowledge and my lasting enthusiasm for its founder, Thomas Mazaryk. Like a hungry wolf, I read and read during those days in Karlsbad because for the first time I could read literature forbidden in Germany. It was an eye-opener and a shock to see how excellent material was available on Nazi atrocities, on their total regime, and how little we in Germany had known that the world was informed about them. We who came out of the meager communication one could get in Germany had forgotten what it meant to have a free press and to get all the news one wanted. I stood for hours in front of newspaper stands relishing the opportunity to read free papers, to read news about different countries! Klein made it possible for me to use the libraries.

He also had contact with the labor unions in France, and he told me that soon I would know what arrangements could be made to stabilize my future.

I took long walks in the beautiful mountainous country surrounding Karlsbad. Once I met a girl collecting firewood. We began to talk. She recognized my German accent and with great eagerness asked me about Germany. I was horrified to realize that this child of poverty was seeing in the Nazi regime hope because she parroted, "They'll take the money from all those rich Jews and then we will have enough." Ignorance and clever propaganda worked together to prepare the soil for another Nazi victory.

I once visited the young Jewish woman whose address I had through Mother. The world I entered there was even more strange to me than Klein's scholarly and gracious home. Here were young happy couples. The woman I visited had just had her first child and was elated with joy. Other young women came to visit and there was a chatter about babies and bottles and breast feeding and young husbands coming and admiring their wives and their children. I was experiencing all this like a stranger looking through a glass wall. Somehow this life did not seem real, and sadly enough, like a Cassandra, I could not help seeing them herded together by the brutal whip of a Gestapo, being torn away from their children in a world that did not put up enough resistance to this. Unfortunately, this Cassandra picture fulfilled itself.

Klein, too, never escaped the Gestapo. A few years later in Paris, I was present when one of his friends received his last letter. Klein always had a calm and serene courage. This last letter was still full of courage, but at the same time—as he wrote—he accepted the inevitable: he wrote that Czechoslovakia at that time had been invaded, that the local hordes had hunted him and his wife and were now coming up the hill to get them. They both had waited to the last moment. They did not want to leave their country; they felt that they were too old for emigration. He ended by saying that he could see them come and that at this moment he and his wife, together, were committing suicide. How this letter got out, I don't know. Klein's suicide was not an easy way out. He did not want to give the victor the pleasure of seeing him or his wife cry out when tortured.

There was one moment of truly great joy in those anxious days in Karlsbad. That was when, for the first time in two years, I held in my hands a letter from Paul. In these past two years we could never even write to each other. Now we poured out our thinking and feeling in long, daily letters.

We hoped so very much to see each other but we both decided to continue the fight against the Nazis even if it kept us separated. Finally, the news came that I should proceed to Bratislava, a city on the Danube, close to Vienna. In Bratislava was a lawyer who had helped many underground fighters who had to flee Germany. It had been decided by the underground movement that I should later go to Austria to help prevent further spread of Nazism. To be able to enter Austria and to live there I would need legal papers. There was one way to get a legal passport which in those troubled times was frequently used, namely to marry a person of that nationality. This is one of the most painful chapters of my life. Though everybody considered this a pure formality (this is all it was), I not only revolted at that time against the idea, but it still makes it painful for me to write about it. It was clear from the beginning that the person I would marry had no claim on me and that we would be divorced or have the marriage annulled as soon as possible. It was purely a paper transaction. Yet still, today, I have a hard time looking at the paper that bears his name or at the divorce papers which came later. Yet, there was no other way out. In fact, there were still many obstacles to overcome before the marriage could be performed. First I had to get from Karlsbad to Bratislava. Though this was in the same country I, as a foreigner, was restricted to only the Karlsbad area. The lawyer finally provided me with a certificate indicating that I had severe arthritis and needed the hot mud baths near Bratislava. As one of my friends jokingly wrote, "You surely seem to deteriorate before our eyes."

Paul, in Paris, knew the man whom I had to marry. This man was also an active union member, an Austrian, who faithfully had worked with the labor unions. He was a thoroughly reliable person but—as Paul wrote—"ugly and disagreeable." I surely had mixed feelings when I read this. On the one hand this seemed like a good protection, but on the other hand, it somehow hurt my pride to be married to someone like this. (One is not really old, even if one is 26 years old!) The lawyer in Bratislava was kind. He arranged for the civil ceremony of marriage. I needed to stay in Bratislava awhile to establish residence. He teased me about my unknown future husband, obviously hoping for a romance. I was not a bit in the mood for joking.

Erna, who had been for awhile in France after leaving Hamburg, had meanwhile gone to Vienna. She, too, had married an Austrian the same as I was to marry one, to be able to live there. In fact, she was the one who had asked for my assignment to that country because she was anxious for us to continue to work together. She came to Bratislava to see me about one week before my "future husband" was to arrive. It was a beautiful spring day, and we walked up to the hills looking down on a peaceful city

buried in flowering fruit trees. There we talked first about our
work and the possibility of bringing anti-Nazi leaflets from
France and from Austria into Germany and also fighting the Nazi
movement in Austria. Then we talked about my approaching fake
marriage. It was only to Erna that I expressed my hatred of it. In
fact, at that moment I broke down and told her that I just couldn't
go through with it. Erna, in her calm and almost matter-of-fact
way, brought me back to the realization of the necessity for it.
Later the lawyer helped by saying half-jokingly, half-seriously,
"In the Middle Ages kings and queens went through marriages of
convenience. Today, it is the underground worker, the king and
queen of the fight for humanity, who must do this." Perhaps this
was a bit sentimental or exaggerated, but it helped.

My future "husband" arrived. Perhaps I saw him with Paul's
eyes. I too thought he was very ugly, and I did not like him. He
made a great effort to be kind. He was much older than I was. He,
too, made a sacrifice just as I did. He, too, took a risk in tying
himself to an unknown person. I lived at that time in the room of
a Slovakian family. When the teen-age daughter realized that I
would be married, I became a romantic figure in her eyes. This
made things even worse. Nobody but the lawyer and Erna were
allowed to know what kind of marriage this was. Before the
marriage ceremony, the secretary of the lawyer said, "I sure am
happy to be asked to be your witness today. I see too many di-
vorces." I cringed inside. We stood before the flag of the
Czechoslovakian Republic which I had learned to love as a symbol of freedom. We heard the rapid words of the man who united
us in marriage and I felt like the most abandoned soul on earth,
desperately trying to tell myself that actually I was a "hero,"
but I surely did not feel like one.

My "husband" walked me back to my room. I had violent
headaches. He put his hand on my forehead, and in the most unkind and disagreeable way I told him sternly that he should
never, ever touch me. (The poor man later was killed during the
war.) He was to return to Vienna, and a few weeks later I fol-

lowed as a new bride with a brand new Austrian passport. I was no longer "stateless."

The next days were a little easier because I knew where I would be going and I began to come to terms with my new life. Paul and I were confident that—if we would ever come out of this mess alive—we could still start a life together. I had to discuss with Erna about the living arrangements in Vienna. We both had no intention of living with our so-called "husbands." Yet we had to make up a reasonable story to the outside world. Erna's husband was a writer in Paris. Therefore, this could be explained as a temporary separation. I was adamant about not wanting to live with my "husband" either and we agreed to make up the story that he was looking for better housing for us while I was staying with her. How long we could keep this up we did not know.

Chapter Sixteen

1937 Austria:
Resistance, Arrest, Prison, Nazi Invasion

*I*t was a beautiful sunny day when I made the boat trip between Bratislava and Vienna on the Danube. There were no problems at the border. On the contrary, even the man who looked at my luggage congratulated me as a new bride. How wonderful it must be to be young and newly married and really in love and see the whole world happy around you. I had to play a part all this time. My "husband" and Erna were present when my boat docked. I had mellowed somewhat and could accept him at least as an ally in our struggle against the forces of darkness.

Vienna, 1937—A beautiful city lying amidst the mountains at the river, the spire of St. Stephen's reaching into the sky. So many stories have been written about Vienna, so many songs sung about it. Some day, I would like to see the city again without the clouded eyes of someone who has left a prison and expects to enter

another one. I also would like to see the city in a different situation than it was at that time, a dying city and a frightened city.
Vienna originally had been the capital of a huge empire and the
riches of the then-known world had poured into it. Yet, at the
time I saw it, it was the capital of a small, dismembered Austria,
and it was threatened by the growing Hitler Germany on the one
hand and the Mussolini Italy on the other. It was desperately
poor, with beggars swarming all over the city. It was under semi-
dictatorship, the dictatorship of Schuschnigg. Schuschnigg was
fighting both the Nazis and the Socialists, both strong in Vienna.
His own government had only a small base.

Erna and I rented an apartment with two rooms. One of the
rooms was a large artist's glassed study. We could see a whole
range of mountains and the evening sun over them. The starry sky
was practically in our room at night.

It was not easy for either of us to find work. Erna did some
typing while I tried to get work with children. There were amusing little incidents, as for instance, my going to an employment
agency and the woman not believing me when I said I was 27
years old. She insisted that I was not even 20. When I showed her
my birth certificate, she exclaimed, "My God, you look young, you
must never have had a worry in your life!"

That same day a young boy of about 17 whistled at me and
followed me. When I walked very fast, he said, "Don't run. I
would like to walk with you."

I laughingly said, "For heaven's sake, kid, find a youngster."

He said, "My God, you aren't much older than I am," and then
blushed furiously when I told him I was close to thirty.

Well, it helped my self-confidence. When you feel terribly
old inside, it makes you feel a little like spring when others don't
think of you this way.

The iron necessity of underground work continued. There were
very few who really understood what the threat of Nazism
meant, yet we had to find them. Since Austria already was a
dictatorial state, this was not easy and many people feared to
talk to strangers. Yet we found a few who were willing to join us.

They were very special people. There was one, (after the Nazi defeat, a high city official) who told us about the heroic fight the Socialists had put up when their homes were bombed and shot at during the time of Dollfuss. Both he and his wife had participated actively in the open resistance. When he described how his wife had held his child's head down when the shooting started so that he would not be hit, I felt the awful breath of war....

There was a woman writer who wrote frivolous stories about love and enjoyment and who looked like a little Meissen figure, pretty and vivacious. But behind this frivolous prettiness she was a fearless person. To her, life should be enjoyed and this should be possible for everybody. Genuine freedom was part of this. And so she joined us in discussions of what could be done to prevent the ever-growing influence of the Nazis. She also helped us distribute leaflets that were not allowed even in Austria because Austria already wanted to keep "peace" with the Nazis.

There was her friend, a young scientist, serious, with prematurely graying hair. He understood that a scientist needs freedom of thought.

There were Gerhard and his sister Jennie. Their lives were most unhappy ones. Today Gerhard lies somewhere, unknown, killed when he was, after a time in a German concentration camp, forced into the German army. They were both originally Austrians but had lived in Germany for many years and had joined the underground movement. Both had been arrested in Germany. After Gerhard had been released from prison, he had stayed in Germany as long as possible to wait until his sister was released. Jennie had three years of a German prison behind her. She looked a gaunt young woman who wanted to live a normal life, but somehow had difficulty finding her way back into a world she had begun to distrust. The prison had done strange things to her, even physically. For three years she had not menstruated. Now she was back "in freedom" but in a freedom that was very insecure. Both had been sent back to Austria, which they never had known. Both were happy to join again the labor union underground with which they felt identified. Both were exceedingly lonely people. All these people were not Jews but actively fought the Nazis.

And there was Inga, a wonderful older person, part of a Jewish working class family, full of fun and enjoyment. People like Inga are the salt of the earth. There was no hatred in Inga. She loved life, food, people around her. When one came into this family home, there was warmth and the smell of good cooking and baking. And yet, everyone in this family knew that life can only be carried on this way when a nation is free. Inga herself had always been active in labor unions. As a young girl she had started in the needle trade and she knew that it was necessary to keep the freedom they had fought for for so many years. I especially enjoyed working with her because she made our work feel again as something alive and human and not something that was born out of the desperate hatred that sometimes assailed me in the concentration camp.

It was not always easy to meet as a group, though it was not yet quite as difficult as in Nazi Germany. I remember, for instance, some of the beautiful evenings we had at the Danube with the stars shining down on our little group sitting near the water, looking toward the mountains and the river. I remember, when we had a meeting for two days and had to stay overnight but there was no money for hotels. We had only two tents and so we had to sleep men and women in the same tents. Our writer said laughingly that only Germans could possibly let young men and young women sleep together in one tent without, as she said, "something happening." We laughed. In all these years under the Nazis, these kinds of situations had occurred over and over again. One considered only the necessity of the situation, hardly other emotions. I remember sleeping that night next to Gerhard, the lonely, unhappy man. I saw his face trembling in the light of the moon that shone through the tent. The next day I wrote:

> In der Nacht
> Ein dunkles Angesicht,

Fremd und voller Trauer.
Steinern fast,
Und dann zuckt es...

Und voll Ohnmacht
senkt die andre Stirne sich,
weil sie brennend
von dem Schmerz des andern
doch nicht helfen kann.
Und wendet sich....

Translation:

In the night
a dark face,
strange and full of sorrow.
Almost stony,
and then it trembles...

And in powerless despair
The other averts her eyes,
Burning with the other's pain,
yet she cannot help

And she turns....

There was a happy interlude in this period. For the first time in years I had a legal passport. For several years now Paul and I had not seen each other. The World Exposition was at that time in Paris, and this offered an opportunity to see him. I had earned a small amount of money through the private lessons I gave. I got some help from friends. It was one of the most exciting trips to ride on a train "legally" to Paris and to feel for a moment the burden of our work falling off my shoulders.

Seeing how Paul lived in Paris was a terrible shock. It was horrible for this active man to be shunted into a country that did not give him permission to work. Paul lived in a room infested with bedbugs. Every night he had to start a hunt to get rid of them. He had little to eat. He worked as an apprentice to a woman who did fine weaving. With his "golden" hands, who could learn anything, he did a beautiful job of weaving, but he earned practically nothing. His "récipissé" (the permit to stay in France) was always valid for only about a month or a few weeks and had to constantly be renewed. His was a desperate existence. Paul wanted to go back to Germany and do some active work against the Nazis since he could not stand the kind of life he was living in Paris. Yet there was a certain discipline required of every underground worker not to decide such a step individually. Unfortunately, inside the immigration movement—as so often among immigrants—there was much quarreling, much disagreement. Opinions among immigrants always are strong and diversified. There is not enough outlet for all the energy of committed people. The group with which we had worked had been a highly idealistic, small group while we had been in Germany and this had lent itself very well to underground work. Individuals are capable of great dedication and sacrifice. Yet, when these same people become immigrants in a country which does not really accept them, they often become quarrelsome and self-seeking.

Inside the group were some strong and ambitious people. They created a form of class society with the highest status given to the intellectual who could write. In this environment there was little room for anyone who was technically or artistically gifted, as Paul. Paul's gifts could have been used in many other ways, but there was too little understanding of this among those who were immigrants at the time. The arrogance of the intellectual—always strong in Germany—actually increased with immigration. One of the women who had a comparatively high position in the movement, shook her head when she realized that Paul and I were close.

She said arrogantly, "Well, what can you find in him? He can't write articles!"

Paul was very lonely. He did some magnificent carving and weaving, unknown to most of the others.

Immigration also frequently increased dictatorial attitudes among immigrants—partially out of necessity (problems had to be solved quickly) but partially because one got used to quick dictatorial decisions. I saw all this in those days I visited in France.

Yet for us there was the happiness of seeing each other again. We visited the Van Gogh Exhibit. There were rooms and rooms full of the glowing marvelous colors of his paintings. Standing before these wonderful pictures full of life, we would sometimes feel some hope. Had not Van Gogh lived and created this beauty while he was tortured with inner and outer misery? Perhaps something could change for us, too. I wrote about a picture of Van Gogh:

> Wenn wild der Wind weht über dunkle Felder,
> Wir fühlen nur den weiten klaren Raum.
> Und ballen dunkle Wolken sich zusammen—
> In uns wächst nun die Ruhe wie ein Baum.

Translation

> When wild the wind blows over darkened fields
> We only feel the clear wide space.
> When darkened clouds crowd full of threat
> In us now grows a calm, strong as a tree.

It was terribly hard to separate again. I could not stay in France. Paul gave me as a "good-bye" a poem written by Zoroaster 900 years before the birth of Christ:

> When will it start
> the dawn of the day
> when humanity
> turns to the light
> of Truth,

when the call of the helper
finally will be heard
and will be acted upon?

Yet it may be, whenever it will be.
I will work hard
as if the time has come today.

New Year, 1938: Erna had gone to Paris to renew contact with
the leadership of our underground movement there and also to
meet her friend from whom she too was separated.

I was alone in Vienna but I do not remember this New Year as
a lonely one. The snow lay white on the ground and was crunching
under my feet when I walked home in the early evening. All the
people I really wanted to see, my family, Paul, his family, were
far away. Yet somehow the few new friends in Vienna seemed to
give a special warmth to that night. We met for a small New
Year's party. We talked about the state of the world and what
we could do. There was love in what we were talking about and
not hatred. We began to sing some of the beautiful Viennese folk
songs. We listened to the street musicians who came around, even
on that cold winter night. They were called "The Singing Misery"
because it was hard to make a living this way. But the "Singing
Misery" did not seem like misery that night. It was beautiful.

Erna was supposed to return in early spring of 1938. I went to
the station to pick her up. When I looked into her face I recoiled.
It was white and her eyes looked frightened. She quickly whispered to me that she had been caught with anti-Nazi leaflets at
the border between Germany and Austria. She had not been arrested, but she was sure that this would happen soon. We hurried
back to the apartment and immediately began to burn
incriminating material. We had hardly done this when there
was the familiar knock at the door. Two Austrian policemen in
civilian clothes entered. The interrogations started: the nightmare of a year ago was repeated, only in a somewhat milder
form. The two men made a careful search of the apartment.

Actually there was not much left that could raise their suspicions and the warm stove was not unusual in the chilly spring days. There was an incident, a comedy-like interlude: They found—as they thought—some strange code. Erna, I have to explain, sang beautifully, and loved music, but she could not read notes. She therefore had invented her own system of writing notes using a modified alphabet to write her own compositions. To the men who made the search this aroused their suspicion. They began to grill her and me about the meaning. Erna finally brought out her guitar and began to play the tunes to prove that it was written music, but I doubt that she really convinced them. During the search they also found some of my writing of short stories. I could find an outlet of unhappiness and despair in writing poetry and short stories. A few I have saved and I enclose them here.

BLIND

Again these pains in the eyes! Again this veil which sometimes covers everything. That means I'll *have* to go to the oculist, but when...Rather not finish thinking. How old had I been at that time? Ten, no twelve years old, and I heard how the doctor said: "Yes, we have to do something, otherwise the child will become blind." And then there were the strange shots which were so painful, I still don't know what they were and the nights full of anxiety with this awful child's fear that maybe in the morning it will be as dark before the eyes as at night! But now it is long ago...Oh, these spider webs! I have to go to the doctor.

There is the doctor's office. He looks kind, trustworthy. How thoroughly he examines. What strong, reassuring hands. That is good. Such physician's hands are good. I constantly look at the hands. One can have confidence in them. Damned, it is so dark. I cannot see the face, whether it looks matter-of-fact, calm, or even concerned. But I have no fear. The fear is gone. That is what these hands can do. Such hands one could also *feel*, couldn't one? One wouldn't need to *see* them. One could feel them even when blind. But worry, worry in his eyes—one can only *see* those. What is he saying? Oh yes, turn my head. Yes, of course, but what will he say at the end? Nothing, certainly nothing. The doctors never tell you when things look really bad. But I *must* know. It will be better when I know. Otherwise, I shall be afraid; afraid of what *could* be. Only of this I am always afraid: of what could be, not of what really *is*. He ought to tell me. I demand it. Look to the left...yes, now to the right.. .yes. If only I could see his eyes.

Done. The light has returned into the room. But I hardly see a thing. The veil is back again. "Well, doctor?" He is writing. No, I won't have any of this. I am all by myself. There are no parents to whom "it" could be told, no relatives. Thank God. He *must* tell me. I am not hysterical and I shall have no fits. "Please, doctor, tell me the honest truth. I must know because I shall have to plan my life accordingly. I am no coward." Well, it is out now. I am really no coward, I am quite calm. He looks out of the window. He is still not speaking. Then he turns around, and he puts his hand on mine. How good this feels! It is true, one can feel these hands. It is hard for him to talk. (This I can hear, I don't need my eyes for that, I am thinking.) "There will be four weeks left at the most before complete blindness will set in, and there is no other possibility." He is holding my hand firmly. Now he is afraid, because he has said something one usually doesn't tell patients. But I am calm. Now I *know*. "Thank you." I am wanting to leave. "You will not do anything foolish?" "But no," I am even smiling. I am on the street. An early spring day; moist pavement. Still bare branches, but the air is warm. I don't want to go home now, into my room where only books are waiting for me. I walk into the park. This bench is almost dry. One can *feel* that! I am noticing again how I am asking of all things whether they can be experienced without eyes. I sit down. I am so gloomy inside. Four more weeks, then everything will be dark.

But I don't want this to happen, do I? Suddenly it wells up, the calm is gone. And I love colors and light, light! And I had in mind to become a painter—naturally, I could have made it. Nonsense, don't talk yourself into such nonsense now. Sure, I could have made it. I shall have to let myself be led, and I shall be helpless, I, who have so much pride. And I am still young! I shall not be able to hike, and, and...the darkness! This is an uproar—wild, and desperate.

"You look so pale, is something the matter?" Anne is standing beside me, Anne, who always has so much to worry about, who has to make a living for herself and three sisters, and who only has these two hours at noon to get some rest. "No, Anne, it's nothing." I am getting hold of myself again. Quietly, we sit side by side. We sit often this way. Both of us are working, and we are tired at noon. There are also blind people who work. I can type when I'm blind. I shall learn braille...The light, the light! It goes through me like a bolt: "Anne, I'll go away tomorrow. Into the mountains." "You? Were you not going to take your vacations in the summer?" "Yes, but I'll like it better now. I'll be back in four weeks."

In four weeks...Four weeks are left for me. Four more weeks of light. I'll see the mountains and snow and green meadows and children off and on, yes, children's faces and the sun, yellow and brilliant, and red and soft. And then, some day, the night will be here, this everlasting night. Then I'll see how I can stand up to it. And I am sure some hand will be there to lead me back from the mountains—back to work. I'll have to rely on hands. And it will depend on those hands whether I shall master or repudiate life.

MASKS

Jeanne is looking fresh and tanned. She has just come back from an ocean trip. She has seen the steep rocks of the fjords and the green meadows in Sweden; her last stop was in Kopenhagen. She has so much to tell. All have questions for her; mostly those three of us who have traveled North the year before. They are all happy that one of them has returned again. And it's their turn to tell her what they had done in the meantime: working hard at painting in the academy, and hiking. "Now we are making masks. Death masks." Suddenly, there is general seriousness. "How people look different then."

"Because they otherwise always wear masks in life," the little sculptor with the sad eyes told us seriously. "That is not true, Hilde," Jeanne puts her arm around her friend's shoulder, "you only imagine that." "No, no. When I sit in the train, for instance, and all the faces look alike, with eyes staring into space, it makes me think: *You* would like to *cry* now, *you* would like to shout, and *you* would like to put your head on someone's shoulder to rest; but all of you sit stiff and straight: Masks."

"By the way, have you met Ernst in Kopenhagen, Jeanne?" "Yes, I naturally looked him up, because of you. And he looks fresh and healthy and he talked so happily. You need not worry about him." "When was that, Jeanne?" "Well, on my return trip. "Do you remember the date?" "Why?" Jeanne looks up surprised. "I'm just asking." "Well, it was on August 11." "I see."

In her room Hilde picks up a letter: "Kopenhagen, August 11. It is a great day today, I want to go down to the ocean, to paint, to try to get *some* rest. I cannot write much today, I only want to send you this Rilke poem:

> Ich wollt, sie hätten statt der Wiege
> mir einen kleinen Sarg gemacht,
> dann wär mir besser wohl, dann schwiege
> die Lippe längst in feuchter Nacht.
>
> Dann hätte nie ein wilder Wille
> die bange Brust durchzittert,—dann
> wär's in dem kleinen Körper stille,
> so still, wie's niemand denken kann.
>
> Nur eine Kinderseele stiege
> zum Himmel hoch, so sacht—ganz sacht:

Was haben sie mir statt der Wiege
nicht einen kleinen Sarg gemacht?

Ernst"

Translation:

"I wished, instead of a cradle
they would have built me a small coffin,
then I would feel easier, then my lip
would long be silent in the moist night.

Then never would have trembled a wild wish
through a fearful breast—then
it would be silent in the little body,
as silent as no one could imagine.

Only a child's soul
would rise to heaven, so softly, very softly:
Why haven't they instead of a cradle
built a small coffin for me?

Ernst"

He wrote that on August 11...Masks!"

The policeman looked up at me, shook his head and said, "I surely hate to arrest you. This is beautiful."

Nevertheless, at the end of their search and after some of the interrogation they decided that we both had to be arrested. I was frightened. What could this mean? It might mean extradition to Germany for both of us and that would mean torture and certain death. We said goodbye to our kind landlady. She was a lively, dark-haired woman, a devout Catholic who had always be-friended us. We had never talked to her about political issues because we never wanted to involve anyone. Yet she had always

shown understanding and friendship. We had sometimes wondered why she had been so friendly. Later I found out that she
was in love with a Jewish man and that she knew what would
happen if the Nazis came to power.

I was alone with the police in the police station. Erna and I
had been separated. I stood in the office of a police station surrounded by men in uniform. I was asked to remove anything that
could be used for a suicide. A policeman reached for my eye
glasses to take them away. I refused. He insisted. For the first
time I lost my calm. I knew that I would be so helpless without
glasses. It would influence my whole attitude, because I could not
see the person confronting me. I struggled. A few policemen said
finally, "Oh, let that poor 'Hascherl' go. The glasses don't harm
her."

A fat policeman was supposed to bring me into one of the cells.
We walked through a long, dark corridor. He began to make sexual advances. I stiffened. No use to call for help—no one could
hear me here anyhow—I could only let this big fat man feel that
I was not a bit interested in him and that I had no intention of
giving in. Big hands grabbed all over my body while I was
becoming rigid like a piece of wood. He got angry. "For heaven's
sake, what's the matter with you? Don't you want to enjoy yourself a bit before something worse happens to you?"

I said quietly that I was married—did he not know? He
swore under his breath, but let me go. He pushed me into a huge,
very dirty cell. It was one of the dirtiest places I had ever seen.
The dirt was some sticky substance that was all over the floor
and the wooden board which served as seat and as bed. The policeman threw into the room a filthy blanket which smelled of
the vomit of the drunk. As I was lying fully clothed on the dirty
wooden board I felt again reduced to the level of an animal. All I
wanted was water to wash, water, water, water and soap! Night
fell and slowly I began to think again. I felt depressed, but I remember that I fell asleep on a reassuring note: I had told mother
that this had not been the end of the fight. She would understand.

I stayed in this incredibly dirty cell for three days without change of clothes and without any opportunity to get washed. On the third day I heard outside the cell door the loud voice of my landlady. She was angry. Her insults of the police expressed in true Viennese dialect sounded like music in my ears. She was berating them for keeping a young woman in a place like this without allowing her to clean up. She had brought clean clothes, a wash cloth and soap and a wonderfully fresh loaf of bread. She succeeded in leaving all this for me. I still can feel the coolness of the tap water, the rubbing of the wash cloth against my skin. I can feel the cake of soap and the joy when I saw the dirt coming off my hands. Washing was such a relief that I would have loved to spend a long time at this little spigot. Yet I was soon sent back into my cell.

On Saturday, something strange happened. There was a loud hubbub around the corridor. Several fat older women with huge featherbeds under their arms came into my cell. They had a friendly chat with the policemen and then made themselves comfortable on the dirty boards spreading out their featherbeds and their clean sheets. The cell became a strange looking dormitory room. Soon they told me their story. These were women selling apples in the streets of Vienna. They were the breadwinners in the family, since the men could not find work. According to a city ordinance the women were supposed to not move around after they had occupied a spot in the street. All of them knew that one sells better if one moves from one place to another, and so they did. They usually were charged a fine when they were moving about. Since they could not pay the fine, they were sentenced to two or three days in jail. These days accumulated, because they violated constantly the ordinance. The court recognized that they were the only support of the family and allowed them to fulfill their sentence by staying in jail for the weekends. Some women spent every single weekend in jail. They were used to it and it had become almost a social occasion for them. They chattered and told each other their troubles and their joy. In the morning their children came and brought them coffee. I learned much

about "justice to the poor." I was treated by those women as somebody one had to pity. I was the "armes Hascherl," the poor little
thing. They knew that a political offense was much worse than
offenses against a city ordinance. They did not take a political
stand, but they shared a feeling of kinship with me. And I felt
kinship with them! There were some amusing little interludes: I
had learned, in the concentration camp, to keep my body "fit" by
doing exercises. Now I had started this again. Even while the
women were in the cell I did my morning exercises. They got
interested in this, and asked me to teach them those exercises.
There they were, a group of women, most of them in their fifties
and over, most of them worn out from hard work, large from
childbearing, all sitting on the wooden benches and trying to bend
and touch their toes. Twice policemen came into the cell, shook
their heads and laughed. There was good-natured banter with
them. Even the fat fellow who had frightened me so much in the
beginning became quite a different human being when he was
with them.

When the women had gone by Sunday evening, I was again
alone. The next day a young girl was placed into my cell. From
her I learned much about human misery. The young girl was
pretty, but her face was disfigured by a swollen black eye. She
had run away with a young man to get away from an abusing father. She pulled up her sleeves and showed me the welts on her
arm. They had been caused by her father's strap. The black eye
had been caused by the young man who also had abused her.
"But" she said softly, "I'll go back to him. He is the only one who
is sometimes kind to me."

Here she was, with a black eye, welts all over her body and
yet she felt sorry for *me* because she knew that I was in a much
graver situation than she was. There was a sweetness and kindness about this girl who would, I am sure, be adjudicated as a
delinquent. I also learned about the strength in her. Somehow
there was some hope in her for something better, something that
would come along some day and help her get out of all this. She
told me that she picked flowers in the mountains and sold them

to make a little money. She was sure that some day she could start a little store. She would never have told an "outsider" about these little dreams, but she opened up to someone "in the same boat."

After she left, I again was alone. Several days had passed. One morning I heard the voices of several policemen arguing. I realized that they were arguing about me. Several of them insisted that I should be transferred to another place and not stay in the police jail, because it wasn't right to have one young woman alone in this place. Their conversation was interrupted by loud, inhuman cries. I could look through a small opening in the door and saw a young, beautiful girl held by two policemen. She shouted in a deep and strange voice insisting that she was the Messiah and that she would bring good to all humanity and they should let her go. The policemen held down the obviously mentally sick girl but were unable to understand what to do with her. They were not unkind but they fought her. The ignorant treatment of mental illness made a deep impression on me. The girl finally broke down sobbing after she had screamed for a long time.

Shortly after this incident, the door opened and one of the policemen, angrily, told me to come out. He said that he would not let me be exposed to anything like this again. He telephoned and insisted on my transfer to a regular prison or concentration camp. The request was granted.

Late afternoon, one of the men who had searched our room, came to accompany me to—where? I did not know and I got no answer. He was a cold person who reminded me of the Gestapo. But the streets looked beautiful to me! I felt the warmth of the sun as I had felt it when I was released in Hamburg. I knew I was still under arrest and I had no idea what would happen to me. I asked my guard whether I could buy some toothpaste. He first wanted to refuse but then he shrugged his shoulders and went with me into a store to buy it. There was something odd about going into the drugstore looking as though I were just a young woman being accompanied by a not so bad looking young man. Yet I knew that this young man was guarding me and that I was a prisoner...

The concentration camp to which I was transferred lay in the middle of Vienna. At the time I entered it I knew very little about Viennese concentration camps and I knew only that it probably was full of both Socialists and Nazis. The situation was very different from the concentration camp in Germany. When I arrived, I was brought into the room of the commander. He looked like a figure out of a Strauss operetta. He had a little mustache and in his uniform he reminded me of the "Chocolate Soldier." He was exceedingly polite but he looked harassed. He asked the policeman what they thought he should do with one woman in a concentration camp filled only with men. The investigator shrugged his shoulders and said that that was none of his business; he was told to deliver me here, and that was it. He also said that at one time or another I would be called for interrogation. The commander looked more harassed. He asked one of the guards who was standing outside to send for his wife so that she could take me downstairs for a shower, since I had not had one for a long time. The walk through the corridor was memorable. There were hundreds of men milling around who suddenly stopped, staring as if a creature from the moon had appeared. Here I was, a young woman (I surely do not consider myself beautiful, and I doubt that I looked very good having slept in my clothes for several days), but they looked at me like an apparition. There were whistles. The woman guard hurried me through quickly. After I had cleaned up I felt much better. The friendly but taciturn woman took me upstairs. Before I got into the corridors which previously had been full of men, I heard a loud command, shouting: "She is coming, everybody back into the cell." I heard much shuffling of feet. When I entered the corridor it was empty but every door was ajar and hundreds of eyes stared at me while I walked down the corridor.

I was led into a big cell which was pleasant looking. It was a large room on the second floor of a house in the city, though it had bars at the window. The room apparently was designated for a number of people. There were several mattresses on the floor. Otherwise it was totally empty. I thought: "Oh, there is sunshine, and it is not so dirty!" I asked whether I could have a pencil and some paper and some reading material, but this was refused. I sat on one of the mattresses waiting to see what would happen. I heard the clanging of the doors which meant the evening meal was carried around. My door opened and a young man, a prisoner, called in Austria the "Fazi," came in. He had a tray on which was a big mug with hot tea, and, oddly enough, a big slice of cake. He was accompanied by a policeman. The "Fazi" said that the men had sent me that piece of cake. I should not feel that I was in a place that did not appreciate a woman. He also turned to the policeman in my presence and said that it was a disgrace that a woman should drink tea out of a mug. Did I have a cup? I said I had none and I didn't mind drinking the tea out of the mug. He shook his head and only fifteen minutes later he appeared with a china cup. I did not know what to make of that situation.

The moment the "Fazi" left, a tightly rolled piece of paper was thrown through the spyhole of my cell. Several questions were written on it: "Who are you? What are you? Are you Nazi or Sozi? Here in the camp we are so and so many Nazis and so and so many Sozis. If you need anything, just let us know. You can smuggle a piece of paper into the hands of the "Fazi." He is a good friend. He will get you whatever you need, including special food or smuggle something out for you." I did not answer. For one, I could not answer because I had no pencil and paper, but I had also learned in the bitter years of underground work that one cannot trust anybody and cannot put anything into writing under such circumstances. As if the men had guessed my plight, I heard a short time later a noise and saw a pencil and a piece of paper flying through the spyhole. I still did not answer and when the "Fazi" came in to pick up my tray, I just shook my head. Shortly after this I had to go to the washroom. This became as much a production as my former walk across the corridor. There was a loud shout that the men had to return to the cells. I again passed by the half-open doors with the many eyes staring at me. In the washroom I found a small message saying, "We understand if you

don't answer, but let us at least know who you are. Nazi or Sozi?"
I left a message saying, "Definitely not Nazi. I am under investi-
gation and cannot talk." This seemed to satisfy those who wanted
to know about me.

Quiet settled down over my cell. I had nothing but the little
pencil and a piece of paper. I used it to write down a few names of
the ones I love, looking at them and thinking that maybe I would
never see them again. Suddenly the cell door opened and the
commander and a man in civilian clothes entered. He was the
physician of the camp and asked solicitously how I felt and if
everything was all right. Again, this struck me as very strange
under the circumstances. In spite of all this friendliness, I knew
that I was a prisoner.

The sun had disappeared and it was time for me to settle
down for the night. I lay down on one of the many mattresses in
the room and pulled a blanket over me. The light overhead shone
right into my face. There was no escape from it. I don't think that
it was especially arranged this way to torture the prisoner, but it
had the effect of torture. The only way to sleep was to pull the
blanket over my face. I felt not as full of terror as I had in the
German concentration camp. Though realistically the situation
was very serious, the human contacts had warmed me and had
made me feel more secure.

I was awakened early in the morning—first by a knock and
then one of the guards entered. He bent over me and whispered
that I should get up earlier than the others. He explained that
this way I could wash myself real well. He added soberly, "I'm a
family man and a father of seven children, so you don't have to be
ashamed to wash in front of me, but I certainly wouldn't want you
to do it in front of all those other men." He added wistfully,
"Always remember, many have been in prison for a long time and
they can tear a woman to pieces when she is here alone with
them."

While I was washing he carefully turned his back to me.
Later he told me how he himself was concerned with the situation in Austria. He insisted that he was a good Schuschnigg man

but that he was worried that there was not enough resistance to the Nazis and that some day they would come. He also thought that Schuschnigg should not have alienated everybody else. He felt sorry for the decent Sozis sitting in the prison. It was strange to find the man who was guarding me confiding his worries. I had the impression he was glad that he could talk to someone who would listen, but I remained silent.

It was cold during the day and I was shivering. Again the kind Fazi must have seen that. Around noon a loud knock at the door announced a guard accompanied by a tall, good-looking prisoner who was carrying two pails of coal. While they worked on the stove, the prisoner spoke loudly to the guard, obviously trying to convey what he was saying, also, to me. He said that it was wrong to have a young girl shivering here and why wasn't she released? Surely she did not look like someone who would overthrow the Austrian government. The guard grumbled but did not say much. The man also told the guard that it must be awfully boring for a young woman to sit around doing nothing. Doesn't she get anything to read? The guard answered that I was not allowed to get any printed material, and he therefore could not give it to me. The young prisoner shook his head and suggested that the guard at least could give me the prison rules. (In fact, this the guard later did, and I studied them with interest.)

When the two left, a folded newspaper was left near the stove by the young prisoner. This was a break and I realized that he had left it there purposely so that I had something to read. When I opened the newspaper, tears sprang into my eyes: everywhere, at the margin of the paper, he had marked down some encouraging words. It was as if somebody spoke to me, the same as the scribbled little note on the wall in the concentration camp had spoken to me. There on the margin of the paper were comments like: "Don't despair. All of us will get out of this some day." Or, "Look, keep up your courage, we are all standing for what humanity needs." I read and re-read that newspaper and I thought, "If I only could keep these little notes. If I only could keep them so that I would remember, that—in a most desolate spot, where I knew no one—some human being felt my fear and despair, understood and knew how to bring me encouragement." I certainly could not keep these notes on paper, but I kept them locked in my heart. Later whenever I was hurt by people, the margins of that newspaper with those finely written words appeared before me. I never saw the man again. I will never know who he was. He gave hope and courage to a person who felt alone, without any hope of reward. Thank you, unknown stranger!

I cannot tell you how long I stayed in this Viennese prison. I know it was not too long, and yet it seemed endless. I was finally brought back to the police station in which I had first been booked. A short interrogation started. It still puzzles me why during all this time my German experiences were never mentioned. I am sure that they were known, but for some reason they were not brought up. I can only explain it by the strange political situation in Austria at that time. One never was certain who was in charge and who was interrogating. Perhaps it was an anti-Nazi in my case. At the end of this interrogation, I was suddenly told that I could go home, but my passport would be withheld and I would not get it back until the trial of Erna—who was still being held in prison—was finished.

Once again I went out into the world "free" in the sense that I could walk outside of prison walls. Yet again I was confined within the borders of a hostile country. The passport for which I had made the sacrifice of a sham marriage was gone.

There was much to be done after my return. I had first of all to contact the families with whose children I had worked. One of them did not want me to work with their children anymore, but two others gladly accepted me again.

I also had to contact some of our underground friends to let them know what had happened, to find out whether we could do something for Erna. We did find a lawyer who took her case. I cannot remember his name, but I remember his kindness and willingness to listen to someone who could not offer him any money for the services he gave so generously. I also remember, like a picture flashing out of a confused background, the funeral of Adler in

Vienna. He had been one of the great Socialists. His funeral became a demonstration by those who believed in the ideals for which he stood. I see before me the long silent line of people following the coffin. They stood at the grave for a long time.

During this time the tension with Germany increased. For awhile Schuschnigg had hoped for some kind of understanding with Hitler, and had not actively fought him. He also had hoped for Mussolini's help in case Hitler tried to attack. Yet now, the Nazi's demand for "Anschluss" was increasing and Schuschnigg was pressed by Hitler to fulfill his demands. When Schuschnigg did not agree with this the situation became critical. In those final days, Schuschnigg must have felt that he needed the support of a total country, including the Socialists he had fought for too long a time. He, therefore, pronounced an amnesty. Unfortunately, in this amnesty, the Nazis too were freed.

Erna was released. Her passport was returned to her while I was still without mine. Whispering at night, because we were afraid that hidden microphones might be in our room, she would tell me about her experiences in prison. She had had a hard time. After this Erna could not find work. I continued my tutoring of a few children.

It was a late spring afternoon when I, as usual, went to the home of one of my little Jewish pupils. The young mother greeted me almost hysterically. She had heard that the Nazis would invade Vienna. She cried she could never live anywhere but Vienna. This was her home; this was her beautiful city. I spoke quietly to her, saying that these were rumors and one shouldn't listen to them. In the course of the afternoon she seemed to calm down a bit. Dusk fell over the city when I left the family. I slowly walked back to my room. Some leaflets lay on the pavement. I picked one up. I stared at it. The big letters announced that Nazi troops were entering Vienna and that Vienna should welcome them. While I started at this, an older woman grabbed my hand, looked at the leaflet and started to cry. Sobbing she said, "What will happen now? We will all die together."

I walked on, my face like stone. Turning around a street corner I heard the familiar song I had not heard for over a year: it came with voices of young men "und wenn das Judenblut vom Messer spritzt." The young men came straight towards me. In the dusk I could not see faces, but I could see the bright red armbands and the swastika on white. The Nazis had arrived, and they had arrived swiftly and efficiently. I had to hide. Erna had to be saved. She had a passport. She could get out. What would happen to all of us?

I still see before me the peaceful scene that offered itself in our studio when I returned from this nightmare. Erna was in the room talking with my "husband," who had come to visit. I said, "Erna, you must pack and leave for Paris immediately."

She looked at me, "Don't panic so quickly; you are always exaggerating. What's the matter?"

"The Nazis are here," I said, and I held the leaflet before their eyes. For a minute they did not want to believe it. An odd droning filled the sky. There was enough window space in our study so one could see the sky wide around us. I pointed to it. There, up in the sky, German planes with the big swastika painted on them, circled, circled, and circled over Vienna. Erna began to pack immediately. While she packed we discussed where she should go. Should she go across the Czechoslovakian border? It was only a short way from Vienna, and therefore the easiest and quickest to reach. After much deliberation we decided against this. Maybe the Nazis were already closing the borders. The one most accessible would be guarded with the greatest care. It was best for her to go to Paris, since she had a legal passport. It was a chance to take. We also knew that it would be a hard experience for her, because she had to meet Nazi troops moving directly toward Austria. Today, I am glad that we made this decision. Erna arrived safely in Paris the next day, but many other leading anti-Nazis who fled that night over the Czechoslovakian border were caught by the Nazis. Many of them were killed immediately; some of them were tortured and kept prisoners. Very few of them live today.

The landlady arrived, sobbing, while Erna was packing. She said that this was really the end of her Vienna. She turned on the radio. The voice of the traitor Seys-Inquart repeated constantly, "Viennese, do not resist the German troops who are coming. They are coming as friends." After Erna left—she had held back the tears again, one must not cry—we started to burn books and letters to be sure that nothing would fall into the hands of the Nazis which could incriminate anyone. Again Paul's beloved letters went up in flame. Here again some of the wonderful books that I loved, like Jacob Wassermann's, had to be burned. While we were doing this we looked up at the sky. It looked like a signal of doom. It was filled with smoke, sparks coming out of many chimneys; many people were obviously doing the same thing that we were doing. And above the smoke the German airplanes were circling, circling, circling the skies of Vienna.

The next morning came up bleakly. The maid of one of the homes in which I worked with the children arrived, crying, saying that the family was desperate and I must not come back to work.

I went to the family where I had been the afternoon before. The mother was lying on a couch amidst an apartment that was in shambles. During the preceding night, some of the "good neighbors" who had only waited for the Nazis to come to power, expressed their hatred towards a Jewish family by entering the home (this was legal now!) and hacking to pieces most of the furniture. The three children huddled around the mother. They cried when they saw me. The oldest one came running towards me, saying that his mother did not let him go to school any more and he loved school, why couldn't he go? Before I could answer, his mother shouted that she couldn't let him go because the children would treat him badly and they might spit at him.

He said angrily, "Well, then I'll just spit back at them!" The mother turned more pale, "Oh, you mustn't, you mustn't! You must let them spit at you and not even move because otherwise they will arrest your father."

Bewildered, the child looked at me and looked at his mother, not understanding why he should not defend himself when he thought it was only right and honest to do so. I could feel how cowardice and bitterness were implanted into a child....There was not much one could do here. Perhaps the only help that I could give was to say that somehow we must all be prepared for the worst and yet we must remember that we are standing for a decent world, and the others did not. But was this really helpful to an anxious mother who saw her children banned from all future opportunities and who knew that they might end up in a concentration camp? I have never heard of this family again. I don't know what happened to them. Probably the gas chambers of Theresienstadt have destroyed their bodies as they have destroyed many I have known....

I cannot remember details of the days that followed. I do remember "pictures" as sharp and clear as if they were etched in my memory. I see people dragged out of their homes, beaten and kicked and then thrown on a wagon where they were lying like dead with others, one piled on top of another. I see Jewish pregnant women scrubbing the streets where there were slogans written by the Schuschnigg regime. Young Nazi soldiers with swastika armbands were standing over them. They laughed at the women with the heavy bodies doing this work, spitting at them or pushing them if they did not scrub hard enough.

I see two young Jewish girls coming back into the house with white faces and limping. They had been made to carry heavy carpets into the Gestapo headquarters, and had to work that way the whole day.

I see the Vienna market, beautiful, with the lovely colorful vegetables, and I see people recoiling suddenly and staring, because four "brown shirts" passed through with a girl between them. Her forehead bore a stamp, reading, "I slept with a Jew." The eyes of the girl were burning and yet cold. She was not crying...

I see jubilant Nazi demonstrations everywhere. The Gestapo had brought tables and chairs for their offices into the city, so efficiently had they prepared everything. The swastika armbands were blossoming on almost every arm in Vienna.

I walked through all this like a person dream-walking. Most Jewish people did not enter the streets. I was so certain I would be dead soon that I felt no fear, only numbness. I constantly said to myself, "You must know it, you must know how it looks when a whole population goes insane. You must know how it looks when the inferno is beginning on earth. And if I ever get out of this I must shout, I must tell, I must never, never forget."

I had to move. There was no money to pay the rent for the place that Erna and I had. I rented a room with a family I did not know. Under the circumstances, this was frightening. Would they spy on me? Were they Nazi? After we got to know each other a bit, we admitted to each other that I was standing behind the door trying to listen to what they were saying and they were listening in when my "husband" came to visit me to find out what kind of a person I was. I soon found out that they were Spanish Jews of Turkish nationality. They hoped to leave Vienna soon. (I heard later that they had succeeded.) The girls in the family had dark hair and were afraid to leave the house. I volunteered to do the marketing for the family. For this they shared some potatoes with me. This meant much to me, since I had no money left with the exception of a few shillings I saved for an emergency. My rent had been paid in advance. I ate only those potatoes and some bread. I cannot tell how many days this was or how many weeks. A strange phenomenon occurred in me. While I usually am a very active person, I slept in those days almost constantly. I withdrew by sleeping seventeen, eighteen hours a day. I did not want to wake up. I went to bed, curled up like an embryo and slept, tightly, without dreams. All the terror dreams came later, when I was safe. At that time I slept and slept, tightly. The days were without food and without hope.

Chapter Seventeen

Escape from Austria

One day a letter from Ruth, my sister in England, arrived. In the letter was some money which made it possible to buy food, but it contained something much more important. It contained coded messages from Paul, of his thinking of me and wanting to see me, and it contained directions from our underground organization in Paris of how I could be helped to escape from Austria. My first reaction was "No. No, I don't want to run any more. I have run once, and that is enough. Why should I leave?" I had seen Paul and what immigration had done to him, and I had no taste for it. I felt sure that the effort would be futile anyhow, and somehow the Nazis would get hold of me at the border. I was afraid to act. I was tired and just wished to not think, to die. But this was only one side of me. The other side was beginning to wake up, warmed by the way in which Ruth had communicated with me. It showed that my friends in France and England had told her how to use our underground way of writing so that she could bring this message to me without having it be detected by the Nazis. It meant that people were really concerned about me and had made an effort to help me. And then there was Paul. I loved him so much! We had counted on never seeing each other again and on never having a happy life together, but perhaps there was some hope?

Many people I knew committed suicide. This was not what I wanted to do. The knife that had been lying on the table before me in the concentration camp in Hamburg arose like a symbol again and strengthened my stubbornness—"I will not do them this favor. If they want to do the dirty work of killing, they will have to do it themselves." And so, I decided to try to escape. Another letter came giving me specific directions. I was to travel by train to Innsbruck. At a certain given time in the morning I had to be at a certain place wearing white gloves. There someone would help me over the border. I did not know which border nor who it would be.

The Austrian writer's friend was the only person I could contact during this time. He was not in much danger. I told him about my impending disappearance, but also how I hesitated, and how I was afraid. He looked at me, this man with the graying hair and the young eyes and smiled. In all this horror it was so good to find somebody who could smile. He said, "Say, Gisa, what's the matter? Don't you like cold showers?" I laughed and said that I actually liked them. "Fine," he said, "it's just like taking a cold shower. Just do it. It will work." And he added kindly, "I'll watch you get on the train, I'll be in that crowd milling around. You can be sure of that."

The day of my departure came. Again I had to leave everything. It can't be helped, but wherever they are, human beings seem to accumulate things they love. I had tried not to acquire too many things, knowing that there wasn't much room for worldly possessions for people like us. But I did have books again, and a friend had shipped from Hamburg the beautiful bookcase Paul had so lovingly made for me in the early days of our courtship. It was my most precious possession. It seemed such a long time ago that he had scoured the Hamburg harbor for wood from the interior of old ships, and had built this bookcase. Now, a second time, I had to leave it behind. There were dresses I was fond of. There were some pretty vases. There were knives and forks that mother so kindly had sent me as a "wedding present" though she had suffered with me knowing that this had not been a true wedding. There were beddings and blankets, things we considered very precious in Europe, because we had too little of them. Again I left with empty hands. The only thing I could take with me was my pocketbook, my identification papers and the etching Fritz Husman had given me. The feeling of tenderness in it had so much meaning to me that I took it with me wherever I went.

My train for Innsbruck left late. The station was full of people. They wore swastikas, all of them jubilant because the Nazis had taken over the country. I saw my friend in the crowd. We gave no sign of recognizing each other, but it gave me reassurance to see him. Yet my heart was heavy realizing that I left him behind, not knowing what would happen to him.

The compartment in which I rode to Innsbruck was as all compartments of German trains, a small one with wooden benches. In it were two Nazis in brown shirts, a young girl, a little man in civilian clothes, and myself. The Nazis were drunk and triumphant. They grabbed the girl, pulled her on their laps, pushing her from one to the other, and shouting, "Heil Hitler." They also grabbed me. I said quietly that I was a married woman, showing them my wedding ring. One of them said, "Oh, girlie, don't be stiff today. This is a day of jubilation." There was nothing I could say, without screaming at them that I was actually an underground worker now leaving the country, a Jew too and that I hated them, their faces, their hands, their ugly thoughts! I silently walked outside to the small corridor combining the different compartments of the train. They thought I was a bit too "faithful to my husband" and made jokes about it. I thought angrily, "Obviously they don't smell that I am a Jew."

The little man began to speak after a while. He said that he surely welcomed the Nazis, but life was very complicated. Here he was a "Beamter," a civil servant. "It is so difficult," he said. "What can I do? When I started my career, I gave my oath to be eternally faithful to Franz Josef, the Austrian Emperor. Then the Revolution came and I pledged my allegiance to the new Austrian Republic. Well, then Schuschnigg came and I had to be sworn in on the Schuschnigg regime and now I am travelling to pledge allegiance to the 'Fuehrer.' It surely is complicated." He sighed in bewilderment.

I shuddered. Here was someone who was not really a Nazi, but someone who thought he did his duty by mechanically doing what authorities asked of him. Alfred Kerr's verse came into my mind:

"Der Täter war der Schlimmste nicht.
Der, der alles verschuldet hat, war der,
Der alles geduldet hat."

Translation:

"The ones who committed the deeds were
not the worst. The one who really is guilty is the
one who has tolerated everything."

It was early in the morning when the train stopped at Innsbruck. A fine rain fell making the landscape look dreary and unreal. The mountains were almost hidden by the rain clouds. I walked around for a while, keeping near houses so that I would not be drenched by the rain. Finally it was time to meet the stranger. I put on the white gloves and moved toward the designated building. I was standing there only a second when a pretty young girl approached me. She too, wore white gloves, the sign that was given to us for recognition of each other. She threw her arms around me as if I were a friend she had expected. She whispered to me that we had to go first to a hotel. In this hotel room then, I learned to know this stranger whose name I will never know. She was a minister's daughter, a Swiss girl. She shyly told me that she was afraid, that she was not skilled in lying and deception, but she was convinced that it was important to get people like myself out of the hands of the Nazis and she could not have a clear conscience if she did not help.

She handed me a passport. I stared at it incredulously. It had my picture and it had a signature in my handwriting, but another name. For a short time anti-Nazis had crossed the mountains to France, but this had become too dangerous because guards were stationed everywhere. Many were sent back to Austria condemned to death because Switzerland had suddenly decided not to become involved with its powerful neighbor, Germany. The young girl told this with a sense of shame. Courage, in nations as well as in individuals, is rare. She then explained the plan of escape for me. I had to take a train that would bring me back through Germany. In Germany there would be a delay of several hours in Munich where I would have to get off the train, stay in the waiting room and then continue on another train to Paris. My courage suddenly failed me. I was frightened to death. I just could not go through Germany again! I couldn't! I could not bear to hear the word "Germany." How could I bring myself to sit at the same table with all these people who were celebrating victory while Nazi victims were beaten to death and tortured in the nearby Dachau. I just could not! I said nothing, stared at the passport— the key to freedom? The young girl looked up suddenly. In her face I saw a mixture of pity, of hero worship and fear. No, I could not disappoint her. I could not disappoint those who had worked so hard to get me out of this. I put the passport into my pocket and thanked her for having worked out everything so well.

Now came the technical part. She had to tell me the story of the woman whose name appeared on my passport. I rehearsed the name, the history and the different trips the woman had taken which appeared on the passport entry. Then came another painful moment. The young woman told me that every evidence which showed my true identity had to be destroyed. This hurt. It seems strange that we are attached to those "papers" that indicate who we are. But it was not only a sentimental attachment.

The truth struck me that—if something should happen to me now at the border, nobody would ever know. The person arrested would be another person, another name. All my loved ones would know that I had disappeared, but they would never know where I was. Perhaps it is the yearning of every human being for his own identity that makes us cling to these things that should be so unimportant at a time when life and death are involved. I chided myself, "Why are you so sorry for yourself? There are already mass graves in the concentration camps. You will be just one of them, so don't think that you are anything so special." It is good to be stern with oneself at such times.

When everything was clear, we left the hotel. The girl accompanied me to the train. At the station she whispered, "I admire you, and I am so afraid for you. Are you all right?" Yet it was she who was the hero, who had taken inconvenience and danger upon herself! I felt very humble and deeply grateful.

Today I can only say, "Thank you, little Swiss minister's daughter, wherever you are, and whatever you are doing, for not only having helped somebody to escape, but for having given this person at a time of greatest need the proof that there are people who will think more of others than of themselves."

The train I took was a vacation train, full of young people, laughing and happy because they had had a wonderful time in the Austrian mountains. Most of them were Germans. I could see how elated they were because Hitler had achieved the "Anschluss." They talked about mountain climbing in the same spirit as they talked about this political event. I drew back slightly when I entered the compartment. It was filled with young people from Hamburg. I knew the accent. What would happen if somebody recognized me? But this also passed. The border control was perfunctory because now all this was "our Great Germany." The girl next to me saw my Swiss passport, was fascinated by it and began to involve me in a conversation about the Alps. She said, "Oh, I love Switzerland," and then, "But you don't have a Swiss accent." I quickly responded with the remark that my mother had been German but I vowed not to talk much with people on the train.

The train stopped at Munich—I had a few hours to spend waiting for the train to Paris. People were drunk with victory. Everybody, but everybody wore the swastika, more than I had ever seen in the first days of Nazism in Germany. Everybody was laughing and jubilant. Beer was flowing in the waiting rooms. While I was sitting there, I saw before me the face of Ludwig, another Jewish resistance fighter who had to dig his own grave while he was in Dachau and who was buried alive by laughing Nazi guards and was only dug out when he was almost dead. (He later died in the camp.)

In the compartment of the train to Paris I was alone with a young Frenchman. He was homeward bound after winter sports in Bavaria. He was elated by his vacation and not touched at all by the political situation. I was silent and he was disappointed by his travelling companion. The more we approached the French border, the more anxious I became. It was evening when the train stopped near the border at Strassbourg. The man who handled the passport control walked through the train, looked at our passports. Everything seemed to be all right, and he moved on. I heaved an inner sigh of relief. At this moment the custom officer returned and the Frenchman was called to the border police. Now, what would happen? What was the matter with him? Had I misjudged him? Was he someone who was sought by the Gestapo? He stayed for a long time and the train was held up. Finally he returned laughingly. He had tried to smuggle some liquor out of the country and had been caught. This certainly was not as bad a crime as political resistance, and he was permitted to continue his journey with just a warning and without the liquor. I almost hated him at this moment for having acted so carelessly.

The train began to roll again. While I am writing this I still hear the wheels clicking over the bridge that led to France. I held my breath—click, click, roll, roll—it seemed as if the wheels were singing, "Freedom, Life, Paul, Freedom, Life, Paul, Freedom, Life, Paul." The words sounded so real!

Beyond the bridge I became a different person. I could not understand what happened to me. It was as if ice had been broken, as if I woke up, not only my emotions, but also my whole body. I could not sit still. I was running to the window, back to the seat, again to the window. I could hardly wait. I began to believe that I would see Paul! It was as if the bonds of a sickness were breaking. The need to sleep suddenly left me. There were things I had to do; there were things I had to feel; there were things that waited for me. And—perhaps there could be love again, perhaps work! How I loved love and work, and perhaps, perhaps there could even be a family and children! It was like a song of life! The melody of it was as strong and jubilant as the great symphonies.

Nobody was at the station in Paris when I arrived. This did not disappoint me because nobody knew about the time of my arrival. I had not expected anyone.

Chapter Eighteen

Refugee in France

I would like to tell how Paul and I reunited, what the first moments were like—yet memory fails again. There are some stretches of this story that I can tell in an orderly sequence and yet there are others where memory blacks out. I cannot remember how we two greeted each other. I do remember later lying quietly beside him, having his head cradled in my arms, or cradling mine in his. He had been so terribly hurt during the time he was in the immigration that he was not the strong person I knew all my life. At this time we both had been hurt so badly that we had to comfort each other. I still feel his hand holding mine as we gave each other the feeling of life again.

These flashes of memory include some sad insensitive remarks made by those immigrants who had been away too long. There were remarks like, "Oh, Austria was not so bad, was it, huh?" And there were remarks deploring the increase of refugees. The horrible realization struck me: Now I was a refugee, too. I wasn't what I had been the summer before, a visitor who returned to the important underground work. Now I also was a nuisance to everyone. This realization came suddenly and was constantly intensified. This happened through many small experiences. It came first with my hunt for papers, for permission to stay, this "hunt" that engulfed every refugee in Paris. Once, I accompanied Paul to the Prefecture de Police when he had to apply for the prolongation of his récipissé (permission to stay). There were hundreds of refugees waiting to get in. The "flic," the French policeman, was standing there watching them. When the doors opened those people, most of them emaciated, ran into the courtyard trying to get up the stairs. The flic laughed at their struggle to keep their place in the line. His laughter and his eyes had the same cruelty as the young Nazis who had looked laughingly at the pregnant women scrubbing the streets of Vienna.

The refugees stood in line in the corridor to get a stamp in their papers to allow them to stay in France for another four weeks though there was no other place for them to go. I saw women fainting, children crying. I ran downstairs to a Bistro (restaurant) to ask for water. The man shook his head, said he could not lend me a glass. I, "There are women fainting and I need the water."

He, "It happens every day. What's the matter?"

I shouted,"If it happens every day then they need water every day." Perhaps it was my insistence that made him give me the water. People were treated like things in a place that was supposed to be their refuge from oppression.

Later I learned even more what it meant to be a refugee. My first encounter was with the Austrian Refugee Committee. We waited for hours: No appointments were made, one just waited. We filled out long questionnaires. One of the leading men on the Committee—he looked like the fat policeman in the police station in Vienna—asked me to stay while he held his fat hand on my knee. Alone with me, he pressed closer, his fat hand pawing all over me. Another employee entered. The fat man gave me the official paper he had to give me but asked me to meet him the next day. He promised to go to the prefecture with me to get a permanent permission to stay in Paris (such a paper was very important and was practically impossible to obtain.) He gave me a sly wink and said, "We'll make out well, my little one." I said little being very bewildered by the situation. I felt degraded, but I did not know what to do.

It was as if I was thrown into a world that I did not understand. It was not the fact that I was in another country. I had visited Paris before and I did not feel helpless in those surroundings. It was more that I had come from the deep feeling of friendship among those who fought the Nazis and lived almost cloistered in the countries of dictatorship. There was a closeness of feeling and a real concern for one another. Here I suddenly saw strife between different political factions that meant nothing anymore in the country from which we came. I heard petty accusations and I saw ambitions among people who had no way for outlet of these ambitions and therefore were fighting each other. There was also little understanding of the newcomer. I remember how some of my refugee friends had laughed about my Racine French which I had learned in school.

Paul seldom spoke French because of the cruel taunts coming from refugees who made fun of the way he pronounced it. French people themselves acted less in that way, but refugees had little contact with them. Those refugees who had contact with native Frenchmen tried jealously to guard that relationship and keep it for themselves.

Paul waited for me outside the Austrian Committee. I told him what had happened. He blew up in a way I had seldom seen him do. All the frustration of those years had accumulated in him. He shouted that no récipissé should be bought by sleeping with a man and even letting him touch me. He was ready to denounce him publicly. Yet, we both knew that this would be useless. The Austrian official had the power. All I could do was not to meet him as suggested and not take advantage of his offer.

I never got the coveted permanent permission to stay. The endless days of petitions began: temporary papers, promises, no results. Financially I was helped by the refugee committee, eating mostly only one meal a day. I earned some money by cleaning for others. Paul, meanwhile, moved away from the infested room and got a smaller room which was at least clean. The room was almost completely filled by a weaving loom he had built for himself. While he was still working as an apprentice for the woman who had a large weaving establishment he did weaving on his own at home. He made beautiful scarves but he was not a salesman. I sold some of them for him. I still have one of them.

The story of refugee life is endlessly dreary. It was only our love that kept Paul and me from being thoroughly demoralized. The "great cause" looked shabby in the light of what was going on among refugees in Paris. Paul and I could not get married because French law forbade people to get married on the soil of France when they did not have permission for permanent stay or for a year at least. The golden hope for a family disappeared. In addition to that, the political situation looked so bad that we were sure the Nazis would start a war. Who wanted to bring children into a world that would only mean their destruction?

One day Paul did not appear at the place where we ate. He had been arrested. Paul had had to appear about every second week at the Prefecture to ask for another récipissé. One day the extension was refused and he was asked to immigrate to another country. We walked from the consulate of one country to another asking for asylum. Each one refused to accept a refugee who had nothing but his hands and his brains but no worldly goods. Each time he got a sip of paper proving that he could not immigrate to that country. Nevertheless, the French Court decided to make an example of people who stayed in France without the official permission, though there was no other way out for them. In Court, therefore, Paul was sentenced to four weeks in prison because he was a refugee and could not go anyplace else.

Despite being innocent of any crime, the conditions under which Paul served his sentence were not much better than mine had been in the concentration camps. His first ten days and the last seven of his term he was not permitted any activity. No book, no chance to write, or make anything. To have something to do, Paul investigated his cell minutely. In the corner beside the door were two shelves with a wash basin, a food bowl, a mug, and even a tablespoon, all of tin. On the top shelf, stuffed into a corner, he found 13 joke books evidently left by the former occupant of the cell as a way of greeting the next prisoner. The jokes had been clipped from weekly newspapers and Paul found reading them a pleasure. Under his table top there was a dull knife, its blade fastened to the handle with string. He never used it. The table top had a chess board scratched on it in fine lines and Paul made chess figures out of bread and played his own kind of game, not being familiar with chess and having no partner. His game called for having two sides as parties. One of them he called the king's party and the other the peasants. He wanted to be objective but it didn't work. An invisible hand always pushed the peasant party on to the winning field. He gave up his game. He had sucked hatred against the kings with his mother's milk and could not prevail against it even when he wished to.

Like me, Paul tried every way to overcome the boredom of confinement in a single cell. He walked round and round, to be moving. After awhile his feet moved faster. Then faster and faster. When he saw he was attaining speed, he put one foot in front of the other, measured the cell across many times, made a figure walk, a numbers walk, dancing steps. At last he discovered that he was dancing! He performed many dances after that, alone in his cell. These performances brought him relaxation and pleasure. It is not easy to restrain a man like Paul. Singing and whistling were prohibited in prison but he did both anyway, in very low tones. Windows were to be opened only for an hour mornings and evenings but he had his open almost all day. The prison trustees ordered him to close his window but he let them scold and rave and no one enforced the rule.

Paul had learned at the Prefecture's office that his left middle finger measured exactly four inches. He used his finger to measure everything in his room, to make the hours pass. A chair in his room was chained so that it could not be moved more than a yard. Someone had converted it from a stool into a chair by making a backrest for it and some prisoner in 1904 had carved his initials in it. Paul decided that he should free this poor chair from its chain. It wasn't easy, because he had to be sure he was not being observed through the spyhole in the cell door. He managed to open the S-link at one end of the chain. The chair was free! Paul, taking the chair as a kind of symbol, snatched it up and whirled around his cell in a dance of joy. Afterward he replaced the chain.

Mice visited Paul in his cell and he welcomed them. He even placed some of his meat ration at the hole through which a visiting mouse came. The meat was too large for the hole but in the morning, Paul was delighted to find that the intelligent mouse had chewed off half of the piece of meat and disappeared with it. The other half, still too large for the mouse hole, lay beside the hole.

Paul's prison had a library from which he could borrow one book each week. One of the books he was able to borrow was the Jewish Yearbook 1860-62. Although not Jewish himself, he found the story of the persecution of the Jews very interesting. He also read a book about the life of Spinoza.

After ten days in prison, Paul was given a job pasting cellophane bags, for which he was paid a small amount. With this work he could lay hands on writing materials. At first he used a button, later he got a needle. On the cellophane bags he wrote an account of his imprisonment and smuggled it out. It is from this account I have filled in the details of the story he told me.*

Three days before Paul was due to be released, he went through a bad depression, yearning for the outdoors, for leaves and sky and me. He tried to sing cheerful songs but they turned into dirges. He tried to exercise his muscles but they stayed limp. In anger he picked up a stupid love story he had tried to read and hurled it into a corner. Finally, he calmed himself and with his

---

* Laura Nelson Baker helped to do this.

needle began to write letters on the cellophane. The last days of his confinement seemed endless, but by an effort of will he conquered his depression and lessened his own tension. He was able to laugh at himself, at the beard he had grown in prison, over the whole "unholy mess" as he referred to it.

Gaby, a friendly French trade-union member, tapped me on the shoulder, "Hallo, Gisèle, Paul has just been released. He waits for you in one of the boulevard cafes." She grinned, "And you might not recognize him, he looks so different with his long beard." I went to the designated spot. I walked around several times looking at this person in a shabby dirty coat with a long flaming red beard, not being sure whether this really was Paul. When I finally approached him and saw his smiling kind blue eyes, I finally knew that it was he. We could not help but laugh in spite of the sad weeks that had passed. He had not known that his beard would be red. (The hair on his head was blond.) With his wonderful sense of humor he had, right after release from prison, gone to a photo automat so as to remember how he looked in this odd disguise. I had to persuade him to shave the beard. It was quite a change when he got out of the barber's chair.

During this time of waiting for my papers to be issued, I participated in a small international institute near Paris. This was shortly before Munich and Chamberlain's disastrous "Averting of a War" which really meant giving in to Hitler. War was in the air. We had violent discussions with our friends from England with whom we agreed in many other areas. These English friends insisted that war must be avoided at any price, especially since England had not proved that it treated people right. Several of these English union members had been active in the struggle for India's freedom and felt strongly about the demeaning colonial practices of the English government. Some of them had been in India. They described how the native Indian population was not allowed to use the same sidewalks as the English. They argued that England had no right to pretend it was better than Nazi Germany. Those of us who had just come out of Nazi-dominated countries disagreed violently. We agreed that no country ever is free from guilt, that English colonial practices were to be condemned. Nevertheless, we thought that our English friends overlooked that Nazi dictatorship condoned this kind of behavior everywhere. In England one could at least speak up against those practices. This was impossible in Nazi-dominated countries. We were not calm in our discussions as one can be when one is farther removed from the problem. We shouted. Some were crying because we felt that we could not convince each other.

The French countryside was calm and beautiful. One evening we saw an unusually huge red moon. One of the younger French participants said quietly, "The farmer says that kind of red moon at this time of the year means war." We realists, usually above such "superstitions," became very quiet and stared at the red moon.

The news of the invasion of Czechoslovakia by the Germans occurred when I was at this institute. Everybody sat silently. We suggested that our English friends should leave because war would break out imminently. Two nights after this the village crier appeared and shouted that Chamberlain had made peace with Hitler. Our violent discussions became more violent.

I was very unhappy during this time. I felt increasingly my resistance to refugee life. There was a split between the "old" and the "new" refugees. All this came to a head during this institute and there were sharp fights. My personal unhappiness increased when I heard the news of several of my friends whom I had known during my childhood having been killed by the Nazis. One of them was Hans Litten, of whom I spoke earlier. And there were others...I walked in the blinding sun along a French acre feeling numb. I constantly repeated to myself, "What is the use, what's the use?" Perhaps it was best to end life. It was not during the time that I was attacked, it was not in prison, when I thought of suicide. It was when it seemed that nothing could be done any more. I lay down on the ground and looked up into the sky. The blue sky had not a single cloud, and around me was a great and soothing silence. I felt small, helpless. Paul was not with me at that institute. I resented our being forced to be separated again.

I had to leave Paris. There was no longer any hope that I would ever get a permit to stay and time was running out. My sister in England knew someone in Lyon who wanted a maid and she made this contact for me.

In Lyon I served as a maid in the home of a woman teacher. Her husband was retired. He was a kind older man. He made me feel that I was a human being, in spite of being a maid. His wife was intent on exploiting this refugee as much as she could. I had to get up every morning at four o'clock to fill the coal bin. Every night I had to scrub the parquet wood floors with steelwool. I had only half a day off once a week. Nevertheless, this half day brought me in contact with some unusually fine people. I got to know some of the small Hugenot Community in Lyon which was very helpful to refugees. André Phillipe who, after the war became a well-known statesman in the French government, was a deputy in the Lyon government. He helped me to gain papers which allowed me to stay in France. Through him, Paul finally got the kind of papers that kept him from being sent to prison again. But, again, we two were separated.

Refugees constantly streamed into the country. I met an Austrian family living in a poor hotel, hoping for the American visa to arrive to remove them from their miserable situation. They had a little boy, a thin child who had lived through Nazi terror and who had the hunted look that I saw in so many children. He had to go to school and he was very frightened of it. He cried because he could not understand teacher or children and he expected punishment. I was the only one in his environment who could speak French and so I went to school with him. How good to meet one of the wonderful French teachers! He was a young man. When I told him about the fear of the child, he smiled and said reassuringly that he knew how these children must feel, but soon he would know French. He told other children in the class that the little boy had gone through difficult experiences and that they should talk to him, even if he could not understand them. And children (bless them) always understand if an adult really takes them into their confidence. They smiled at the little boy and pulled him into their games. In addition to that the teacher himself gave extra time to him, talking to him slowly in French, once in awhile translating it into some German which he knew. Within two weeks this little boy was not only playing happily and talking French with his friends, but he could do the shopping for the family!

While I was working in this cold Lyon household, I "saved my sanity" by much reading or writing. On the anniversary of Mazaryk's birthday, I collected excerpts from his writings which were published in a refugee publication. I received a letter from his son, Jan Mazaryk, then in exile, thanking me for this article.

The situation in the household in which I worked became more and more intolerable. I fortunately found a position as governess to two young girls in a castle near Lyon. This was a very new experience. It was a completely different life from anything I had ever known before or later. I had known life among laborers, factory workers, office workers; among students, among middle class business men, among professional people, among the prostitutes of Vienna streets and the poverty stricken apple sellers. But I had not known nobility and its life. The castle was spacious and lay in a beautiful landscape. The children were spoiled, beautiful, lovable. For the first time in many years I had the great satisfaction of being again with young people and using my skill as a teacher. They learned languages from me, but they came frequently with their problems: Young Jeanne (16) with her first boy problems and serious religious doubts, little Monique (11) with her beginning rebellious thoughts. They adored their young mother (the parents were divorced) who supervised the personnel. She was cold and haughty. I learned how naive I was about people. The mother had often asked me to sit with her in the evening and do some sewing, but she quickly sent me away each time when a young man came to visit. It took me a while to learn that he was her lover, came regularly, that the children knew this, but must never talk about it or mention it. Behind the respectable facade of the household lay much hypocrisy.

During the summer the family went by car to the south of France. I saw the French landscape in its full beauty. In Hendaye, a city at the border of Spain, the mother left to live in a hotel while I stayed with the children in a camp, sleeping in tents. It was a wonderful opportunity to meet many French people. The children and I enjoyed our close companionship. We also learned much about the nearest, cruel dictatorship. Franco had recently come to power and he suppressed every opposition to his regime. Almost every night we heard the shots at the border and we knew that some refugee who had tried to cross the border into the freedom of France was caught. On our walks we found half-naked people crouching in the bushes. They were Spaniards who had swum across the river to freedom. The Basque farmers were kind and took them in. They spoke a similar language to the Spaniards on the other side of the river and they understood each other. Among these farmers and shepherds there existed a quiet sort of helpfulness. If those who fought for freedom were in need, one shared bread and room.

The refugees brought with them the experience of torture and suppression by Franco and also of the curse of their so-called "allies," the Communists, who played their own game and harmed the true freedom fighters.

Again a picture: A man trying to swim to freedom in the early morning with strong strokes. On the other side the police were firing at him. The bullets did not reach him but a boat dispatched after him went faster than the man could swim. I saw him fighting those who were dragging him into the boat; in full view of all of us on the other side of the river, he was beaten with sticks by the fascist police.

For the first time in many years I got a "paid vacation." I brought the children back to the north of France near Paris where their father had a summer house. They adored their father and were happy to be with him. Paul and I decided to spend these two weeks of vacation together. We had not seen each other for a long time. We were sure that war would soon reach us and there was very little hope in us for ever having a normal life together, so we had these few days of respite. We had Paul's tent that he had taken with him on the bicycle when he fled Germany. We had two borrowed bicycles. It was not expensive to live on fruit and bread and some soup. We spent wonderful days at Deauville camping on top of the cliffs, seeing the yacht of the millionaire Morgan and feeling like millionaires ourselves. We visited Mt. Saint Michèle, its beautiful cathedral cut out of rocks mirrored in the ocean. We talked about the marvelous energy and faith that those monks must have had by bringing the material from the mainland and building this beautiful church. We bicycled through Rouen and saw the cathedral and Jeanne d'Arc's statue. There were lovely quiet evenings in front of the tent, with Paul playing the mouth organ softly and I listening and feeling that this was something like a "normal life."

I wrote:

> Leise steht die Nacht vor meinem Herzen
> Und ich fürchte nichts
> und nichts tut weh.
> Über all den grossen, dunklen Schmerzen
> liegt die Ruhe
> wie ein tiefer See.

Translation:

> Softly stands the night before my heart
> I am not afraid
> and nothing hurts.
> Over all the dark suffering
> lies calm
> like a deep sea.

At the end of this time, Paul had to return to his little room in Paris and I went back to the suburb where I was to meet the children to bring them back to Lyon.

The Russian-German Pact was closed, when Germany was ready to invade Poland. The Communist party line was changed immediately from fight against Fascist Germany to friendship with it. Inside of Germany, communists denounced active anti-Nazis, who were not communists, to the Nazis, and there were new arrests. The same occurred in France. Even some who had prison experience under the Nazis behind them, were suddenly denounced by the communists to the French government as dangerous Fascists. The communists knew that they were lying. They wanted to get real anti-Nazis out of the way since the party line made the Nazis their friends.

There was Eric, for instance, who had been in a German prison for several years. Eric was suddenly denounced by communists to the Daladier government as a Nazi. He who had had a permanent permission to stay in France was brought to the border and told to leave immediately for Germany. He could not do this since certain death threatened him there. Eric was shunted from one border to another, constantly sleeping on the ground of no-man's-land between borders. It was only with the help of friends in the labor unions that, after shuttling between France, Belgium, Holland and back and over again, he finally got to England and settled there. He later served in the English Army.

Paul and I returned to Paris the day the war blackout began. As yet there was no declaration of war, but war was close and everybody knew it. Some German refugee children we knew who attended an international boarding school in England had visited their parents in France during the summer. Those children had to be sent quickly back to England because it was not sure how long trains could run between Paris and the north of France, and boats cross the Channel. Paul and I picked up two of them to bring them to the train. It was sad to see the two serious little boys being torn away from their parents. They had had that experience before; it had happened in Germany, and now it was happening again. The Gare St Lazare loomed before us, dark, totally blacked out. Only small blue light bulbs were burning inside the station. The children looked like ghosts, their faces white and drawn, exaggerated by the blue light. We waved goodbye. We went to the little telegraph office in the station to send a telegram to the mother of a Swiss child whom we also had brought to the train. When we handed the telegram over to the operator, he looked up and asked, "Where are your papers?" Oh, no, both of us almost fainted. Paul had no papers at that time. My papers were made out for Lyon, but what would happen if this was found out? While we hesitated for just a second, another customer pressed against us and impatiently held out his message to be sent. The operator said, "Oh, well, this concerns one of the kids you sent off, doesn't it?" We said it did and with this he waved us on.

Chapter Nineteen

1939. War Begins in France

*G*as masks were distributed in Paris. General mobilization started. Men were streaming out of their homes with little bags in their hands, going to the stations where they were put into uniforms. It was a silent, large mass, moving deliberately and yet one began to get the feeling of something frightening, something ominous. Women were standing in the doors of the houses crying. Children looked at their fathers with wondering eyes, not understanding what was really happening.

The refugee organization in Paris and individual refugees immediately announced to the French government that they were glad to help in their fight against the Nazis. In fact, there was real hope among refugees that they finally could participate in this fight they had fought alone for so long. Yet, unfortunately and incomprehensibly, France did not use these allies; all the men who were of "alien" origin were called to the big stadium in

Paris to be ready for internment. The pretended reason was that it was too difficult to sort out the Nazis from the non-Nazis, but most of us knew that this could have been done quite easily. Immigrants knew each other well. For we women, it was a horrible thought that now the men were gone but not into battle as they had wanted.

I had no communication with Paul for a long time to follow. Later he told me that he felt much better at that time because they were all in the same boat. He became a force of hope in the internment camp. His old courage and resourcefulness and his basic health returned. He had brought along a sleeping bag. The stone steps of the large stadium were hard, but he undressed for the night and crawled into this bag. Others had slept in their day clothes, but Paul felt that it was a morale booster to change for the night. It was quite cold, but he woke up refreshed the next morning, having slept soundly. To the surprise of those around him, he vigorously threw off the sleeping bag and started to do exercises in his shorts. Others joined him and felt refreshed.

I myself had to go back to work with the children for whom I was responsible. This was no more in Lyons, but in the vicinity of Paris. The family was badly frightened with the exception of the father. He was a calm, handsome, tall man with a strange mixture of kindness and aloofness.

The first alert sounded and the German planes were overhead the first day I was with this family. The mother begged me to give my gas mask to the children—they had none—and I did. I felt much more hopeful than for a long time. War had given us allies in the fight against the Nazis.

The children had to return to Lyon to go to school, but the city of Lyon and its environment had been declared a "Zone Interdit." This meant that no alien could live there. Paris, too, was "Zone Interdit." That meant that there was no place for me to stay permanently. I went to Paris to find some of my friends in different refugee committees to find out what I could do. A few of the men were not interned because they had been residents of Paris for a long time, and were well known as anti-Nazis. One of the leading men was Erich, a Jewish lawyer who had stood up courageously against the Nazis during the first days of the Nazi regime, and who had to flee when they searched for him. It was sad to see what time had done to him. He was so afraid to fall between two chairs, the Nazis on the one hand and the French government who had allowed him to stay at home, on the other side, that he did not dare to let me stay overnight at his family home. He said he could not give me any help. Another refugee, Hanna, who had always seemed a rather withdrawn woman, quietly offered to let me stay at her place any time I had any business in Paris.

In spite of many contacts at the prefecture, legal permission to stay in Paris could not be obtained. To stay illegally was taking too great a risk and would involve others. I returned to the house of the father of my charges, telling him about my plight and saying that I had to try to find lodging somewhere. He invited me to stay at his house. He vouched for me at the police station. He asked me to take care of the house, clean it, and have it ready for week-ends which he intended to spend there. During the week-ends I should also cook for him. I would not receive any salary, but I would have a roof over my head and food. There was no alternative, and so I accepted.

These were strange and lonely days. I was alone in this house with little news from anyone else. The "drôle de guerre" as the French called the "phony war" started in September 1939. There were blackouts; there were planes coming overhead; but there was no shooting war. There were desperate and yet encouraging letters from my sister, Ruth, in England.

Gisa, my dearest friend,

A letter from you! You know, I am usually the only one in the house who can sleep well during the day and generally wake up refreshed and feel like singing. Well—it hasn't been like that during the last weeks. One was too upset and too busy listening to the wireless to sleep during the day and accordingly I would wake up after 3 hours' sleep with heavy head and eyes and a pain in my heart. Today it was all different. I slept like a

log from 11:45 till 6:45, I woke up, and before I had cleaned my
teeth I was humming some silly song. Quite a surprise to myself—until I found your letter downstairs, then I knew why! I
shall feel better now, for a while, I am sure. It wasn't too cheerful
a letter, I know, but it was your writing and your spirit, darling,
and I had been waiting for that more than I can ever tell you.
My heart is so full of grief and worry, Gisa, and I have poured it
all out to you so often (in my heart), that I shan't do it now again,
on paper.

No, darling, I am not courageous, you know I am not. I am,
really, a timid little mouse, and very sad and afraid to death just
now, afraid for the world in general and for everybody I love in
particular and also for myself (I don't make myself any better
than I am, ever). But I am pretending, the best I can, to be as
phlegmatic and thick-skinned as an elephant, and am quite
pleased with myself when I succeed. Mobilization? Not yet for
me. At present I am still considered "Enemy Alien," which I
have printed neatly, red on white, on my registration book. I am
allowed to carry on my present work, but I am not taken for
National Service. Maybe that will be altered in time.

Poor Eri! (This was our name for Paul.) If one could only do
something for him! I wonder what those camps are like. Does
he need anything? But, oh dear! I don't even know if it would be
possible to send anything. Money must certainly not leave the
country. So I cannot keep my promise to pay for your eye-
glasses. That hurts me very much. How are you managing
about it? Is it selfish to think of all sorts of personal things now?
I think it is just human. What a life we have had, Gisa! How true
every word you say! But still: if I see some of the terribly dull
and narrow old maids here, Gisa, then I think life hasn't been
too bad, after all. True, they feel less pain than we do, but surely,
they have felt less joy, too. I have had a taste of all good things
in life: beautiful countries, work, art, and love, and I know they
were good while I had them and I tasted every last drop of
them. I don't think I have had enough, I don't want to die yet
(though theoretically there is no reason why I shouldn't), but

even if I should live to see the end of this war I shall be worn out and tired and old and not fit for enjoying life. But I shall know that I have had something.

Do you see what I mean, dearest? At least life hasn't been empty—But for all this philosophy, how I should like to live to see those beasts down, down in the blackest hell, where they belong and from where they seem to have sprung! No, I am not good. I wish them all the evil in the world, if it could only come quickly to save all the others I should like to save!

What a hopelessly muddled letter, Gisa! And if I don't stop myself I shall go on and on, and I, myself, can't make head or tail of all my emotions and thoughts, how much less could you.

If I could pray, Gisa, I would pray: "Let me meet her again!" But I can't pray, and I can't believe and I can't hope. But I love you, my sister!

Tell Eri, if you can, that I think of him!

The feeling in England, the soldiers without song or flowers, the sense of duty against Hitlerism, the hate for him and not for the German people—it is all the same as you tell from France. Don't let me talk about it any more! One goes crazy if one thinks too long about it.

I shall go on writing weekly. Leave your address behind wherever you go! There was no letter from Palestine for weeks, but I got a newspaper today that Fredi sent me (funny, that that should come through easier than a letter!) So I hope they are all right. How good that I went to see them! Poor Hanna and Mutti! It will be much worse for them than for us. If we could only be together! Oh, hell!

Here is a kiss for you, my sister!

There were Ruth's sad poems, the words of a young woman:

HOPELESS YOUTH

From the tree of life
hangs splendid the fruit:

glimmering, glistening,
gloriously gold.
But the Eternal
within the fold
of his flowing white coat
carries the knife
that will cut it.

And you who are seed,
and you who have in you
the hope and the creed
of new trees and new branches,
new leaves and new gold
you—waiting to grow—
you know and behold,
The Eternal who hidden
in folds of white silk
carries the knife
that will cut you.

BLACK-OUT

I wander through the night to you
The town is strangely hushed and grey
 a scent is in the air—like autumn hay.
And slowly changes gray to grayish-blue.

A soldier's arm across his sweetheart's back
shows blurred and dimly and soon disappears.
A cigarette glow, only marks the way he steers.
A country night wind—and the town is black.

I had little contact with the rest of my family and there was
no longer any contact with anyone inside Germany. Once in
awhile there were a few letters from Paul who had meanwhile
been attached to the French Army as a "prestataire," (refugees

who were considered loyal to France). They were not allowed to be French soldiers carrying arms, but they were part of the French army, used like "pioneers," digging ditches, erecting barracks, etc. Mr. X was at the summer home on week-ends. I had learned to withdraw whenever he arrived and only serve the food I had cooked. He brought with him his pretty little mistress who stayed for the week-end.

One of those evenings he asked me to go to the movies with them. When we left the theater that night, the moon was shining so brightly that the night seemed like day. It was such a clear night, the Seine was glittering like a silver band. Someone said, "A good night for the German bombers to fly over Paris. No blackout can disguise this!" And—as if they had heard those words, suddenly, the bombers were over us; a whole group of beautiful silver bodies, yet with their ominous groan—German planes. Like everyone else, I had learned in those first days of the war to distinguish German bombers from English and French ones, simply by the sound they made. The young woman clung to her lover, sobbing, saying that the world should allow them to live. I was silently standing next to them—very, very alone.

The next morning she begged Mr. X to let her stay in his house for a little while, while he was gone. She just could not go back to Paris. She would make some excuses to her family.

Those days we were alone brought we two young women, from such different worlds, closely together. M. sobbed out the story of a woman whose husband was away in the war and whose child she loved. But, "Oh, I love Mr. X, he is so gentle, so good." Yet when her husband returned, what could she do? He would kill her! And perhaps she loved him, too, but he just wasn't here, and oh, how she loved the baby. But her family wouldn't let her have it if they would find out. War—that was what it meant to the little French girl with the sweet face, the brown eyes and her great passion. There was really no villain in this whole plot. There were just human beings, real and confused in a very confusing world.

Winter came and it was very cold in the house. I could not use fuel when Mr. X was absent. I slept on a mattress on the floor (only two rooms were furnished in the house.) My sheets were often iced over and I dreaded going to bed. I could make a little fire in the fireplace from the wood that I had gathered in the neighboring woods. I pushed the mattress as close to this little fireplace as I dared to and tried to thaw out the sheets before I crawled between them.

There were a few kind neighbors not too far away. They were Polish workers who worked in the fields. They felt with my loneliness, also being foreigners in a foreign country as myself. They suggested that I come over during the night raids which occurred periodically. I accepted their kind offer. Behind windows covered with tape so that no light could shine through them, I found the warmth and the undemanding kindness of a simple and happy family—in spite of the war.

New Year 1940—there still was no shooting war. The French talked about their strong Maginot Line and were sure that nothing really could happen to them. Paul's prestataire company was stationed near Orleans, building barracks for the German prisoners. It is an irony of history that later the Germans used these barracks to keep the French prisoners in them. The wives of the prestataires frequently made petitions to see their husbands since French soldiers did get furloughs. Yet such petitions were never favorably answered. Well—then—one had to go without permission.

The day before the New Year I had arranged to leave the house and to borrow some money for the short trip from where I was to Orleans. The prestataire compound was full of men! At this moment I loved all of them, those men in the ill-fitting uniforms. I knew many, but had not seen them for a long time. They came towards me with outstretched arms and we fell into each other's arms regardless of how our relationships had been previous to this. Much of the old and disagreeable bickering was forgotten because there was now danger and there was a need to stick together.

Paul turned to me slowly. We had not seen each other since the summer, and much had happened to both of us. There was no privacy in this room and somehow one could not but feel embarrassed to show strong emotions. The prestataires were housed in a large school auditorium. Each one of them had tried to build his own little private nook. Over their army beds they had fixed some "headboards" for books or pictures. Most of them were intelligent people who could not just spend their time gambling or staring into space. They had formed discussion groups and kept themselves informed of current events. Paul and one or two others had begun to do some wood carving. Some of the intellectuals considered such work far beneath their dignity. Nevertheless, because of the strange situation in which they found themselves, they did not express their disdain as vehemently as they had in Paris.

Not everyone had visitors, and so almost everybody else shared in each other's visitors. There was always a whole group around each of us. One could not have a private conversation and one could not say that one wanted to be alone, because there was such hunger in the eyes of all the men to see others and to hear about events on the "outside."

Finally night fell and the New Year approached. The auditorium was cold, but because of many people sleeping there it was comparatively warm. Nevertheless, those who wanted some privacy did not want to stay in the large room where everyone was sleeping practically on top of each other. There were some little, very cold rooms under the roof. One was not permitted to be up there, but the French guards had much understanding for the situation and there was silent agreement to make them available for those rare visitors. The men could only go upstairs to meet their wives after the roll call. While waiting for them, we wives huddled under the cold roof, close together. We warmed each other and we talked in low voices. We hardly knew each other but we felt like sisters.

Slowly one man after another came, carrying blankets. It was touching to see that they did not bring only their own, but they brought those from other men who had relinquished them to us.

It was odd to look out from the little room window and see the snow downstairs, the compound rising with the barbed wire around it, and the moon shining on the glittering snow. A French soldier was marching up and down, up and down, as if to protect us.

To Paul

Hell, von tiefer Freude heiss durchglüht
tönt mein Lied.

Jubelt auf and trägt uns stark und weit,
Überfülle aller Seligkeit.

Einmal noch des Leben's Kelch getrunken,
ineinander wie in eins versunken.

Bleibt ein stiller Glanz und Kraft und Schwung,
Dankbar lächelnde Erinnerung.

Translation:

Glowing, deeply warmed by joy
Sounds my song.

Jubilant, it carries us strong and far
overflowing with deepest happiness

Once more we drank of the cup of life
sunk into each other—becoming one.

And with us stays a quiet ray of strength,
a thankful smiling memory.

I later found the poem my sister, Ruth, wrote the same night—how close we were!

New Year's Night's Love—1940

Don't let it go beyond this New Year's night!
Don't lift the veil! Don't let it see the light!
Keep it within the gladness of your heart
and treat it like a thing from all apart,
keep it in dimness like a lovely dream.
And by a lonely fireside let gleam
your fairy castle built of ruby and of jade
and it will never die and never fade.

In the beginning of the New Year I realized that there was some talk about me in the village. Some people had found out that I was a "foreigner" and there were questions about me. Some others considered me Mr. X's second mistress. His ex-wife made comments about this in her letters. I began to look for some other place to live because I realized that I could not stay much longer under the circumstance.

Jacob, a young German refugee I knew had married Yvette, a French young woman some years earlier. They had a farm not too far from Paris. They offered me a room above their barn. Meanwhile, also, the refugee committee had been newly organized. It distributed relief for those who were not allowed to work. I was offered some relief money and the opportunity to work for it as an "investigator." This was an opportunity to do some real work and I gladly accepted.

The evening before leaving Mr. X's house, I packed my few belongings into a bag. Some weeks previous to this a stray dog had attached itself to me. The meager food that I shared with him and a little petting had made him my friend. I knew that I could not take the dog with me, that it would not be welcome where I was going. I hardly dared look at it and I packed secretly. That evening the dog did not move from my side. Suddenly it got on its hind legs and clung to me with its front paws. It held me tightly and whined. I suffered with it. I tried to tell the dog that I had made arrangements with the kind Polish family to take care of it. I walked to this family with the dog and told it that it would get food from them. The dog continued to whine and hold on to me. The next day I had to tear myself away from it. I was told later that it refused food and died.

For a short time life became more normal. I was with a family, in fact one of the few families that was still intact. Some farmers were not called up for service because their work was too vital for the country. The man of the house, Jacob, was therefore still at home. They had a wonderful little girl, Marianne, who became one of my good friends. While living in their place I also became part of the village and got to know people around me and was accepted as one of them. It was a great relief to do a day's work for the refugee relief committee. It did not matter that I did not do it for regular wages, but did it for my relief money. The sad part of it was only that I saw social service being given in a most degrading form. When people came to get their relief, they had to wait for hours in an overcrowded, smelly room. Their names were called out by a man who seemed to make it his special business to insult the poor, calling them lazy or making all other kinds of unfriendly remarks about their being on relief. I, as an investigator, was told to find out whether anybody was cheating. The misery that I saw in those days is almost beyond description. There was a young woman whom I had to visit because I was supposed to find out whether she had some hidden worldly goods and therefore might not need the relief money. The gaunt, drawn woman sat on the bare floor in a completely empty room. She looked at me helplessly and said that the few pieces of furniture she had possessed she had had to sell because she just had to have something to eat. She looked sick and was shaking with cold. There was no fuel, there was no food. And I had been sent to find out whether she had too much!!

There was an old man whom I had to visit. He was lying in his bed, coughing. Just when I was present he had a severe heart attack. I telephoned the relief office and was told that it was all right to get him to a hospital. The old man, as so many Europeans, did not want to go because going to the hospital meant to him that he was dying. I slowly persuaded him. He finally gave in, but only when I promised to ride along in the ambulance with him and hold his hand. He had begun to hallucinate and he thought I was his daughter whom he had not seen for many years. Just as we entered the hospital he cried out and held me tightly. He whispered to me that he had left his jacket in the house and in this jacket was a purse with some money. He could not leave this money there. They would take it away from him and I should bring it to him. I promised this and left him in the hospital. I went back to his room to pick up the jacket and brought him the money. He counted carefully the few francs that were left which meant to him the difference between feeling completely abandoned, and the feeling that he was still a self-respecting person with some security. When I made my report to the committee, I was chided for having brought the money to the man. I was supposed to have brought it to the committee so that it could use it for him. I am still happy that I had not done this. The man died the next night holding in his hand the jacket, the one thing that meant security to him, and the money was in it. It then went to the committee anyhow, but at least he had been spared a last terror.

I myself had comparatively little to eat. I was used to this and always knew how to get along on very little money. One day I stood at the window of my little room above the barn and looked out. Suddenly everything swam before my eyes and the snow in front of me seemed to turn red. I had never fainted in my life. I tried to walk down the stairs leading to the entrance of the barn but I did not quite make it and broke down just as I reached the foot of the stairs. Fortunately Jacob heard the commotion when I fell and came running out. They carried me into their home. For the first time in my life I was unconscious. I did wake up by a

strange pricking at the sole of my feet. I could hardly look above
the bedclothes that were piled on me and I was shivering with
cold. I saw my little friend, Marianne, standing at the foot of the
bed and sticking some old rusty pin into the soles of my feet. I fee-
bly asked her what she was doing and with a solicitous voice she
said that she was giving me some injections to get better. It was
difficult to persuade Marianne that her treatment might not be
the best. I soon recovered, since it had been only prolonged under-
nourishment that had produced the fainting.

Every place in the village had to take in some regiments of
soldiers because they could be housed best in the large barns of
the farmers. The barn over which I lived was soon filled with
French soldiers. They behaved decently and were always courteous towards the stranger who lived under the same roof. The men
were touchingly kind with little Marianne. Many of them were
family men themselves and they yearned for their own children.
Marianne became quite spoiled by constantly getting the attention of a whole regiment of soldiers.

Paul wrote that he had the impression that by spring something serious would happen, and I should keep in touch with my
Paris friends. He did not believe that the Germans would continue indefinitely this "phony" war. How right he was, we did
not know at the time he wrote this prophetic letter. He also
asked me to take all his belongings from his room in Paris and
bring them to the farm. This gave me a more comfortable furnished room and Paul's bicycle which allowed for better transportation.

It was in early spring that I visited a friend in Paris. She was
sick in bed. Suddenly Eva came storming into the room, white in
the face: "The Germans have invaded Belgium." Now the real
war had begun. Eva's fiance had just made a trip for the underground forces to Belgium and was caught in the situation. (Later
we learned that he had been made a prisoner. Since he spoke excellent French he could hide his identity as a former German.)

I immediately returned to the village. It was still peaceful
there. Everyone seemed to be hopeful. The Belgian king was

looked upon as a symbol of strength. Everybody assumed that the Belgian armies and the Dutch dikes would stem the tide of the invaders.

The invasion of Belgium had begun. Now the whole world saw Nazi terror. This was not only a war, this was slaughter and it was ruthless slaughter. The world had seen what happened in Poland. People were killed, gassed. The defenders of Warsaw were killed and humiliated. Thousands were brought into the concentration camps in Germany. Theresienstadt, Auschwitz, became names known to the world, places where thousands and thousands of Jews, Catholics, Socialists, Gypsies were gassed and killed. There was not much hope. Yet the Belgian King Leopold let the invaders enter the country. The Dutch government had to go into exile.

Belgian refugees streamed into France. The air raids on Paris began in earnest. One day when I was in downtown Paris doing some of my committee work, the air raid sounded and we had to go into the big shelters under the boulevards. People were quiet and rather collected. Yet one man was sobbing hysterically. For a moment I did not feel pity. Under such circumstances one became almost stern, expecting that everybody must keep a "stiff upper lip." The man's sobbing persisted. I moved over and asked whether there was anything I could do for him? He almost screamed out his horrible story of having left his home in Belgium with his whole family, wife and five children. They were on the road leaving the bombed city behind them. Nazi planes had followed the refugees. They swooped down and machine-gunned the defenseless civilians. Some of his children fell. He took the baby in his arms, but one of the bullets hit the baby. When he dropped the baby and turned around, his wife too was gone. He, a civilian, had left with a family of five children and a wife and now he was here—all alone

I returned that day by bus, as usual. We always passed a house at the outskirts of the woods. All bus passengers had become familiar with the little six-year-old and his friendly mother who waved daily to the passing bus. When the bus neared this spot there was a sudden silence. All of us stared with horror at the gaping hole in the ground where formerly a house had stood. There was nothing but that hole, and rubble strewn around. No remains of the inhabitants could be found.

All men including Jacob were now called into service. There were more soldiers in our barn. A young pregnant woman whose husband was also in the army moved into one of the lower rooms because she was afraid to stay alone in her house. With her was her 13-year-old brother. How considerate, kind and courageous children can be! The 13-year-old acted like a man towards his sister, taking care of her whenever he could. When the air raid sounded we were supposed to go outside and lean against the wall. This was our only shelter. It was known that it was easier to dig out a victim if he had been standing against an upright wall. The boy carefully guided his sister down the steps when the air raid alarm sounded. He pressed her against the wall and then he stood before her with his arms outstretched as if he could protect her against the falling bombs.

I also learned what it means to a young child to be with those who love her under such frightening circumstances. Little Marianne was always with us. When the bombing started her mother and I took Marianne between us and stood with her against the wall. Sometimes a soldier put his steel helmet on her head and the child felt protected by the people around her. There was no fear.

After one of the heavy bombings in our area, I walked with Marianne along the road after the "all clear" had sounded. Everywhere electric wires had been torn down and some trees were broken. Marianne looked at them questioning and wondering who had done this? I said, "Oh, Marianne, that's war." The child thoughtfully questioned again, "Oh, Gisèle, has the war hands?"

An incendiary bomb had hit one of the greenhouses that belonged to her father and had destroyed it. Marianne stood before it and said, "Oh, what will Dad say, I promised to take care of his plants!"

There were frequent night raids. Our village was close to an airport. The sirens sounded so often, I got quite used to them. In fact, at times, I slept through their screaming and Yvette had to call me. It reminded me of the days in Vienna when I slept so soundly under the worst circumstances. One night I was slow in getting ready when the siren sounded. Usually most of us hurried at the first sound to the big house of Yvette's parents. The family felt that everybody should be together at such a night. This was also important to make it easier for rescuers in case people were buried. Since I was late I had to hurry through a stretch of the woods. By this time, the anti-aircraft fire had started and the bombs were falling. Left and right, and directly above my head the fire was crossing, but I walked straight through it. I was not courageous, I just had got used to it. I simply knew I had to walk this way and arrive at the place where we were supposed to be.

A new and frightening situation occurred. Because of the increasing danger of Nazis entering the country, the French government arrested all German women, mostly anti-Nazi refugees, and sent them to internment camps in the south of France. Since I was not only Austrian by "marriage" but also by birth, I was not interned. Erna who also was Austrian, and I kept contact as much as we could. During this time I heard little from my family, only of Ruth. Mail service was still quite reliable between England and France. Ruth was full of happiness in these dark days. Not only had she been declared a "friendly alien" by the English government and could therefore continue as a nurse, she also fell in love and felt love in return.

9.2.40

Gisa, dear,

...As long as I have money for myself, my dear, I have some for you, too. You see, I am not being "good." I am not offering you my last penny and then go begging for myself. I should consider that stupid. But as long as there are two pennies, one is yours if you need it. And there is no argument about it. All right, pay me back whenever you get enough to do it. I am a purpose and shall not be above it and too "holy" to accept it. But heaven help you if you start sending me things while you can't afford it and while I don't need it: And that is the last word about that.

Darling, of course I understand your letter. I have, in the years since 1933 while never anyone I loved was near me, except Lisa and she is going now, become one of the world's best letter readers. Practice, my dear. Pity I have not also become an equally good letter writer!—But what is the good of reading what people have thought out to make the world a better place, when one has so little hope as I have and finds it a waste of time and energy to try and knock sense into its abominable mankind? I know, I know: to have friends, to love people, to hate war and destruction, to admire art, to adore children, to be a nurse doesn't go hand in hand with this utter hopelessness. But then—I have never yet lived what I considered right in theory, and I am giving up hope of ever doing so. And therefore, when my cold will be gone and my head will be clear again, I might, after all, follow your suggestion and read—perhaps Kant..

...The Tribunal was such an almost "nice" and certainly exciting affair that that's why I kept forgetting to tell you about it. Though the result: that I can work and move about in England as I like, is important enough and really almost incredible. That is one thing I wrote to Palestine about the other day: we will never quite understand the English. They seem so simple, and daily one discovers a new side of their character. They seem dull—and govern the largest world Empire. They seem inartistic, and their galleries and museums are a wealth of beauty, they spend their holidays if ever possible in foreign countries— and are arrogantly proud of their own, and they seem the essence of conservatism and then make an almost revolutionary arrangement as this: letting us go unhindered about our business. Unbelievable and admirable. I had a letter from my matron and a lot of testimonials and one had found out from the House Office, I suppose, what kind of a person I was. So I merely got a compliment (says the presiding gentleman: "If all this is said here about you is true, I wouldn't mind being nursed by you" and my reply, "I hope you won't need it, Sir." Laughter.) and then the restrictions were canceled....

31.3.40

Darling,

Gisa, I must tell you something strange: it has, after all, turned out to be more than just "friendship" between Rich and me. And I am, for the first time in my life, so it seems to me, happy. I think it must be a little as it is with Paul and you. He is so good and warm, tactful and tender, the first man I ever met who can see behind my pretense of being independent and sure of myself, and who has patience and really does things for me—I don't mean giving me presents but things of the heart and soul which matter more. He is, to put it short, the first man who understands "love" just the way I do and is ready to give it to me. How awful all that sounds, but please, Gisa dear, do understand! And we mean it to last, and I think it can last.

Strange, I was so reluctant to let him get near me at all. Rich was just there, all the time, and painfully missed during the few intervals he wasn't there. And then, quite slowly, it changed and here it is. I was so full of it two days ago, I wanted to write and tell mother. But it will hurt her so because he isn't Jewish and now I think I'd better still wait and make quite, quite sure before I tell her. But that I feel at all that this is something I can and want to talk about and want her to know—that is something quite unheard of. And my heart is full to the brim and sings. Oh, Gisa, Gisa, to find somebody in all this mess who makes you feel good, somebody in all the lies and uncertainty who makes you feel safe and as if you can always trust and believe him—it is too good to be true. "Too good to be true"—you see, Gisa, I am, in spite of all and though I talk like a "Backfish," [adolescent] still your very skeptical sister. But God knows if that man doesn't even teach me not to be skeptical....

It was a beautiful summer afternoon when I returned from Paris. I had gone to Paris the day before. I knew I would get a telegram from my union friends if it was necessary to leave Paris. I had just taken a walk—the earth was so beautiful in those spring days, flowers and greens. The woods were full of bluebells. Everything seemed so peaceful with the exception of the soldiers in the barn. It had been a little while since I had news from Ruth or from Paul, but I had always told myself that this was war and others had it worse than I. When I came back from my walk it was twilight and the courtyard was full of soldiers. One of the young soldiers said to me, "There is a telegram for you." Oh, I thought, now I have to go away and I don't want to. At first no one could find the telegram, but then an older farmer who was at that moment working with the pigs pulled it calmly out of his pocket. I did not read it but went into the house where Yvette was sewing. I opened it and then I cried out like a wounded animal, and repeated, "No, no, no!" Yvette looked up frightened, but I just couldn't say a word. There were no tears, I simply ran away. I did not want to see anyone. The telegram said that Ruth was dead, killed in an accident.

To me Ruth had always been more than just a sister. We had been so very close. Never, never again would I find another person to whom I could open up completely. Yes, there was Paul. But I always needed a sister, too, the kind of sister Ruth was! And now she was—gone. I still could not cry. I just ran. The soldiers looked at me surprised. Only after a while, I walked back slowly. I did not want to see faces full of pity. I went into my room. I felt so closed in and so thoroughly alone; it was as if there was nobody, nothing. When I finally left my room, the young pregnant woman and her mother stood at the door and asked me what happened. It was rather dark by this time. I saw the two in the dim light and the faces of the young soldiers crowding around us. What could I say to them? Their eyes drew me out of my isolation, I felt grateful for their compassion and I did not feel that they were only curious.

I told them almost shyly about Ruth's death and how I had loved her. And, looking at these young people who soon also faced death I could not help but add, "I know that many go through much worse and I will not complain." The mother said very simply, "Oh, no, everybody is hurt most because it hits the one he is closest to." The soldiers who usually talked loudly and joked were very quiet and almost reverently let me pass. Only later at night could I finally cry. My only consolation was that Ruth had died at a time when she had found love and when she was happy. Ruth's Will reached me later. It was written on September 4, 1939, at 1:30 a.m., and it starts:

"This is the first night after the declaration of war between England and Germany. I am 25 years old. I have never imagined that I should be so soon in a position where it is advisable to make a will. This may account to whoever may deal with this document for its lack of professionally 'right' form."

And it ends:

"Let me end up by saying: I should like to give many more things to a number of people, some of them not mentioned at all. And it may well be that the arrangements as they stand here are not the wisest. I am sorry. But they are the best I could make in the short space of time I have had to consider this question. Time presses and there is nobody to advise me. So, don't feel hurt, anybody! Be sure I meant well.

I am afraid that is the sum of my whole life:

MEANT WELL BUT ACHIEVED LITTLE.

What a shame! But if there was ever anybody who felt a little happier for my being there—and I believe there were—and if there will be anybody who will feel a little sad whenever she or he feels and remembers that I am no more there, I should think it was worthwhile having lived."

Ruth's will could not be carried out during the war. Many years later, Richard, the man she had loved, found her books in an attic in London and sent them to me. At that time he wrote a beautiful epitaph in a letter:

> "It all seems to belong to another world and a different set of values. How much things have changed and how life has gone on in a frantic speed and everyone has changed so much.
> Yet there is something that remained, the eternal belief in beauty and her never-failing answer to any call for help."

Little Marianne also felt my pain. Her mother had told her that my sister had died. She took my hand and said that she wanted to walk with me. And while we were walking, she said, "Please, don't cry, Gisèle, next time we go to Paris, I'll buy you a new sister."

I wrote a letter to my family in Palestine to let them know that Paul and I were still alive, that probably no news would reach them for a long time. They did get this letter many, many months later. It was smudged by water stains and it bore a stamp saying, "Fished out of the Sea at Gibraltar."

Chapter Twenty

Fall of France

From one of the farm windows one could see trains passing. In the past months those trains were full of ammunition and machine guns. They always went east towards the front. But one particular morning it struck us that the trains were moving in the opposite direction. What was happening? How was it possible that the ammunition was moving west, while the fighting was in the east? This evening the soldiers were assembled and told to prepare to leave for the front. From the window I looked at those young French soldiers whom I had begun to know and appreciate for their sense of humor in spite of knowing death close at hand. They stood in long rows in the evening twilight. The officer spoke explaining that they had to fight this fight to save France from being trampled down by the Nazis. We women watched with tears in our eyes wishing we could do more.

Yet a strange thing happened. These same soldiers appeared in our village again after two days. We did not dare ask questions. They looked so discouraged. Some of them told us that they had marched and marched and marched and then recognized that they were back at the point from which they had started. It seemed more and more that they were sabotaged. There was fear in our hearts.

One afternoon I went to Paris to visit a French teacher. While I was there the telephone rang and she was called out of the room. When she returned she was pale. She told me that I should alert every refugee to leave immediately. She just had been told that the French government had left for Bordeaux and that all civil servants should leave immediately. She realized that this meant that the French government had abandoned Paris. Everybody had hoped that a stand would be made to defend Paris. This was the final blow. She felt ashamed for France, especially because the government did not tell the total population how the situation was but decided for civil servants to leave first, civil servants who should have set an example in courage.

I went to alert some of my refugee friends. Erna insisted that I stay in Paris and that we try to make our way together to southern France. The city of Montauban had been designated by the Austrian Committee as the place where we should go since there was a Socialist mayor, friendly to anti-Nazi refugees. I insisted that I could not stay that day because I had to return to warn Yvette of the impending danger. I felt it was important for her, too, to leave to save the child, especially since she was married to a German-Jewish refugee.

The roads this evening were already full, full of soldiers returning, of people fleeing from the eastern part of France, of animals and of large vehicles. The terrible chaos engulfing France had started. Yvette decided to stay in the village.

I packed the usual little "rucksack" and asked her to burn whatever I left behind and to take good care of the bicycle. A bicycle was a precious possession at that time. In my pocket I had a little paper bag filled with nuts and a lemon. We had been used to carry that with us during the air raids because nuts were nourishing food and lemons quenched the thirst. Again I made my way towards Paris. The roads were more crowded than ever. People were screaming, everywhere were cars with bedding on their top. In the subways women fainted and cried hysterically. Rumors constantly grew. I went to the Gare St. Lazare where I was supposed to meet Erna. It was impossible to find anybody. There were thousands of people trying to get on trains. The iron gates of the fence surrounding the station were locked and everybody was kept out. This added to the confusion. Planes were overhead, circling Paris. They were French planes throwing a smoke screen over the city to hide it from the enemy. People were full of soot and smoke. Panic increased. I did not wait to stay in this hysterical crowd. Anyhow—what use was there in leaving Paris? What would be different somewhere else? I walked back towards the house of a friend. On arrival I was chided by her for even considering to stay. I was told that it was not a question of saving myself, but a question of saving any anti-Nazi who could be saved. I had heard this when I was in Germany, and I had heard it again when I was in Austria and now the same was repeated when I had to leave Paris. It began to seem ridiculous to be "saved" so often. For what? Nevertheless, I returned to the railroad station. I walked across the tracks and saw some trains waiting to go south. Nobody asked for tickets. I got on. The train was full of people. A strange journey began. All these people became one large family. Food was shared, the nuts, the lemon, whatever anyone had. Soldiers told their mournful tales about the retreat. They usually ended with a "Je m'en foux," "I don't care. I'll go home." Demoralization was complete. There was talk about the French government having sold out to the Germans. Anyhow—where was the French government?

The train had to stop constantly because of air raids. Curtains were drawn, the train was blacked out. It was night. At one of the stops several people got off the train to stretch their legs. One of the repairmen said, "Italy has entered the war." This was the final blow. We were going south from where now a new enemy was approaching. People were especially hateful toward the Italians because they had entered the war at a moment when France was "down." But with death seeming now so certain, the first panic was quickly replaced by an amazing calm. In this last part of the journey I saw a France that is not remembered often when the invasion chaos is described. These were French citizens who had refound the strength to suffer, to accept defeat, even to fight if necessary.

The train stopped at Montauban. I recognized several Austrian refugees who had come with either the same train or had arrived earlier. One of the young women, usually alive and strong, seemed dejected and depressed. I gave her a little slip of paper with one of my favorite poems. It was a short verse by the German poet Goethe. "The Gods give everything to those they love, all the joys, the eternal ones, all the suffering, they give it to them—totally." We became friends.

Montauban was a wonderfully helpful town. The mayor had put up large posters all over the city. They reminded the inhabitants of the flood that had threatened Montauban some years earlier. At that time they had received help from many neighboring places. The posters said that now another flood had entered France, the German conqueror. Those refugees arriving had actively stood against the Nazis in their own country. "Frenchmen," it proclaimed, "be helpful to them as you were helped during the flood." The city responded in a warm and generous spirit. Police gave temporary permits which in turn made it possible to obtain ration cards and which gave a feeling of "legality." Treatment at the police station was kind and respectful. (I could not help but compare this with the treatment given to refugees by their own kind at the refugee committee in Paris.) Private citizens offered living quarters. They were paid a small amount by voluntary collections. My Austrian friend and I stayed in the home of an older couple. The man was a retired letter carrier, his wife a motherly woman. Their son was in the Army and yet they welcomed us and understood that in spite of our Austrian and German origin, we were not Nazis.

Days followed of endless listening to the radio and inquiries about the refugee men who were caught in the north in their Prestataire camps. Nobody knew what happened to them. The radio announced that Paris had fallen. We cried. We knew it would happen but the truth was heartrending. There was the awful surrender in the woods of Compiègne (how we shuddered at the sound of the "Deutschland, Deutschland über alles") and the creation of the Pétain Government. We were still in the "free zone" but how long? And what had happened to our men?

One day the roads became alive. The grapevine must have reached some of the prestataire camps where the men stayed to tell them about Montauban's hospitality. Slowly they arrived with bleeding feet, shoes torn off them, with battered clothes and battered faces. They had walked through German lines looking like French refugees, not speaking because their accent would give them away. The stories they told were the stories of a defeated and disorganized country. The French Army to which they had been attached had taken no responsibility for them. They were simply left behind. They were left behind—those people who were most vulnerable and who would have fought the most valiant fight. They walked toward freedom, the Poles, the German anti-Nazis, the Austrians. We women stood alongside the road and saw them come. We embraced them. One day someone said to me in a surprised and incredulous voice, "Gisa, is this you?" It was James whom I knew from the days of my youth.

The Austrian poet, Luitpold Stern, was with us during those days in Montauban. He suffered like all of us, but kept his poetry alive. He got permission to go to the library in the Ingres Museum which was closed during war time. In the evening he read to us his beautiful and courageous poem of Campanella. He helped me to save my own poems. We prepared a metal box into which we were prepared to place them and bury them should it become necessary.

The news got worse. De Gaulle spoke over the radio. It was good to know that somebody kept the resistance alive. The news about Dunkirk that shook the world was good news for us, too, but tinged with bitterness. Refugees, mostly Poles and Germans who had been attached to the English armies in France were abandoned by the English just as the French had abandoned those attached to them. Dunkirk saved the English soldiers but those of another nationality who had fought with the British forces were left behind. They told with bitterness how they woke up one morning and saw that the tents of the English soldiers had been removed.

The last poem I wrote in the German language was written in a night full of despair.

Der Traum

Ich bin von einem Schrei
laut stöhnend aufgewacht.
Ein tiefer Schrecken
und ringsum war Nacht.

Da war der Traum:
Noch floss ganz sanft der Strom,
die Brücke schwang und
ernsthaft stand der Dom.

Und Boote schwammen,
Menschen, Bäume, Wagen
Vom Wasser wie vom
festen Grund getragen.

Ein Rosenzweig
hing über'm Wasser dort,
ich wollt' ihn greifen,
doch es trug ihn fort.

Der Himmel wurde dunkler,
schwer vom dumpfen Drohn,
im Fluss erstand

ein singend grauser Ton.

Der Fluss wild reissend—
Wirbel sah ich drehn,
Nichts auf der weiten Fläche
konnte aufrecht stehn.

Da fielen Bäume,
schrien Kinder, Frauen,
Ich schloss die Augen,
wollt nichts hören, schauen...

Doch unter mir auch
schwankt es,
und der Wagen, der mich bisher
so sicher gut getragen,

er fällt—
schon spüre ich die kalte Flut—
ich sehe Freunde:
"Habt noch Mut, habt Mut."

Doch beim Erwachen
gellt ein böses Wort:
"Der Strom
reisst euch doch alle mit sich fort."

Montauban, August 1940

Translation:

The Dream

I was awakened by a scream
loud groaning
in deep terror

and around me the night.

There was the dream:
Still gently flowing the stream
the bridge swinging and
solemnly standing the cathedral,

And boats floating,
Men, trees, wagons,
carried by the water
as by solid ground.

A rose branch
hanging above the water
I wanted to seize it
but it was carried away.

The sky turned darker
heavy with a stifling threat.
In the river grew
a singing, dreadful tone.

It flowed wildly tearing,
whirlpools circling,
Nothing on the wide surface
could remain erect.

Trees were falling,
children, women crying,
I closed my eyes,
did not want to hear or look...

Yet even below me
it trembled
and the wagon, that up to now
had carried me safely and well

It wavers—
already I begin to feel the cold stream—
I see friends:
"Have courage, have courage."

Yet in awaking
yells an evil word:
"The stream
will yet carry all of you with him."

Chapter Twenty-One

Paul's Story

*T*here was no sign of Paul during all this time. A letter obviously written shortly after I had left Paris, was brought to me by a refugee, but he did not know where he was. I have the letter:

> My dear, very dear Gisa:
>
> Since your last card with the sad news of Ruth's death, I have not heard from you anymore. Since then more than two weeks have passed, and I am very worried. I hope that you are still all right. But perhaps you have written to me and the mail is on the way. Especially, since I have changed my camp twice, this is very possible. Three days ago I passed Lyon; you have known this town for years, and have lived there with the family of Mr. X for a long time, while I lived in Paris. Strange fate, now I am here in the south and you in the north. We passed through the beautiful Rhone Valley. The harbor of Marseille with its many ships reminded me of my home-town Hamburg very

much. All of us were supposed to be shipped to Algeria, but because of Italy's sudden declaration of war against the Allies, the transport was temporarily canceled.

Dearest, you know that at the present time everything is confused and it is impossible for conditions to be normal anywhere. I think very often of the many people who had to flee the enemy overnight! The cursed Hitler! And now there is Mussolini, too, who quickly wants to grab something. Right now it almost looks as if the U.S.A. will actively give aid to the Allies. Let's hope so! The Germans and the Italians must not win the war!

Don't worry about me, dearest! You know, that I am strong and healthy and, therefore, will be able to take it. Yes, I have confidence in our future. Your letter at that time: "We know this kind of life and its cruelties from past experiences" and your calm and your courage give me the assurance that you will survive everything, if humanly possible. I believe, and I feel it, too, that our great pain and the loss of our beloved Ruth will not break you. Did they let you know from London how Ruth's accident happened? And how is your dear mother? What are you doing now? Have you been evacuated? Surely, these arrangements have been made for you. Are Yvette and her little Marianne leaving too? Oh, dearest, I would like to ask you a thousand questions, would like to know so much. You know me.

Inwardly I have the strong feeling that we will see each other again sometime, that both of us will survive all the horror. It is strange, but true. But in spite of everything, I want you to know: In case you should not be anymore and I should never see you again, I will take all my strength and courage to continue our work, to create conditions worthy of humanity. There is nothing more wonderful, than to realize this mission, to live for it. I believe that you have the same strength in you. That you, too, should I not be anymore, continue living like this.

You dear, sweet Gisa, think of our deep love, of our great happiness, to be everything to each other. This will let us forget many a terribly sad hour and give back meaning to our lives.

This war is bringing so many changes with it. It is possible that we may not hear from each other for a long time (months). Count on this and let us keep faith in each other. (I hope this letter will still reach you.)

I am always with you and kiss you dearly.

Yours, Paul

The whole company in which Paul was, was "lost." I was haunted by strange superstitions. I remember, for instance, one day leaving a wooden finger ring, my "wedding ring" Paul had made for me, on a table. A dog jumped up and grabbed it. At that moment I said, "I know Paul is dead."

Yet one morning I woke up with Till Ulenspeegel's happy song in my ears: "Life I wrote on my banner, to live in the light. My first skin is made out of leather, but my second is made out of steel." I felt elated and happy that morning. As usual, Erna and I walked to the post office, always hoping that there would be some news. The post office was a "mecca" for all the refugee women.

There could be mail or perhaps one could see the husband or friend on the road. That morning when I asked for mail the employee offered me a telegram! The last telegram I had received was the one that bore the news of Ruth's death. I trembled when I opened it. My eyes swam. There it said, "I found Paul." An address was given and the date of Paul's arrival in Montauban.

Now we were together again. It was a miracle. Paul looked thin and weary, but I could feel that all his old strength had come back to him. It had done him good to get away from the crowd. When he was alone, he felt his strength.

Here is Paul's story in his own words the way he told it later when he was in this country:

1. THE TRAGIC DAYS

It was at the end of May when I wrote to my fiancée in Paris that the fall of Paris seemed to be close at hand. The German troops had crossed the Somme. There was no hope for serious resistance before Paris. The French General-Staff had declared Paris an open city. All troops had been withdrawn. The Seine would have offered a natural defense-line if the army would have chosen to fight it out. But the army retreated "in order."

June 11th the German army occupied Paris without a shot. I was working at this time forty-four miles south of Paris near Orleans. We were building a huge prisoners' camp for the German prisoners which were expected to be sent soon from the fronts. We had arrived three days ago. The air raid alarm sounded, the anti-air guns roared. German planes had bombed Orleans. Their objectives had been the railroad and the highway to Paris. We continued to build barracks during the morning after the raid. At noon we received the order to pack, as we would leave in two hours. We boarded five busses and travelled back through many small villages until we reached our old camp in Montargie. Here, all those who stayed while we went to Orleans, had already boarded a train. At eleven at night, we also boarded the same train, two hundred of us. The doors were locked and we departed. Nobody knew where we were going. The entire Refugee Camp (Germans and Austrians) and other Prestataires (refugees from the Nazi-conquered nations such as Czechs, Belgians, Poles) were on that train. Noon the next day we arrived in Marseille. Other trains with refugees working for the French army were in the station. Also many trains with French troops, many colonials, among them. We heard that we would be shipped to Africa. This plan was abolished by the French government after Italy had entered the war. They refused to take the responsibility. The government then was in Bordeaux, to where it had escaped from Paris. After two days we were brought into a camp in Miele near Marseille.

Little and contradictory news came from the front. The situation became very dangerous for German political refugees. Something had to be done. We organized a committee consisting of our best people and asked them to discuss with the Commander the possibility of our being transported to a less dangerous zone.

We were threatened from the north by Germany and from the east by Italian troops. After three days of futile discussions, we decided rather to rebel and risk being shot by French mobile-guards, than to fall into the hands of the Nazi. So the next morning, we stayed in the yard and yelled for the commander who had been invisible for quite a few days. The French guards retreated. Then the news came that those who wanted to go should be ready with only the necessary baggage. There were discussions with the commanding general in Marseille about our transport. He sent the order to send us away at noon the next day.

We left. It was like a ghost-train. Nobody knew where we were going. The few guards were glad to get away with us. They did not dare to lock the doors anymore. We travelled six days with provisions for two days and without any possibility to wash, towards the Pyrenean. Then the news arrived that the German authorities had made an agreement with Spain to occupy the border and that nobody could cross anymore. So we travelled back. We went the same way which we had come. The French officers who accompanied us tried to get food and lodging for us. But no town had sufficient provisions for all of us except one small meal (tinned sausage or tinned fish and bread).

The officers did not see a way out and said to us: "Débrouillez-vous" meaning "scram." So I scrammed with three friends into an uncertain liberty. We knew very little French.

2. WITHOUT PAPERS ON THE ROAD

After a night in the fields, we separated. I stood alone on the road, no passport or any other papers; everything had been left somewhere with the Commander in Orleans. I was told that only three weeks after I had left our camp in Orleans, the Germans used it and all other camps, to house their French prisoners. There was no stable government in France anymore. The highways were crowded with refugees from northern France and from Belgium. The small communities in southern France were full of them. Only the most important bridges and highways were guarded by French troops.

Small garrisons of troops were waiting in the villages in order to be released and sent home. The armistice had been signed. One demand in the armistice was that no French commander of any refugee-camp, was permitted to release the refugees unless he submitted the names to the German Commission. We knew only too well what that meant. The Gestapo was looking for victims.

I had in my pocket a small typewritten piece of paper. It said: "Military and civilian authorities are asked to assist the owner of this paper." It was not signed and did not bear a stamp. The French officers did not dare to sign it, as it would have violated the armistice. But on the paper was a photo of me and a certificate signed by a police commissioner that I was a German refugee loyal to France. This paper, insufficient as it was, helped me considerably on my long journey.

I had made up my mind to walk to a person 330 miles away who would most likely be able to tell me what had happened to Gisa and my friends, all refugees, who had stayed in Paris. I turned towards a place 80 miles from Bordeaux. It was a hot day in July. My fare was old, dry bread which I had saved for an emergency ration and green hard grapes which I took from the vineyards. They helped to quench my thirst. The highways were not crowded anymore. Everybody waited for further decisions. Only a few trucks passed, mostly military vehicles which had taken over the food transports. First I was afraid of the open roads. I may meet French Fascists, of which there were many in the army and especially in the guard mobile. I had 18 francs in my pocket, which would last me three days for a normal supply of food. I slept in the field and walked country roads next to the highways in order to avoid being discovered. But finally I had to cross a river and the bridge was guarded by police. I gathered my composure and walked leisurely towards them. It was noon. The guard asked me for my pass as they were looking for deserters. He read it and miraculously did not object. I had crossed the bridge back to civilization. I knew now that I could risk to march the highways. Three hundred miles were in front of me. At night I asked a small farmer for lodging. I showed him my precious papers. He gave me supper, some money and put me up in the barn, after he had made sure that I did not smoke. With new strength I marched on.

3. A PROPOSAL ON THE HIGHWAY

The sun was hot. I perspired. My knapsack, about sixty pounds with all I owned on this earth, became a burden. I had decided to throw things away only in case an emergency or to barter them for food. There were some garments and shoes in it, and I expected that there would soon be a shortage. (Two months later rationing started for garments and shoes and foreigners like myself did not receive ration cards.)

I was four miles out of the last village and had to walk 5-1/2 miles to the next one. A young woman, about 25 years old, in a peasant dress, comes on a bicycle loaded with a basket. She greeted me kindly. And away she went. It was a good experience to be greeted so smilingly after all the bitter days.

Five minutes had passed. I hear in back of me a bicycle. The friendly woman was back. She descended from her bicycle and said again: "Bonjour, Monsieur." I did not know what to say. She asked me where I came from and where I was heading. Then she started to talk. She was a Belgian refugee. Her father and she had bought a farm here and intended to stay. Her mother had been killed in Belgium by a bomb. And then she asked me of all things whether I would not like to get married to her. I would have a good life with her, she asserted. I was embarrassed. Not only was it the first proposal I had received, but that it happened on a French highway out of the skies! War creates strange things. I stammered my regret. I told her I had a girl, that I had not seen her since two months ago and even did not know where she was and whether she was alive. She apologized, told me how sad it was for her and how much she enjoyed having met me, and that I had to know what I wanted.

Smiling, she climbed on the bicycle and departed. I finally re-
gained my composure. I mused that maybe a carefree future
departed with her. But I did not feel regrets. I was too eager to
learn about my friends.

4. THE HELPFUL FRENCH

The next evening I passed the guard near a large village. It
was 8 o'clock. On the bridge of the creek stood an old guard and
three soldiers. On the stone fence of the bridge sat a tired-looking
thin man in a corduroy suit who had a small pack on his side. He
looked frightened. I greeted them and intended to walk on.

The guard said: "Hallo, where are you heading at this hour
of the day?"

I told him the name of the next village.

He exclaimed: "What, thirteen miles more? Through the
night? Come here."

I became frightened.

He said: "Do you have papers?"

"Certainly," was my answer.

He read them and asked for my final goal. After I told him,
he said: "But that is 230 miles. You walk? That is not possible!"

When I told him that I had already come from N., he became
very excited.

"Yes, this morning."

"You mean this morning?"

"Yes."

"How much money do you have?"

"Francs 9.75."

"What, only 9.75?"

"How can anybody let you run around like that?" He turned to
the soldiers very upset. "You stay here tonight" he said, "and
first you eat." He pointed to the tired man. "He is also a refugee;
he comes from Spain. He wants to go to Marseille."

I looked at the feet of the Spaniard. He could not speak
French at all and looked pitiful, thoroughly frightened. His feet

were full of blisters. He had on sneakers and no socks. I put my knapsack down and asked for a pail. I went to the creek and filled it and washed the man's feet. Then I pricked the blisters and took ointment and cotton from my first-aid kit. The soldiers were much surprised. Soon his feet were bandaged. The Spaniard still looked shy and frightened, but in his look was also gratitude.

The guard said to the soldiers: "Look, he himself is out of luck but he does his good deed for others. Now I'll go and fetch him something to eat."

The Spaniard had received a meal before I arrived. I was sitting on a bench when after ten minutes the guard returned with a plate full of potatoes, meat and cheese. From the next farm came a woman, about fifty years old, with a bottle of wine.

She said, "Monsieurs, drink this wine." She was dressed in black, her face very ashen and sunken. On her breast she wore a cross.

The guard talked to her saying it was outrageous that these poor refugees who had helped to preserve the freedom of France were now sent without anything to live on, out into the roads. He told the woman who I was. The woman did not say a word, but her eyes seemed to rest in grief on us. She cried. Then she left.

She returned half an hour later. The Spaniard had spread himself in the hay and was sound asleep. The woman talked to the guard and gave him something. Then both came towards me, and the guard said: "Good news, boys; the woman wants to give you 30 francs," and he put them in front of me.

I jumped up and said: "Oh, no, I will not accept that." The guard yelled at me: "You have to take what this good woman is offering you!"

Then she spoke to me, her voice full of tears and her thoughts far away. "Please, take it. I do not know what to do with the money I have. I do not know anything about politics. That is men's work. But I know that you are hungry, that you have to go far and that you do not have a thing."

She turned away and walked towards her house. I was embarrassed and like a stone. I even did not thank her. The guard
then told me that she had the news two weeks ago that her husband had died on the battlefield. She also had left 30 francs for
the Spaniard.

He said in a rough voice: "I trust you with the 30 francs for
him. You give it to him in the morning. I guess you will do it, for
you bandaged him." Then he left.

He had given the order to the soldiers to stop in the morning
the truck for Marseille and put the Spaniard on it. He also had
wished me well. When I lay down in the hay next to the
Spaniard, he awoke and I gave him the money. I told him that it
came from the woman, but I am afraid he did not understand. The
soldiers put him on the truck the next morning at six o'clock. He
intended to find a boat in Marseille and go over to Africa. When
he was sitting on the truck, he lost for the first time his
frightened look.

He said very softly to me, "Comrade." He waved at me. I
walked in the opposite direction.

5.   THE VILLAGE AND ITS MAYOR

A few days later, it rained. The sky was dark, the air full of
humidity, and dark came sooner than usual. I entered a village of
about 500 people and a company of soldiers. I asked for lodging in
one farm house, for it was too wet to sleep outside. The peasant
woman told me that all available places had been given to the
soldiers and that I should try at the quarter-master's office. She
asked her 12-year old daughter to lead me there. So I could not
avoid going there. Again I tried the straight approach. Later I
discovered that the office of the quarter-master was also the
sheriff's office. All soldiers and the villagers were assembled
there. Higher officers had just arrived for an inspection. They
talked with the mayor. The little girl introduced me to one of the
sheriff's aides and told him what I wanted. He asked for papers,
where I came from and where I wanted to go. A crowd gathered

around me. Against my will I became the center of attention. They wanted to know about the front and how it was in Paris. One of the soldiers was from Mont Parnasse.

I felt embarrassed, my French is so poor. The sheriff's aide had my papers. After half an hour, the officer came outside. The sheriff's aide gave my papers to one of the officers. He read them and turned them back. He was not interested. He climbed into his car and departed. The sheriff's aide called a name. Somebody appeared. He talked to him and left. Somebody told me that that was the mayor. It was dark and the street lamp threw a dim light. The sheriff's aide told me to wait and went inside. The villagers and soldiers pressed me for more news. After half an hour the sheriff's aide came back. I received my papers back.

A young soldier volunteered, "I will bring him there." I did not know what it was all about. Where would they lead me? Was the situation good or bad? Soon I knew. The soldier told me that he would bring me to the house of the mayor. I should not be frightened, everything was all right. We were standing in front of a gate leading into a garden.

Somebody called, "Come in."

The mayor came towards us, introduced himself and led me towards a garden table where I had to take off my knapsack. The table was set.

The mayor called a name and a woman appeared with a plate and a glass. It was his wife. Then I ate. Fried potatoes, fried eggs, lettuce, wine and coffee. It was a kingly meal. The young soldier was his son. He just had returned from the Somme. The second son had been in the Maginot Line but had fled to Switzerland where he had been interned. The mayor himself told me that he had been a prisoner for three years in Germany during World War I. It had not been bad at all; he had worked with a German peasant who liked him and vice versa. He understood my predicament and advised me not to try to stay in towns or large villages as the authorities there frequently were very reactionary and might put me back into a camp in order to conform to the German orders. He himself was a Socialist and

knew well why France collapsed so suddenly. I had to be careful.
It was so heartening to listen to a human being in this wilderness
of chaos. After an hour of good talk he told me he did not know
where he could put me up. The army had control of everything.
There was a possibility of a barn which served as a village
prison. He emphasized that I would, of course, not be considered a
prisoner but just as a guest for the night. I accepted and we went.

6. THE LUSTY PRISON

The barn was at the main street opposite the tavern. There
were two rooms with doors toward the street. Most likely they
have been the home of the horses of the village stage-coach. In
front of one door stood a soldier as guard. A padlock protected the
door. The mayor tried the padlock of the other door. He could not
open it. It was rusty and did not open. What was there to do? He
talked to the guard and then said that I could stay in the
military prison next door. The soldiers were there as prisoners.
That room had to stay locked. But I could leave whenever I chose
to do so as I would not be considered a prisoner. I accepted this
suggestion. The guard opened the door. The mayor asked when I
wanted to get up. I said at six o'clock. He said that coffee would
be ready at seven. He bade me goodbye and shook my hand. I
discovered that he had slipped five francs into my hand.

In the room there was a very large wooden board which
served as a bed. It was covered with straw. The soldiers were sitting there, well provided with wine and quite lusty. One lighted
the candle and asked me what I was in for.

I said, "For nothing. I only board here for the night." At that
they laughed heartily. "Be comfortable," they said and gave me
the space between them.

Then they started to talk. They gave me their canteen filled
with red wine and asked me to suit myself. They had a lot of
wine and could get more. What were their "crimes"? They had
left the village for a few days and had gone to the next town;
there their wives were living as evacuées. The military police

caught up with them and they got fourteen days. They repeated after each sentence: "je m'en fou." ("What do I care?") Then one said that his wife was staying with a farmer in the village and was expecting him tonight. He would leave the prison at midnight and would be back at 4 o'clock. I was not surprised. The same things happened frequently when I was in camp.

There was a knock. A voice said, "Hey you, your wife wants to know whether you will be there."

"Yes," he answered, "I will be there right after midnight." We went on talking. After half an hour, he said, "Hey, will you do something for me?"

"Sure, what?"

"See, after midnight there is no officers' control here anymore. But should I leave my little Jeanne alone till midnight? She is so frightened here. She is from Lille, you know. And it was so hard to get her to come here. I have a splendid idea."

I guessed what he wanted but I played dumb.

"You take my coat and wrap yourself into it and you sleep with your face covered. When the officer checks on me—but he is drunk—he probably will not check. (That was to assure me, as I knew at once.) Then I could leave now and my little Jeanne hasn't to wait. Maybe otherwise she will leave. Will you do it?"

"All right," I said, "but I will be asleep and will not know about anything." He embraced me, told me he would bring in morning coffee and chocolate to me and said, "Bon comarade."

He knocked at the door and told the guard to let him out. The guard told him that the sergeant had taken the key and put it into the office. He was sent to the sergeant but did not find him. Outside a few soldiers were standing. The husband meanwhile investigated the lock and found that he only had to loosen two screws from the inside and the door would open. He asked for pliers. They pushed it under the door. Off went the bird. I had to fasten the screws again and hide the pliers.

The other soldier was already snoring. I wrapped myself in the soldier's coat and fell asleep. I heard noises at the lock. I heard the officer complain about the lock. Finally he opened it. I started to snore. He turned on a flashlight and then left. I returned to sleep. Then a knock. I answered. It was the bird back again. It was five o'clock. I unscrewed the door again. He brought me two squares of chocolate. He was happy. He regretted only that I was leaving this morning, as his wife would stay in the village. She was too afraid alone in the town.

At six on the dot, I was awakened. I went into the street and washed my face in a pail of water. I was led to the school where soldiers were quartered and I got coffee and sandwiches. The soldier whom I understudied had told me before I left that I could come to his place anytime; they always had room and food for me. But I had to walk towards uncertainty.

7. A MIRACULOUS COINCIDENCE

Two days later, I was lying under a tree. I had been very lucky. A milk truck had taken me forty miles; that is the equivalent of two and a half days of walking. I ate my lunch, bread, an apple and water. No human being, no house in sight. There was peace all around. No sign of war anywhere. I thought of my friends in Paris, my girl. She had gone through so many things during the last years and still she was young. She had been in prison, in a concentration camp and finally had to escape. Where was she? Where were my other friends? Where were the three from whom I separated after we left camp? Perhaps some of them were safe. Perhaps they were in another country now, where there was still freedom and no Gestapo.

I stopped thinking. I had to stay hard, not become sentimental. I had a goal; I had to see a Frenchman, still 130 miles away. He might know and tell me; if he was not there, I had further plans. I wanted to try to pass illegally through Spain into Portugal. The fight for freedom was not yet over. I had to go on.

I got up, took my knapsack and marched on. It is a big help to have a definite goal in these hopeless times. There were many farms around now. I crossed a bridge but the soldiers who guarded it only looked at me. They did not ask for papers. There a bus to

Toulouse passed by. If I had some money, I would have taken it; I had to let it pass.

Towards me came a bicycle rider, like a racer he appeared. He was about 100 yards away. But, for heaven's sake, don't I know this figure and these movements? Certainly, I could not believe it, but it was he. An old friend of mine! He came nearer; he did not recognize me. Was he dreaming?

I called out: "René!"

He looked at me and called: "Paul, boy!"

I was the first of the four who left camp together to arrive. René knew about my friends in Paris and he knew about Gisa. A few days later I joined all of them in a small town in southern France. What luck! What joy! What reunion!

If I had not met René, my fate would have been very uncertain. The Frenchman did not live in Toulouse anymore. My road would have led through the town where my friends stayed, but who knows, I may have passed it without meeting any of them."

Chapter Twenty-Two

Refugee in Southern France

The situation in France was becoming more and more serious. The Nazi terror increased in northern France. Many French were shot when they were found resisting the Nazis. We saw the first Nazi troops in the streets of southern France in spite of its being the so-called "free zone." When we heard the first German words spoken in the streets of France, our blood turned to ice. It was as if the language itself conveyed the terror. The Germans had their troops everywhere and they were looting the country almost to death. Soon there was practically no food in southern France.

German anti-Nazis were constantly searched for by the invaders. When they were found, they were shipped back to Germany or killed instantly. The borders were tightly closed.

It became evident that all of us would have to go into hiding for a long time. Montauban was surrounded by small farming communities. Some of their courageous mayors—farmers themselves—understood the situation and were willing to risk their necks by taking in German and Austrian refugees. Montauban itself could not keep all of them.

We, Paul and I, found such a mayor who was willing to let us stay in his village if we agreed to pretend to be Belgian. This was not too difficult since my French was good. Paul (with his knowledge of low German) could be of Flemish origin. We rode 5 hours by bicycle to the little village. The road was mountainous. It started to rain and the pavement was slippery. My hand brake failed. I lost control of the bicycle riding down a steep hill. Paul later told me that I cried out loud, but I did not know this. A soft wheat field cushioned the fall and we continued....

It became very hot. I could hardly breathe, pedaling uphill. Yet, there was Paul's strong hand on the back of the saddle, pushing me while he himself worked hard to get up the mountain.

We came to a shady fig tree, the first one I had ever seen. It greeted us from a hill like a symbol of refuge and peace. It stood at the entrance to the village. We rested awhile overlooking Lavit, the little place which was to give us shelter for a long time. There it lay, one street and the square market place with a water pump on one side.

The village was full of Belgian refugees. One day of each month they had to present themselves to the mayor to get ration cards. This was such a day, chosen for our arrival so that we went unnoticed among the crowd. The mayor made out our récipissé (credentials) with a Belgian name and then said to us, "From now on you are Monsieur and Madam X. and forget everything else." He offered us a little room inside an abandoned stable as living quarters. To enter it, we had to crawl through a small opening that had been used by animals. The room was clean enough, although apparently unused for a long time. At night noisy rats played hide and seek above us. One night they seemed closer. Paul got up to find out what was happening. I admonished him to kill any rat that would get at the only food we had, some bread and milk.

He was very quiet at first when he came back, and then he said with some embarrassment, "Oh, it was just a little mouse. When I directed the beam of my flashlight at the milk jug, it just sat there and looked at me with its shiny black eyes. It looked so scared. I had to think of my mice friends in prison and I could not kill it."

Our food consisted almost exclusively of dry bread and milk. I tried to heat the milk in the evening so as to have something warm in our stomachs. We had no fuel. I used a little hay I found to make an open fire and held a pot with milk over it. The blackberries ripened along the roads. We ate them morning, noon, and night, squashed on bread in the morning, whole with a little milk at noon, and squashed in the evening. (Paul never wanted to eat a blackberry again in his life.) Once, a boy appeared at our stable announcing that the mayor had sent him. All Belgian refugees could get some food sent from the United States. It was five pounds of bacon fat, and two pounds of dried prunes. It was heaven to get this! We saved the fat for months, eating as little as possible of it at each time. We spread it on bread and—when we could get an egg—we fried it! We rationed the prunes carefully to have something different from blackberries every other day.

In the beginning of our stay in the village we kept ourselves isolated, being afraid to talk to people. We did not know them and did not know their feelings and their attitudes. But slowly, this began to change. There was, for instance, the farm woman across the street. She had seen me knitting a pair of underpants. She admired my skill, bought some wool and asked me whether I could knit some warm pants for her. Wool was scarce at the time and there was no choice of color. The farm woman soon wore bright red underpants while mine were light green, but they kept us warm in winter.

There were not many men in the village, almost all the men were taken prisoners by the Germans. Labor was needed. Paul had no permit to work, so he did not dare ask for it. But soon the villagers discovered his skills. They saw him make soles for our broken down shoes from old automobile tires he found on the dump heap. The farmers wore wooden shoes, but they liked to have rubber soles for them. They asked whether he could fix their shoes for them and soon he became the "master shoemaker." Nobody paid in cash, but we began to get eggs and potatoes. Soon we could share those with friends in Montauban to whom potatoes were welcome riches. In a neighboring village lived another refugee couple who were in the same situation as we were. A close friendship developed between us and we exchanged what goods and skills we had. Paul began to learn more French, because the farmers were kind and no one made fun of him for the way he talked. We became more and more a part of village life. It seemed as if the war was far away.

I watched "grandma" doing the laundry in a way it had been done for centuries. She took the huge bed sheets and soaked them for a whole week in a big tub under which a tiny fire was made. She had a piece of cloth stretched across this tub and she covered it constantly with clean birchwood ashes. Then she slowly poured hot water over them. After that week she put the sheets into a wheelbarrow and went to the village pond. There they were scrubbed and beaten. The wash then was wheeled back, put into pails and well water was used to rinse off the dirt from the pond. Finally the laundry was spread out in the sun. I myself did not have so much washing to do. My whole wardrobe consisted of one skirt, two blouses and a nightgown that began to fall apart and that I had to sew constantly. Paul had also very little. Lack of clothing disturbed us less than the lack of soap. We had brought from Paris one piece of good soap, but it was used only for special occasions. We had to "make do" with soapcakes which seemed to be made of sand.

We became friends of old "Milus Dios." He was called this because of his constant swearing in the southern patois. His swearing was kind. It was his language, his way of talking to his cattle. We spent wonderful evenings with him sitting in his room filled with the smell of garlic cloves warmed in a big pan over the open hearth fire. We heard him talk about the glory of France. To him this glory would be revived some day, there was no question about it. When Milus Dios said, "We stormed the Bastille, we will again do away with the suppressors," it seemed as if he had been one of those who stormed the Bastille and we could believe him.

In the fall the mayor offered to allow us to move into an abandoned house. It was quite broken down, no glass panes in the windows. We found old sacks and placed them over the openings to keep out the cold wind. Yet this was better than the stable, and we became more a part of the village community. Milus Dios promised us fondly to help us plant a garden the coming spring. During the wine harvest we worked hard in the fields and the farmers were grateful for our help. The grapes were beautiful and one could eat as many as one wished. We were not paid, but for the first time we ate complete and warm meals. It felt so good eating the delicious chicken dinners at the farmers tables, and feeling part of this life. The farmers gave us grapes to take home. We learned to put them into a paper bag and hang them on a string, to keep them for many weeks without spoilage. We watched the men making the grapes into wine, trampling on them and—to our surprise—jumping into the big barrels, standing in the wine juice up to their waists.

This was almost an idyllic time. For the first time in years we were together, in an almost "normal" life. I wrote in the soft French summer:

Abend

Nun wird es still um uns
Und all das laute Treiben
sinkt weit ins Dunkel leise jetzt herab.
Es ist, als ob von allem nur wir beide bleiben
Und alles Schwere fällt leicht von uns ab.

Jetzt wird es dunkel...
Und ich kann nicht sehen
die Züge Deines lieben Angesichts,

ich höre leise nur den Atem gehen,
und Deinen Mund, der gute Worte spricht.

Und wie Musik umtönt es uns,
Erfüllt uns tief mit beben...
Belädt uns mit so köstlich froher Last...
Ach, Liebster, herrlich, herrlich ist das Leben,
Und wenn es auch nur diesen Tag umfasst.

Translation:

Evening

Now it is quiet around us
and all the busy bustle
sinks far and softly into the dark.
It is as if only we two are left
and all sorrow falls off our shoulders.

Now evening falls...
I cannot see
the lines of your beloved face,
I only hear softly your breathing
and see your mouth which can speak such good words.

Around us it is like music,
filling us deeply with joy,
loading us with precious happiness.
Oh, my love, life is so wonderful
even if it has only this one day.

The Germans called on all Belgians to return to their country. Many followed this call. We certainly had to stay and we became more conspicuous because of this. After awhile only we and an older Belgian refugee, who rarely spoke, remained. One day the grocery woman, a kind person who kept her business going with the help of her daughter and her ten-year-old grandchild, while her son-in-law was a prisoner in Germany, invited us to listen to her radio. When Paul and I went there in the evening, this other refugee was also present. When he greeted us, we recognized that his French, too, had a strange accent, a strongly British one. As an English citizen he was as much in danger as we were—therefore his disguise as Belgian refugee. Bad news came over the radio. The Germans contemplated movement into the unoccupied zone. Many people of German origin, found in France, had been arrested. We recognized several names. I gasped when I heard them, then checked myself, remembering that I was supposed to be a Belgian. I felt the eyes of the grocery woman on me, but she said nothing. Listening together to the clandestine radio produced a strong bond between us. Nothing needed to be said.

It became more and more clear that we had to resign ourselves to staying in France for the duration of the war, perhaps longer. Work had to be found. We could not always live on these odd jobs that we were doing. This could be done during the summer, but with winter approaching some provision for fuel and warm clothing became necessary. Wood cutters were needed. Aliens usually got work permits if they were willing to become wood cutters. Paul, who felt he was strong and healthy, wanted to do this. But he needed working papers in his real name.

We bicycled through the woods to one of the farmers who lived some distance away. He needed a wood cutter. He was a man we had once seen on the market place when the farmers from nearby communities came to buy. He had a good and intelligent face. He was lame and could not walk well. When we arrived, the farmer was in the woods cutting some branches. We asked whether he would hire Paul. He was very happy to, because he needed someone badly and had heard how skilled Paul was. We discussed wages and hours, and he was ready to go into the house to sign the contract.

He asked, "Oh, yes, by the way, what is your name?"
This was the crucial moment. Since I spoke better French than Paul, I spoke up and said, "Monsieur, you now have us in your

hands and you can deliver us to the German police. We are not Belgian refugees as we are known in the village, and our name is not the name under which we are known. We are German anti-Nazi refugees. My husband has fought on the side of the French Army as a Prestataire, but we had to hide here after the defeat of France. Do you still want to have him as a wood cutter?"

He said nothing for a moment, and we waited. A beautiful smile appeared on his face. He looked up and said, "We are brothers, aren't we? We have fought the same enemy. We are still fighting it. Don't worry." He pointed to his lame leg. "It was a German bullet that did this in World War I, and it was a German bullet that killed my brother. But I know it is not the question of Germany, of France, it is the question of Kaisers and Dictators and we fight them, not the individual Germans."

We walked together into his house. He nodded to us and said that he would not tell anyone and he would address Paul by his assumed Belgian name, but, "My wife has to know about it. She is part of all this."

After he had explained the situation to his wife, she shook hands with us and said quietly, "Together we will help make France and the world free again."

From then on Paul worked as a wood cutter. It was not easy work. It was not easy in summer, but it was especially hard work in winter. The winter was cold and we had only poor clothing and no gloves. His hands froze. The skin cracked and bled. Every evening I wrapped some old rags we had found in the house around Paul's hands. Every day when he left I soaked the bloody bandages in cold water so that we could use them again.

I had a little stove in the house. We were very fortunate now that Paul had become a wood cutter. He brought home odds and ends of wood. I could make a fire and I usually had a pot of water boiling on the stove. The hot water was something very precious and helped a bit over the lack of soap. We missed real soap. Like the other farm women I did my cleaning with cold water that I got from the pump a short distance away. I carried heavy pails of water that froze before I could reach the house.

There was a constant stream of refugees coming from the northern part of France. They could not remain in the village, but we served as a kind of underground railroad station. They would stop on their way to a final hiding place. There was always room in our bed (we were at times 4 or 5 people in it) and some hot milk to warm up.

One raw winter day I heard someone crying outside our door. There was a little girl, sobs shaking her. When I asked her what was wrong, she was silent and looked frightened. I remembered that I had seen her with her parents next door, who kept very much to themselves. They were Spanish refugees. I gently made her understand that I knew who she was and she finally sobbed out her story: the teacher had told the children that in the afternoon she would check the feet of all the children to find out whether they were clean. But how could she have clean feet? She would be punished! I looked at her feet. Her shoes had big holes cut into them so the toes could stick out. This had to be done because they were too short for her and there was no money with which to buy new shoes. She had no socks and her feet could not avoid the muddy road. They had no soap in the house! She also could not get into their house because it was locked. Her father was working as a wood cutter and her mother went from one place to another to help with some sewing. Spanish refugees were in the worst situation in southern France. Most of them were so mutilated that they could not work. They were dependent on the little help they got from the American Friends Service, the Quakers. This was the only group in the world that cared about them. French authorities were too afraid to lose their good relationship with Franco-Spain to do anything for them. Many of the Spanish refugees lived in camps of the worst kind. This family was fortunate that they were together as a family and that they could do some work, but they were very poor.

I asked little Marie-Thérèse, whether she would mind coming into the house. I would not hurt her, and I could help her get clean. She came in slowly, this beautiful little six-year-old, dressed in rags. Carefully I undressed her, letting her stand close to the warm stove. She stopped crying and her big dark eyes grew more quiet. I wrapped a towel around her, warmed at the little wood stove. I poured our precious warm water into a basin and gave her a bath. Our "special occasion soap" came out of hiding. (Many, many years later, after the Nazis were defeated and we were in the United States, we sent our first package to Marie and her family. I will never forget the excited letter, and I will always cherish her comment, "You did remember the little girl to whom you gave a warm bath. I will never forget that." Now Marie is a happy mother of a little girl.) After "the bath" I searched among my few belongings for a pair of socks. I was usually knitting something from old wool yarn that people gave me. The socks were too big for her little feet, but it didn't matter because of the open shoes. We both were so happy! She could get to school with clean feet!

Marie and I became close friends. We did many things together. She learned how to cut out paper dolls which made up for all the toys this little girl could not have. I remember Christmas, when we visited with the family. Paul and I had saved our sugar ration which was distributed in lump sugar for several months. We had collected colored paper. We wrapped the lump sugar in this paper so that it looked like candy. We put the pieces into a little basket that I had made out of paper and on which Paul had drawn pictures. And they were topped by something very, very special: Two beautiful candy bees full of honey that a friend of ours had found in another village. The excitement of this little girl! She had almost forgotten how candy looked! I also had made a rag doll for her. She hugged and hugged that doll and then ran out of the house. Her mother looked after her. I wondered what had happened because Marie had looked as if she would cry. Her mother told me in her broken French that the doll probably had brought back harsh memories. When the Civil War broke out and the family had to leave its home, the child carried her doll with her. But the planes came, and killed many civilians.

The mother continued in a monotonous voice trying to hold back her emotions, "You can't imagine the blood running into the gutter! My child's hand lost the grip on the doll; it fell into this stream of blood. She cried out, but we could not let her fish it out, it was too horrible."

Christmas Eve we spent also with our beloved "Milus Dios," sitting at his fireplace with his family. The room was filled with the smell of garlic which Paul disliked, but which belonged to "Milus Dios" as did his swearing and his kind eyes. He talked again about the old times and about the freedom that would come to France just as freedom had once come at Christmas to people who were suppressed by the Romans. Late that evening we returned to our little house. There we gave each other our gifts. They meant so much to us! I had knitted gloves for Paul, gloves he needed so badly. I had written some poems for him, good or bad, but they expressed what I felt at this time. Paul had carved out of wood a little dish and had repaired my "wedding ring." And we were together!

The other refugee couple who lived in the nearby village visited us on Christmas Day. Amy had baked a cake! This was something very, very special! We drank the horrible coffee made of roasted Spanish peas and the fruit of the oak tree, and felt like kings.

The New Year, 1941, brought nothing new. We kept contact with the underground. We, in southern France, were of some help by distributing vital news and smuggling people out of France who were in danger. Worldly goods were shared among the refugees. We brought food into the town and we got some money if we needed it. With Paul doing the woodcutting, we were better off than before. Yet the shared poverty did not make us "good" all the time. Actually nerves were often on edge and lack of food made people easily irritated. There were petty jealousies. For instance, candles became scarce. Electricity and gas light had not been available for quite a while. We measured the pieces of candle that everybody could have. Accusations arose that somebody had cheated and had hidden a little piece of candle without telling about it. The conflict around this was out of proportion—one became petty and angry.

There was a funny incident around this lack of fuel. We had discovered that carbite could be used to lighten the dark evenings. A farmer had given us some pieces of carbite. Paul found an old carbite lamp in the dump and was fixing it one evening. When he tried it out, it exploded and we were plunged into darkness. Nobody said a word. Out of the silent darkness came my frightened voice, "Oh, Paul, are you dead?" No, he was not, he had been wondering why the lamp exploded.

Two important news flashes came to us around February. One was that the United States began to take interest in the fate of refugees in the war-stricken countries and that President Roosevelt had established a special committee which gave emergency visas to refugees in mortal danger. The other one was very disquieting. It appeared that more and more "commissions" of the Nazis appeared in southern France and the government of Pétain became more and more collaborator.

Danger of arrest grew and with it hopelessness. I saw this in Annie, a lovely 15-year-old Austrian girl who lived with her parents in Montauban. She was—as most of these youngsters—mature beyond her age, after having lived through so much hardship. Once, we walked together over the bridge spanning the yellow, churning Tarn river.

She looked down and said sadly, "You know I think that the best way for all of us would be to go down there. At least it would be a clean end. What is the use of all this?" And—in an outburst of despair—"I am an anti-Nazi as my parents are, but to the French girls I am an Austrian, and so I have no friends—what is life worth living for without friends?"

I am still haunted by the thought that I tried to give her hope. Our beautiful Annie died in a concentration camp after having been raped by Nazi soldiers. The river would have been a more merciful and "cleaner" end for her.

The only hope among all of us was the possibility that the United States would enter the war. I even dreamed one night that

I was back in the house where I grew up as a child: I was sent upstairs to call the neighbor to the telephone. I was very afraid to do this because I knew that upstairs were Nazi soldiers. Yet I had to go. I went upstairs, left the message and ran downstairs feeling the eyes of the Nazi soldiers on me. At the foot of the stairs stood a big man with kind eyes and somebody behind me said, "Oh, he just moved into the house. Now we are safe." I looked at the nameplate of the door where he stood. It read, "Potato-King Roosevelt." I woke up. Roosevelt's name meant to us help against fear and hunger.

A few U.S. visas finally arrived and a few refugees could leave for the United States. It was difficult to leave France. It was almost impossible to get a "visa de sortie," the permit to leave the country. Refugees had to illegally cross the rugged Pyrienees. This was a perilous trip. They did it, sometimes with small children on their backs.

We ourselves did not think that we would ever be among those who would get to the United States. We were resigned to stay in France for the rest of the war. We knew, though, that we would have to hide soon in a place where we were even less known. Underground workers of the labor union had made contact with some French people who had farms in southern France to arrange for isolated hideouts. We were to visit such a place to prepare for our disappearance if the situation became more dangerous. This was a farm belonging to two women in southern France. They needed tenant farmers. We felt a mixture of relief and resentment when we met those women in their home. They apparently were friendly to underground fighters, but at the same time they had selfishly hoarded food and other goods. There was no sign of deprivation as in the rest of France. There were big tubs of lard, grain, butter, soap, and balls of cloth. They had outwitted the Germans, but they kept all this for themselves, while others were dying from hunger.

We discussed the possibilities of becoming tenant farmers and I began to look forward to this life. I saw us as a farm couple surrounded by our children and enjoying the company of southern

French farmers we had learned to love. We were about to seal the agreement when the ladies decided that they had better first to check with the mayor of the village. Unfortunately, the mayor, though also hating the Nazis, was afraid to give active help to the underground by harboring foreigners. This shattered our hope for a farm existence in southern France. We returned to our village and decided that we would stay there as long as possible and see what the future would bring.

Chapter Twenty-Three

U.S. Visas Arrive

*I*t was early spring. "Milus Dios" had just given us seeds for a little garden in the back of the house, when one of the underground workers arrived informing us that my visa had arrived from the United States. I did not want to accept it. Paul and I had been together for almost a year. Now the ocean would come between us. Separation again! I saw no sense in this. I felt that I had run enough. There had been the day at the cemetery in Hamburg, when we had to separate because Paul had to leave; there had been the time when I had to go to Vienna to do underground work in Austria; there had been the flight to Paris, seeing Paul again, and then again separation because I could not get the permission to stay in Paris; there had been the outbreak of the war when we had lost each other. Finally we had succeeded in being together again. I did not want to leave him and did not want to leave the possibility of actively fighting the Nazis.

I did not want the visa! But Paul as well as other underground workers insisted on my accepting it. They argued that we had no right to let personal wishes interfere with what had to be done. In a world where there were so few people who fought for what we stood for, those who had convictions had to be alive to continue standing up for them. I had difficulties in accepting these arguments. It seemed to me that I would go into a country that was safe and comfortable while Paul and others were left behind. I was also afraid that my leaving might actually endanger Paul. While we had lived together we could pretend that we were Belgians because of the way I spoke French. What would happen when I left? What would the village say? Again it was Paul who had a simple answer. He discussed the problem with the farmer who knew who we really were.

This wonderful man said calmly, "This is a fight of life and death, and each has to fight it wherever he is. Don't worry, he will be safe here. We know who he is. If the Nazis come around, he will be safe with us and there will be nobody, but nobody, who will denounce him. Come, I will show you something."

This was the first time he showed us "the secret" of the village. He took us into the woods. Well hidden in the ground and under trees was enough food to take care of the whole village if a serious invasion should come. All of the villagers had prepared this together—and yet we had not known about it.

He said, "Look, there is room enough for one or two people to live down there, too. We have thought of the Englishman and you. We know what would happen to you and that you are in greater danger than any Frenchman is around here." He smiled at Paul and said, "You fought once with the French Army, and I do know that you are in contact with the French underground. So here you are—one of us."

He suggested we tell the grocery woman our particular situation. She was an underground worker. She was willing to spread anything we wanted to say officially about my leaving. She was "the village newspaper" and could influence opinions. We went to see her. We told her who we were.

She said quietly, "I knew."

We wondered whether the farmer had told her, but she shook her head and said, "No, you can be sure that any secret is safe with him."

The day we had listened to the radio, she had known. She also reassured me that Paul would be safe. She knew about the stored food and the hiding place: "You are one of us," was also her attitude. I wanted to stay even more after this, but she too urged me to go. She insisted that it was important for everybody to stay alive, and that it was important for people who had seen the situation in France to let the United States know that this was not just any war, but a fight for life or death of freedom. I felt humble, realizing what was expected of those of us who could go to safety. Later, after the war, letters came telling us more about the Nazi horrors. Here are two:

....However, in December 1944 Hans was still taken to Sachsenhausen (Concentration Camp) and there he was beaten half to death. In these six months he had to suffer more than I had to within two years. In one day he received 160 strokes (he was strapped to a block). He was beaten alternately by 2 men with a 4-1/2 x 6-foot long leathercase filled with lead slugs. Then he was put into a straight-jacket for one week and was deprived of food and drink and repeatedly awakened during the night to keep him from sleeping. Besides he was frequently offered saltwater...

Belsen.

I had seen the newsreel, and a padre who had come back to us earlier had said: "It is far, far worse than pictures can ever tell!" Naturally I did not want to see the place. Then a question was put to me and it seemed I would have to go, I still hesitated and it took me some time to make up my mind and go to see the survivors six weeks after their liberation. I could only spend a few hours, talking mainly to a Polish family, the Jewish doctor, his wife and several nurses. What I heard in these hours made me jump out of my sleep and I found myself wandering around the barrack room.

There the nurse, very pale in her white apron, was leaning against the wall and in an even, toneless voice she told of incidents as they came into her mind. The doctor sitting on the table, nervously moving his arms, scribbling something, getting up and running up and down the room, he interrupted and gave one or two other facts. His wife sat in the corner, silent and very recollected, she added some more information while she carried on mending a dress. Other nurses came in, confirmed an incident, added another and quickly disappeared. All of them had their prison-number tattooed in their arms.

"Belsen was a camp for women, you find here all nations, Jewish people, who had no right to live anymore, and most of them come from Poland.

"Yes, some babies have been born here, but a child is something so precious to us, that we would not wish to part with a single one, look, my wife here has given birth to a son, and I have killed him with my own hands. I did not want the SS to kill him. This was in a camp in Silesia where we were allowed to be together. You have no idea what they have done to our children. No, we want to keep every little child of our community, there are so few, so few who survived, and shall I be able to have a child again?

"I myself can't believe that I have gone through all this. Look: they have killed all the Jewish children in Poland, they have thrown them out of the windows, they have gassed and burned them by the hundreds, in one orphanage the SS man made the little children put their heads on the table and then they shot them with a pistol one by one. We have hidden our children wherever we could and when deportation came our women did not take any food, but in their rucksacks they put their little children of two, four and six years. And then a mother comes to me in Silesia with her 10-months old baby and asks me for an injection. I could not do it, she went on her knees and begged me. She said she can't hide the baby anymore and the SS would kill it so brutally. So I gave an injection to this child and I don't know to how many.

"Oh, if I could only have gone with this transport to Sweden, but the list is closed. I want to get out to start a life again. Yes, I have everything I need, and I am so lucky to have found my wife again. I have work to do, I did work all these years, but after nearly six years imprisonment I can't even stand the fences anymore. But where could I go to? Poland is impossible; from the town we come from only 50 to 60 people are still alive. My relatives, all my relatives are dead. I can't go back to such a dead place and here in Germany I cannot stay either. Yes, if we could have a place where we could work in peace and can be free men again, many of us would, yes, would stay in Germany, but I really want to start a new life, in a new country, I want to get rid of all that is behind me. Here I wanted to do so much, but I have no patience, I can't concentrate."

Silence followed this outburst and I was near the point of crying, so I looked out of the window and saw the shadows of women, dressed in gay colors, wandering along the square.

After a while I asked the wife how she did come to Belsen, and I had no idea what this question would bring back to her mind.

"We were rounded up in Poland and went through several camps, went along Auschwitz, Hindenburg, Vienna, Prague, Nordhausen, Eger, till we got finally here. We were put 150 women in one open railway-truck. We were packed like sardines, one standing and leaning on each other. In this way we went once 10 days and nights, another time 21. My best friend here, I had to beat once terribly, because she started to faint and whoever fell would have been killed by the footsteps. We tried to change places, so that everyone could have a place leaning against the sides for some time. And four times she started to faint, but here she is alive."

"When we passed a station and the train stopped, the SS went out and if there were people standing on the platform we had to duck down so that they could not see our heads, but we cried, of course, and they must have heard our cries. In CRS people threw bread, but in Germany we never got anything. Oh yes, people must have seen our transports. But this poor girl, I had to hit her so hard that it hurt my hands."

Here the doctor fell in, "During these transports many men died but not a single woman. Everywhere I noticed that women can bear more than men, also while we had to work 14 hours a day with hardly any food and with very bad food."

Only now the nurse started to talk: "Nobody will ever believe what the hospital looked like, this dirt, these lice and then the patients lying there with all their clothes on and simply waiting till they died. Patients came in and when they saw those on the floor, without blankets, they said: 'Sister, give me something to do, if I start to sit down I shall die,' and then they would work for a week or ten days, one day they fell down, laid there for a day or two and then died. In a room as small as this (it was a very small living room) I had 62 patients and there was not enough room for everyone to lie down, they had to sit or else I could not get them all in. Out of these 62 patients I had in the last time, only two are still alive. And how many out of your room?"—"I had 60, but they all died."—"Whoever had not had typhoid in the ghetto, died of it here, and 60% of all who came here were soon down with TB."—"Wait a moment, even now there are 20% TB cases in my ward and this after so many have died."

"And do you remember when the new Oberarzt came, a few days before the Allies were here?" He called a meeting of all doctors and nurses and said: 'I have no bread, but I shall give flour soup, this is all I can do. I have no medicine, but you must try to nurse the patients with good words; when I was in Russia in the last war I experienced how much a good word can do even when nothing else can be done. Nobody is allowed to beat any of the sick and if I hear of bad treatment I shall have the sister punished! The soup we got for the hospital for one day."

"For three weeks we were without bread and I don't know for how long without water. One of my patients said to me: 'I don't want anything to eat, if I could only have a bath, a clean sheet, then I could die happily.'"

Winding up the doctor said: "It was all a part of a systematic process of extermination of the Jewish population. As long as they could still work, they had to work, when they became ill, they had to die. They died in the gas chambers, they gave them injections, where they died one minute afterwards or else they just left them lying, in the end they could not cope with all the bodies in the chimneys so the corpses remained where they were."

"I was in Buchenwald and there were also German political prisoners; in the last days 20,000 of the Jewish prisoners should have been killed. But they could not find us. The political prisoners helped us, we deserted our bunks and lived with them, they hid us everywhere they could and so 3,500 of us remained alive."

I had heard and seen enough. How could I get out of this camp again, which stretches over miles? Finally the doctor took me to his TB ward; from underneath their blankets they looked at me as if I were someone from another world, a world they did not know about.

What kind of hope could I give to the man, his wife and his helpers? Only that I would let his relatives know that they were still alive and that I hoped a place could be found soon where they could live. "Yes, if I could have only gone to Sweden or perhaps to America?"

On my way home I passed the old camp, not bigger than an enlarged football ground and there they had lived and died, tens of thousands. In the far end we found the graves and it said: Grave Nr. 9, appr. 1000, Grave Nr. 8, appr. 2000, Grave Nr. 7, appr. 1000, Grave Nr. 10, appr. 800 and then all the others came with Nr. unknown.

When I came home and my comrades heard that I had been all the way to Belsen instead of going to a holiday camp, one of them said: "I wished you had not gone to Belsen, now you and we shall talk about it and I don't want to hear it."—"Then let those hear who are not afraid of the truth and don't worry I shall not talk too much, but I want that something is done to let people start a new life and that the TB ones shall have a place with enough sun and the best treatment anyone can provide."

(Written by Eric Innis)

The saddest goodbye was the one with our Spanish friends. The picture is vividly before my eyes. They asked us to come to supper. They usually had little food, but this time there was plenty to honor us. We talked about the hopes for freedom and for the defeat of inhumanity. The husband spoke for the first time freely about the battles in northern Spain. He spoke with great bitterness of the communists who played both sides against each other to gain credit for themselves. His voice was full of anger and sorrow when he said, "Povres Communistos, they will not live if we ever come to power." During the evening he left the room and came back with a little box. He opened it solemnly and took a small flag out of it. He said, "Nobody but you has seen this. This is holy to us. It is our flag. My wife carried it across the border at a time when blood was running in the streets. It is the symbol for what we stand." He placed the little flag back into the box with gentle hands as a father puts a baby to bed. We were very, very quiet. Marie stood in the corner and I could see that she was trying not to cry.

It was especially hard for me to leave this child whom I loved dearly. She too tried not to be overcome by her emotions. When it was time to say the final goodbye, she turned away from me, bent over her book and began to study her algebra. I knew I had to respect her withdrawal. There was new hurt in her already sad young life.

The Americans gave me a temporary passport, since none of us could get official passports. Yet, I did need the "visa de sorti," which now—after the first refugees had left the country illegally—was given by the French police. I had been warned by other refugee women that the price for a "visa de sortie" was to sleep with one of the officers who had the power to issue those visas. (Many years later I saw in the United States the film "Casablanca." It shows with great realism those practices.) The officer whom I asked for the "visa de sorti" was a young, handsome Frenchman. He made the expected demand: "You can get the permit. How about it tonight?" Perhaps it was my own feeling of indifference whether I left or not, but I felt no fear this time. I looked straight into his face and said, "Can't you find a prettier and younger girl for that?" I must have taken him by surprise. He laughed and stamped my papers with the precious visa.

Chapter Twenty-Four

Leaving France for the U.S.A.

The last day at Montauban: Several friends had come to the station. There were James and his friend. They pressed two volumes of Stendahl's "La Chartreuse de Parme" into my hands as a "goodbye." Paul was very quiet. I was depressed. I waved goodbye. All I could think of was that I was leaving him for always. Oh, Paul!

A young French friend rode with me part of the way. After she got off the train she waited on the platform until it left. She stood against a column in the station, her soft, brown hair waving in the wind. She forced a smile on her face. Through smiling tears she sang in a sweet voice "A la claire fontaine." Its refrain meant so much "Il y a longtemps que je t'aime jamais je ne t'oblierai" (for a long time I've loved you and I will never forget you).

The train rolled on towards Marseille. I had to appear before the American Consul on a certain day to get my visa, a visitor's

329

visa which allowed a time-limited stay in the United States without permission to work. Soon the train was supposed to arrive in Arles. To me the name of Arles evoked the beautiful sunshine of Van Gogh's painting and I looked forward eagerly to see it, in spite of my distress. Shortly before the train reached Arles, the sky darkened. A snow storm—very unusual for that part of France—arose. The train was short of fuel, and stopped for a long time. It became ice cold in all the compartments. No food. Some soldiers riding on this train began to look sick. Only then did we realize that they were wearing torn footwear and that their feet were frozen. I remember holding the dirty blue feet of those soldiers in my hands, rubbing them for hours to get the blood circulation going. Finally soldiers from a nearby base arrived and brought some canned food.

The delay had been long enough to miss my appointment with the American Consul. It seemed to me that fate had decided I should stay in France and not go to the United States.

The train finally arrived in Marseille. I remember the huge staircase leading to the station. The very first thing I saw on those steps were booted feet of German soldiers, the German Military Commission!

The refugee committee of the trade unions was well organized in Marseille. They worked closely with the American Unitarian Service Committee. I was told in the office that the Consul had been informed about the snow storm at Arles and I would be excused for being late. This was important, since—unfortunately—the then American Consul in Marseille showed little understanding of the desperate plight of refugees. For instance, one of the women had arrived to pick up her visa in her shabby clothes. The Consul had given her only one look and had shouted that beggars were not needed in America and that if she didn't know how to dress decently, she did not need to expect a visa. She finally got it, but only after others spoke for her. The refugee committee had learned from this experience and was prepared from then on. The moment I arrived, I was dressed in a well-pressed clean coat, a hat and gloves. This outfit made its rounds among almost every woman who had to present herself at the Consul. The coat was constantly shortened and lengthened. At least the Consul was spared seeing us the way we actually looked when we came out of hiding places.

When I arrived at the embassy, I was told that I had to go back once more and bring along several photos. I was surprised that the refugee committee had not known this beforehand and had not prepared me for this. I returned to the committee and reported this. Surprised exclamations: "What, several photos? That's something new. Those are only needed for immigration visa!" There was frantic telephoning. The person in charge came into the room, beaming all over.

He grabbed both of my hands and shouted, "You lucky girl. You know what you will get? An immigration visa!"

Amazing! For the first time in years there was hope to live in a country, legally, and not temporarily, with the permission to work: The telegram from the U. S. State Department allowing them to issue immigration visas to refugees had just arrived that morning. If the snow storm had not come up, I would have only received a visitor's visa. A miracle!

I had to travel through Spain and to Lisbon to take a Portuguese boat for the U.S. This was the only way open at this time. Refugees were assured safe travel through Spain if they promised not to stay overnight. There were difficulties in providing the refugees with money so that they could get their tickets. All this was worked out by the committee while I waited in Marseille. Another miracle occurred. A letter from Paul told me that he, too, got his visa and that he soon could follow me to the United States. I knew that there might be many obstacles, but there was hope.

The day before leaving Marseille I was asked to see the chairman of the American Unitarian Committee. This was unusual. I have a vague memory of a serious face and a kind, gentle voice which asked me whether I was willing once more to risk myself. He explained to me that the Nazis had recently issued a list of what they considered the most dangerous anti-Nazis and that they were hunting those people. Underground forces had got hold of this list. It was very, very important to get it to the United States to help save them. They could not send it by direct mail nor through diplomatic channels. Would I be willing to hide this list, bring it safely to Lisbon, from whence it could get to the U.S.? I welcomed this request. It somehow relieved my feeling of guilt at leaving. In spite of what everybody else said, I felt like a deserter. This gave my leaving some meaning. The list went with me in a special hiding place.

The trip from France to Spain: The mountains were glowing in the evening sun when we, a few fortunate refugees, passed them by train. We had several hours in Madrid. I had time to walk through the city and see the famous Prado. It seemed incongruous that at a time when we were under such pressures I thought of visiting the art gallery, but I said to myself, "Remember what you thought in the concentration camp and the Austrian prison? You often felt 'This they can never take away from me.'" And "this" were memories of kindness and memories of beauty and memories of places I had seen. In the Prado, Greco's paintings meant most to me. His tortured colors were part of myself. Even in the Prado I could not forget the horror of Spain's Fascist Government. There were empty spots of pictures that had been taken away or sold. When I walked through the streets I saw many destroyed quarters. I saw hungry children, emaciated. France, too, had been robbed of food, but children were not actually dying in the streets. Yet, here they were. Small children were lying in the streets, too weak to move, with the large bellies and the thin arms of starvation. Often, directly behind these children were stores full of food. Goods were available, but not for everybody.

We had to buy our tickets for the trip to Lisbon. The ticket vendor insisted that there were no tickets for Lisbon. One of the refugee men next to me pulled out his cigarettes and shoved them through the opening of the counter—immediately the tickets were available.

I remember vividly the last stop at the Spanish-Portuguese border. The woman custom officer looked also starved. She searched my whole body, and then said, "You won't need bread in the United States."

I realized that she was so famished that the few pieces of bread that I had taken along from France to eat on the trip meant much to her. I gave her the bread. When we were settled in the compartment in the train, we heard the clamor of voices on the tracks behind us. There was a swarm of children with thin arms reaching out to us begging for bread. Here we were, people who had nothing, but at least the hope to get to a land of plenty. There were those who had to stay behind, and they were children! We threw out of the window every bit of food that we had saved, telling each other that soon we would be in Lisbon and we could wait to eat. Those hungry eyes, the horribly thin bodies and the outstretched arms!

The train crossed the border to Portugal. It seemed strange to see people working in the fields and looking healthy and well dressed.

We reached Lisbon. It was full of refugees. Ships did not leave regularly and there was not always space for the many refugees. Here refugees from all the countries overrun by the Nazis met. This was also the city of spies. We were warned not to discuss anything in the streets that might give any information to the Nazis. We were told that everywhere were ears to pick up information. We were also instructed to speak exclusively to people we knew; never, never, to a stranger even if he said that he was a refugee waiting for a boat. It was sad and frightening. Yet Lisbon was a most beautiful city full of sunshine, of gleaming colored tile on the outside walls of buildings, of terraces rising out of the blue Mediterranean.

The refugee committee that took care of us housed us with families. I stayed with a young Portuguese woman who lived alone with a housekeeper. I became acquainted with the strange sheltered life that this young woman led. She was never allowed to leave the house alone or to speak with a stranger when she was outside the home. We became friends in spite of our not speaking the same language. We communicated by my speaking in a slow French and she in a slow Portuguese. Somehow we seemed to understand each other. She felt so badly about my poor outfit that she insisted on making a beautiful dress for me, a beige dress with blue and red trimmings. It meant *so* much to me to have a new dress!

Before I left Europe, I had the great joy to meet Hilde Monte again. We went to Escorial and lay in the sand dunes looking out on the Mediterranean. We had watched carefully that nobody was behind us because of the possibilities of spies. Hilde Monte had been the youngest in my youth group when I was 17 years old. She was then a little 11-year-old, the same age as my younger sister. She was an exceedingly intelligent child who matured rapidly. She was interested in and committed to the work of the labor unions and our small idealistic group. At the age of 16, she wrote articles on economics which were published in a daily newspaper. Her parents were not in accord with her ideas and, to remove her from those associations, took her on long trips. Each time when she returned to Berlin, she called me, her older friend and confidant. Hilde had to go into exile when the Nazis came to power because she was very well known by the articles she had written. She was then not quite 20 years old.

When she was in London, she wrote several books, one on economics and one on the fight for freedom in Germany. Both were introduced by Jenny Lind, a British member of the Parliament. Hilde combined a scientific mind with many artistic talents. She wrote poetry and painted beautifully. Unfortunately there was jealousy among some of the older immigrants against a young girl who was so gifted. They tried to make it impossible for her to write or to keep contact with the German underground. The worst was that they began to question her motives and spread rumors about her. Hilde told me that she had overheard one of the leading older refugees say about her that she was getting a too "swelled head" and "I surely will break her, I'll tell you that." Being young, idealistic and trusting, this had been a great blow to her. These people drove her into imprudent action. She could not sit still without being actively involved in the fight for justice. As far as I know, or as others have told me she instigated the first—almost successful—bombing attempt on Hitler. She did not tell me this, but she did tell me that she was on a mission to go back into Nazi countries to try to help underground workers and that she would continue doing this through the help of the labor unions with whom she worked closely.

That day she was no more "my little girl" in the group. We were equals. I spoke about my concern of leaving Europe and how I would prefer to stay. As all the others, Hilde made it clear to me that this was impossible. I had already been twice in the hands of the Nazi police, and was much too well known by them. She, too, tried to convince me that I could do more in the United States to help the cause of human justice than if I stayed. She was the first one I met who knew something about this new country to which I was going, and spoke about it in a much more positive way than most of the others who saw it only as a short time gap before we would defeat the Nazis and return to our own countries. Before we separated she gave me a book she had made for me, bound in felt with pictures of Portugal. She had written into it for me,

> "Die bleiben haben die Heimat
> Aber die ausziehen, haben die Welt."

Translation:

> Those who stay have their homeland,
> but those who leave, have the world.

(Hilde was killed in 1945 shortly before the end of the war. She had been on an important secret mission to Austria, which she had fulfilled successfully. On her return, when she was trying to cross between Austria and Switzerland, Nazi border guards shot her. Swiss border guards wanted to come to her rescue, since she was lying in No-Man's land. The Nazi prevented them from doing this. For hours, before their eyes, this young, gifted woman bled slowly to death....Later, Austrian youth marked her grave with a simple cross. She lives in the memory of all those who were her friends and for whom she fought courageously.)

Many refugees left on the Portuguese boat that brought me to the new country. Boats had to be overcrowded because time seemed to run out. Room, usually used for baggage storage, was now filled with people. Ships moved slowly because they had to circle mine fields and observe black-out regulations at night. It took 14 days to get from Lisbon to New York. I was very seasick during this trip. I remember only some people on it: An impatient 17-year-old, who had not wanted to leave France because she left behind her friends and because she too wanted to be an active part of the fight against the Nazi. She traveled with her family, with parents who understood the unhappiness of their daughter and tolerated it. Another beautiful 15-year-old, who had responsibility for her mother and her younger brother. She looked like a fairy princess. She was strong and capable. And another teenager, who talked in an excited voice about the great wonders that were waiting for her in the United States, especially "painted fingernails and $50 a week!"

In general, adults were rather silent on this trip. There were too many memories and nobody knew what the future would bring. Many of us had little knowledge about the country to which we went. America was only known to us by stories about the big cities, New York or Chicago. We were afraid of oceans of stone, of cold impersonality. We knew of race discrimination. Nobody had told us of the wonderful warmth and generosity of Americans we later got to know, white and Black.

The boat docked early in the morning in New York Harbor. Stories tell about the view of the Statue of Liberty at arrival. But I do remember: Trees! Green trees! This was the first time (and many others followed) that a stereotype of America was shattered. There were green trees; New York consisted not only of huge skyscrapers!

Newspaper photographers crowded on the boat to take photos. Many of us who had been active in underground work were hiding from them because we were afraid that our pictures would appear and harm others who were left behind.

The labor union committee that had sponsored us came on board. For the first time I met Americans. I remember the kindness and gentleness of those older men who walked among us making us feel that we were important people, that we were not a nuisance as we had been as refugees everywhere else; that we were one of them.

A gangplank led to the land. There was the officer on duty who asked, "Anything to declare?" A very simple question.

I said, "No;" he waved us on.

And suddenly I was filled with a jubilant joy I had not felt for a long time. I turned around to the person following me, "Did you see this?" I said, "They believe us!!" Relief washed over me, relief, not because of a safer or more comfortable life, but because of a new promise,

"In this country—no more lies!"

Only one more thing I must tell, one more picture: Paul standing behind the partition of the custom office, just after his disembarking, about two months after I had arrived. There was the beloved face, thin, tanned, drawn—the voyage had been a harassing one. Yet his eyes sparkled. And before the gate opened, I called out jubilantly, "Here, in this country, we can get married in three days!"

And we were married three days later, I, in my one Portuguese dress and a hat I had bought for fifty cents and Paul in his one pair of pants and shirt he possessed. Yet I did hold flowers in my hand (we had bought them for our last 25 cents) and our witness, our new American friend, the landlord, took us on a wedding trip for 5 cents, on the Staten Island Ferry and sang the wedding march when we came into his house! And a new life started—together!!